ORGANIZING AMERICA

Also by Erik Loomis

A History of America in Ten Strikes

Empire of Timber

Out of Sight

ORGANIZING AMERICA

STORIES OF AMERICANS WHO FOUGHT FOR JUSTICE

ERIK LOOMIS

NEW YORK
LONDON

Published in the United States by The New Press, New York, 2025

Distributed by Two Rivers Distribution

ISBN 978-1-62097-787-3 (hc)
ISBN 978-1-62097-897-9 (ebook)

CIP data is available

The New Press publishes books that promote and enrich public discussion and understanding of the issues vital to our democracy and to a more equitable world. These books are made possible by the enthusiasm of our readers; the support of a committed group of donors, large and small; the collaboration of our many partners in the independent media and the not-for-profit sector; booksellers, who often hand-sell New Press books; librarians; and above all by our authors.

www.thenewpress.com

Composition by Dix Digital Prepress and Design
This book was set in Bembo Std and Gotham

Printed in the United States of America

10 9 8 7 6 5 4 3 2 1

Contents

Introduction

For several years, I taught a course called "Protest and Resistance in America" for the honors program at the University of Rhode Island. On five different occasions, I've had semester-long conversations with smart students about the world and how to change it. I wanted to take students who already had a good sense about politics and teach them how to use their power more effectively, whatever their politics.

I found out that students needed more than just political knowledge. They needed hope. Many felt desperation as they face a mountain of student debt, watch the Supreme Court crush abortion rights and other core human rights, despair over the endless massacres of students with high-powered guns, and wonder if they should have children because of the inevitability of climate change.

I tried to redirect them away from their despair. I posed a question to the class and I will ask it to readers of this book: What are we going to do about it? Mainstream Democrats just tell us to vote, and yes that's important. In fact, in a winner-take-all political system, we have to vote for whichever of the two major parties are closest to our positions. But we need so, so much more than just voting to create change. We need organizing.

But who knows how to organize? How do you create a social

movement? It's not like you contact someone and get a playbook. It's hard and intimidating!

Yet people do it all the time. For whatever problems we have in our society, we have also seen tremendously positive victories in our lifetimes. Maybe a small example can shed light here. I wrote the beginning of this book one day in the library of the University of Oregon. I walked into the men's bathroom and looked at the tampons available for transgender students, staff, and faculty. When I went to Oregon as an undergraduate student back in the 1990s, even though it had a leftist reputation, the idea of such a thing would have been unthinkable. This might seem small but it took committed people with a strong political vision and goal to make it happen. Yes, queer and transgender people continue to face tremendous hate and backlash, but we can marvel at the victories that have been won even as we engage in the next round of the struggle.

Part of what students needed were stories of struggle and success to inspire them. I struggled one year to break through their depression until I had them read two books. The first was Pramila Jayapal's *Using the Power You Have: A Brown Woman's Guide to Politics and Political Change*. Jayapal, one of the most progressive members of Congress and an Indian immigrant, powerfully speaks of her history, her organizing experiences, and her attempts to reach out to politicians who don't agree with her and find something they can work on together. The second was Alicia Garza's *The Purpose of Power: How We Come Together When We Fall Apart*. Garza, one of the founders of Black Lives Matter, shows how to build a powerful movement, while also openly sharing her own mistakes and the challenges of organizing today. She showed that she wasn't so different from my students, as flawed people trying to make the world a better place.[1]

These books inspired my students because they combined a how-to approach to organizing with an honest discussion of contemporary problems that spoke to my students' lives and beliefs. The students needed stories of organizers that went beyond cheap talking points or ideology or mythology, and that presented real people working on real problems.

As a historian, I started thinking about how I might apply what I learned teaching my students to how we as Americans learn about our past. With regard to social movements, I think the history we teach is all wrong. We weigh down our current young people by creating myths about the greats of the past. We turn Rosa Parks,

Martin Luther King Jr., Malcolm X, and Cesar Chavez into our own Mount Rushmore of social change. We look upon them as heroes rather than as humans. When we cannot live up to what these legends did, we feel like we have failed. We may say, "King would have known how to build a giant social movement today and we don't know how." I don't think that's true. I think we can accomplish just as much as any great activist leader did in their time. In fact, I think we can accomplish more.

Part of my belief about this is that I know the stories of these great organizers' failures as well as I do of their successes. The truth about past greats of our history is that they barely knew what they were doing any more than we do. They tried and failed. They screwed up. They had personal flaws that got in the way of the movement. They had egos and political miscues and losing campaigns. We can be like these greats because they were people, not mythological heroes. Learning from their success *and* their mistakes can help us win today.

What should we gain from studying history? First, let me disabuse you of one notion. The past never repeats itself. Never. That cliché has annoyed historians for decades. Don't say it. More importantly, history gives you stories of humans trying to make change. They succeed, they fail, or more likely a combination of the two. Every social movement in this country has an incredibly rich historical record. Sometimes, activists will say that no one has taught them the "real" history they want to know about this nation. That might be true, but don't blame historians! We have written literally thousands of great books in the last several decades on Black history, women's history, Native history, environmental history, the history of slavery, labor history, nonviolent organizing campaigns, armed self-defense organizing campaigns, almost every issue you can think of. Today, historians publish groundbreaking new works on trans history and disability history, reflecting new social movements. Some history books today are written only for other historians and are not that fun to read. But many new histories do engage the public. I hope to do that with this book.

Learning the stories of our organizing past teaches us many things. They teach us why this nation has the problems that remain so hard to solve. They teach us how people of the past have tried to change things for the better. They demonstrate different methods for making change. They help us understand the interplay between government and grassroots social movements in these strategies.

They inspire us to do better. They infuriate us about our history of slavery, genocide, and other forms of oppression. But maybe the most important thing they do is give us the knowledge and context we need today to make change. We don't have to reinvent the wheel with every campaign. We can learn what worked and what did not work. We can learn why. We can learn how to build campaigns, how to create community that sustains us through the hard times. It can make us question some of the ideas we have about making change today. It gives us examples.

Basically, reading histories of organizing and justice turns us into better Americans and citizens of the world who know more about how to see the world we want turn into reality. It might also help us figure out how to fight collectively. We've seen some great struggles in recent years. A surge in labor organizing at companies such as Starbucks and Amazon has demonstrated that a lot of people, especially younger people, are seeing the need for unions as an agent of change. Higher education has seen a lot of this as well—from student workers to graduate students to professors, unions have formed rapidly in the last several years.

But we often struggle as modern Americans to act collectively. We are not connected with one another. We don't hang out together in public much anymore. We often do not talk to people who have different beliefs than we do. In 2000, Robert Putnam noted this phenomenon in his famous book *Bowling Alone* and, in the time since, the problem has only gotten worse. Online communities might fill some of that gap, but surveys consistently show greater isolation and anxiety than in previous decades.[2]

This problem has even more importance now that we are dealing with another Donald Trump administration. I am as sad, horrified, and outraged as you are that Americans chose this authoritarian imbecile with hate in his heart and greed on his brain to be president again. The reasons why this happened are too complicated to go into here. But there is only one way for us to deal with this, and that is to organize. In the aftermath of Trump's election, the media published story after story about how liberals had no answer, were not going to protest, had mostly given up on resistance.

If that happens, then shame on us.

Why would we give up in the face of Donald Trump? The stories in this book suggest that such an attitude is foolishness and selfishness. Do we have it worse than Ida Wells did after the lynching of her friends in 1892? Do we have it worse than Eugene Debs did after the government threw him in prison for organizing the Pullman boycott in 1894? Are the challenges we face more difficult than what Robert Moses faced when three activists organizing Black residents of Mississippi were murdered by the Ku Klux Klan in 1964?

Of course not. These people kept up the fight.

We must keep up the fight too. What right do we have to be too tired to organize? Maybe less doomscrolling and more working with our friends and neighbors for actual on the ground change would reinvigorate us. Organizing isn't easy and I make no claims otherwise. It's hard work. But we can all contribute a little bit to resisting the forthcoming human rights violations of Trump and his appointees. It's not just that we have an opportunity to resist. It's that we have an obligation to our fellow human beings.

This book gives you twenty stories of great American organizers and activists, with all their success and their failures, their bold characters and their personal failings. You will learn about amazing campaigns in astounding lives. You will also learn some disturbing details about them. Don't cancel them when you do. Remember that we are all flawed humans. We can't expect perfection from ourselves or anyone else. When we organize, we build movements that include a diversity of people, from different backgrounds, perspectives, and ideas. Solidarity requires working with and for people who might not think as you do. That was true in the past and it is true in the present.

People say they want to learn from the past. I wrote this book with that in mind. Each chapter attempts to provide a lesson about change in the present by looking at an issue from the past. Some of the people profiled made change through grassroots organizing. Others did it through their writing or their teaching. Some made a difference through negotiating in a board room, others died for their beliefs. Some started their activism as children, others in middle age. They have diverse stories and represent diverse identities. Each of their lives can help us understand our own lives today.

This is not a definitive history of organizing in America. Nor is this my list of the twenty greatest Americans or twenty greatest leftists. One could easily come up with a book that covered a different twenty people. But each of these chapters provides a piece of the past I think we could learn from today. I cover most of our social movements, but not quite all. You will find many of these stories interconnect. Some of the profiled people knew each other. Some organized each other. Hopefully, in the future, I can share more stories of America's great organizing past with you.

Read the stories of Americans who fought to create justice and crush oppression, think about these people and what they did. Let them seep into your lives and think about what we can learn from them. Let the stories of past Americans organize you into an agent of change for the future.

1

Benjamin Lay

The First Anti-Slavery Crusader

We might think everyone in the past was racist, sexist, misogynist, homophobic, and so on. It's true that decades and centuries ago, most people didn't have today's progressive values. Nor should we expect that of them. Ideas about human rights had only begun to develop at the time of the American Revolution. Even those who did articulate them, such as Thomas Jefferson, applied them only to elite white men. Jefferson did not only own slaves; he raped at least one, as did so many of the so-called Founding Fathers. Women could not vote; men could beat women to the point of death without any legal consequences; Americans engaged in the genocide of Native Americans. After looking back at the distant past, it's easy to damn it all.[1]

This is a mistake, if an understandable one. But it is not completely correct to say we should not project our values onto the past. It's true that people in the past thought differently than us today. But making such an observation can also serve to sweep the horrors of the past under the rug. The question we need to ask ourselves is: Who can we look to in the past who can inspire us in our own fight for equality? Who did the hard work of organizing when no one wanted to listen to them? Who made the world better through their hard work?

These people existed in early America. Not everyone was a racist, a sexist, or a supporter of genocide. Benjamin Lay, a disabled Quaker, spent his life fighting against slavery at a time when almost no white people thought it was wrong. You have probably never heard of Benjamin Lay. I hadn't either until a few years ago, when the historian Marcus Rediker rescued Lay from obscurity with his book *The Fearless Benjamin Lay.*[2] This is what many historians do: they dive deep into the past and tell us stories that we likely have not heard, stories that might help us understand both the past and the present in a useful way.

Lay was born in 1682 in the village of Copford, Essex, England, to Quaker parents who were part of the Protestant Reformation that transformed England. Lay grew up in the center of religious dissent going back to the Lollard Revolt of the fifteenth century. Quakers believed that no minister or other authority had the right to dictate someone's beliefs in matters of faith, a stance that was radical even during the Reformation. Not all Quakers applied that radicalism to every facet of their lives, but Benjamin Lay sure did.[3]

The Quakers' core beliefs caused them to consider the evils of slavery before other denominations did. They embraced pacifism and spiritual equality, believing that everyone could receive God's word and that the inner light of God was in each person. This democratic sensibility planted the seeds for questioning society's ills. A few Quakers initially took steps toward condemning slavery and other inequalities, but it would take until the eighteenth century for someone to articulate this into a full-fledged attack on an institution that a lot of Quakers used to get rich.[4]

Lay spent his young years doing hard work, first on his older brother's farm and then as an apprentice to a glovemaker—a filthy, smelly line of work, as was the rest of the leather industry in these days. He hated being a glovemaker, so he ran away to sea as a common sailor, but eventually ended up back in England in the glove trade.[5]

Lay had dwarfism. He was about four feet tall and had a hunched back, with short legs and long arms. Many people had disabilities in this era, a time when medicine had not advanced much since the Middle Ages. People made fun of his appearance, but Lay was not intimidated, likening himself to David and his many enemies to Goliath. He did not lack for confidence. He stood up to bullies, using his verbal mastery to bring them to heel. The disability activist Eugene Grant urges us today to think of Lay not just as a role model, but as "a *dwarf* role model." [6]

Lay would not let his disabilities obstruct his crusade for justice. His time at sea allowed him to see different parts of the world, which spurred him to significantly rethink his society. He jumped ship in the Holy Land and explored the home of his religious beliefs. He also first saw slavery while at sea. It got him thinking. Lay developed a feel for the ideals of personal freedom and liberty and began to reject religious institutions that interfered with those ideals. The Quakers were far from the most repressive religious institution in the eighteenth-century world, but he frequently got in trouble with his fellow Quakers for questioning their ideas and claiming that they were not being guided by the Holy Spirit.[7]

In 1718, Lay and his wife, Sarah, moved to the Caribbean island of Barbados, where they operated a store. At this time, Barbados played a big role in the British sugar empire, which depended entirely on slavery. The international slave trade, one of the cruelest events in human history, reached its peak during these decades. Slave traders rounded up millions of Africans, put them on slave ships owned by Europeans, forced them across the Middle Passage to the Americas, and then dragged them out to plantations to grow and harvest crops for the export market.[8]

Plantations on Barbados were effectively death camps, working African slaves up to eighteen hours a day until they dropped dead. These planters had gotten so wealthy and the price of slaves had dropped so much that planters could just kill them and buy more. The brutality should have turned more people against the institution of slavery, but most Europeans didn't care. The history of slavery is filled with whites who did not grow up around slavery and then became brutal slavers once they married into slave-owning families, for example. Quakers were no better than their peers, using torture as a routine form of punishment.[9] While in Barbados, Lay even used corporal punishment himself, whipping Africans he had caught stealing from his store.[10]

Lay never forgave himself for whipping other humans. Contemplating his sins, he began to develop a strong opposition to the institution of slavery. He later wrote of the terrible tortures the slaves faced, from being starved and whipped to suffering inhumane working conditions where their body parts would get caught in the sugar factories and dissolve into the sugar. Lay and Sarah started hosting gatherings of Africans in their home. Soon, hundreds of Africans visited them. Lay railed against slavery and urged them to resist. The island's ruling class tried to banish the Lays from Barbados, and after eighteen months on the island they returned to England, deeply disturbed by their experiences in the slave colony.[11]

The Lays spent the next twelve years back home. Lay continued to question Quaker ministers and rejected their religious authority entirely. Slavery remained a subject of his critique of society, but now, far away from slavery's daily horrors, he usually attacked Quaker leaders on doctrinal points. That changed in 1732, when he and Sarah again moved to the Americas, this time to Philadelphia, the colonial center of Quakerism, where Lay opened a bookstore.[12]

Pennsylvania was not Barbados, but the Quaker colony had plenty of slaves too. It did occur to some Quaker thinkers that human bondage was not consistent with the core tenets of the faith. But most just put it out of their head and made the compromises that people always make to justify their participation in unjust systems.[13]

The majority of Quakers who had no compunction saw slavery as natural, as did most Europeans. Benjamin Lay told them that it was not.[14]

In 1738, Lay spoke at the Philadelphia Yearly Meeting, the Quakers' biggest annual event in North America. Over half the members of the meeting owned slaves. In his big, loud voice, Lay announced that God saw all people as equal, regardless of race, gender, or income. He told the audience that slavery was the greatest sin in the world. Then, in dramatic fashion, he tore off his coat, tossed it aside, and revealed the military uniform he wore underneath, complete with sword, presenting himself a soldier for the equality that God demanded. He also held a book, which he had hollowed out and in the empty space inserted an animal bladder filled with pokeberry juice. He shouted, "Thus shall God shed the blood of those who enslave their fellow creatures!" He took the sword and plunged it into the book. The juice, which to the astonished onlookers appeared as blood, squirted everywhere. This was guerrilla theater in its purest form.[15]

No one had spoken words like this before. The audience was outraged and furious. The Quakers of Philadelphia had previously allowed anyone to preach who felt the need to do so. After Lay's incendiary speech, they changed their policy to stop him from speaking again.

But Lay was not bothered by their reactions. He spent the rest of his life railing against slavery's evils and building the first organized anti-slavery movement in American history.

Lay had some allies in Philadelphia. A merchant named Ralph Sandiford wrote an attack on slavery in 1729 that he published himself when no one else would. He and Lay became friends shortly after the latter arrived in Philadelphia in 1732. Lay honed his critique and increased the aggression of his attacks over the next five years before the infamous fake-blood incident. Other Quakers started taking his ideas seriously and began to question their faith's approval of slavery. He began to make a difference, small as it might have seemed at the time.[16]

Sarah died of unknown causes in 1735. The tragedy seems to have made Benjamin's anti-slavery fervor even more intense. After her death, Lay started writing his ideas down. He gave the manuscript of the book, *All Slave-Keepers That Keep the Innocent in Bondage, Apostates,* to the printer Benjamin Franklin, then a young but rising figure in colonial America. Franklin owned slaves himself and accepted advertisements for slave sales in his newspaper. In 1757, when he became America's chief colonial diplomat in London, he brought two slaves with him. But Franklin also believed in the freedom of ideas. He at least was open to hearing Lay's critique. Later in life, influenced by Lay, Franklin realized that he had been wrong. In 1787, a half century after meeting Lay, Franklin became president of the Society for the Relief of Free Negroes Unlawfully Held in Bondage, better known as the Pennsylvania Abolition Society.[17]

Lay had inspired one of the most iconic of the so-called Founding Fathers to critique and then call for the end of slavery.

Benjamin Lay's lifestyle reflected his values. For starters, he lived in a cave. He and Sarah had refused to buy land and live in a regular house, so he turned a cave on some friends' property into a small home, making it a comfortable abode that even featured a large library. Also opposed to allowing either people or animals to work for him, he made his own clothing on a spinning jenny in the back of the cave and refused to wear wool because he believed it oppressed sheep. He planted fruit trees and tended beehives. He refused to eat meat, but he would eat honey. He would drink only milk and water, in an era when neither beverage was particularly safe for consumers. He also refused to buy anything associated with slavery, especially sugar, the ultimate slave crop. A typical meal for him was roasted turnips with water.[18]

Lay was one of the first committed known vegetarians in American history. He believed in animal rights. He opposed the death penalty. He showed concern for the environment at a time when most English colonists thought it either was an evil wilderness that must be tamed for God or entailed only worthless forests and swamps to be cleared for plantations and profit. He strongly believed in the power of the printed word and spent much of his limited funds on books on biblical analysis and ancient philosophy, which shaped his anti-slavery and other reformist arguments. He fought the censorship he faced and championed the principle of free speech, a new idea in the eighteenth century.[19]

Lay wrote as a prophet, framing his opposition as a single man speaking out against the establishment, consequences be damned. Some Quakers had told him that they personally did not approve of slavery but feared speaking out against their religious elites. Lacking this fear, Lay channeled the anger he observed in other anti-slavery Quakers.[20]

Lay said that slaveholders, including those who were Quaker ministers and ministers from other denominations, were "in League with the Devil" and must be thrown out of the church. He also said that slavery was the "mark of the beast," quoting the Book of Revelation, which influenced Lay and about which he wrote extensively. The existence of slavery was a sign of the end times, brought on by enslavers' eagerness to get in bed with the Devil. He quoted the Old Testament prophets extensively as well, feeling a strong identification with men who preached fire and damnation to sinners who did not want to hear such prophetic words. Compromise was not in Lay's playbook. He would tell your sin to your face and demand you repent. In this case, repentance was giving up ownership of human beings even if that meant risking one's economic position.[21]

People really hated Benjamin Lay. They made fun of him. They thought he was a lunatic; anyone who opposed slavery to that extent must be mentally deranged—or so they thought.[22]

Lay had few allies. Sometimes, you try to organize people, but they do not want to hear your message, regardless of whether it is true. We see this today on many issues—climate change, genocide, imperialism, gun violence. But Lay teaches us that you have to keep up the fight. No matter how much opposition you face, how much others make fun of you, how much your family rejects you, your fight for justice is the most important thing. Plus, you never know when change will take place. People fight and struggle their whole lives, then something happens and the world changes. Sometimes, by the time you are old, new generations have embraced your ideas and you get to enjoy having witnessed that. Benjamin Lay experienced a bit of that joy.

It took decades for mainstream Quakers to embrace Lay's legacy. In 1754, Quaker reformers gathered to demand a return to the simplicity of the early days of the church and the eventual end of slavery. By this time, Lay's already dodgy health had declined. He could not actively participate in the anti-slavery struggle any longer. In 1758, the Philadelphia Yearly Meeting, where twenty years earlier Lay had pulled his fake-blood stunt, decided that Quakers who sold slaves would be disciplined. When Lay heard the news, he said, "I can now die in peace."[23] London followed Philadelphia's lead in 1761, making opposition to the slave trade a core tenet of the Quaker faith.[24]

Lay died in 1759, at the age of seventy-seven, before he could see the Quaker church become an international leader against slavery and, in 1776, ban slavery in its community. But his beliefs had achieved their impact. It took nearly his entire life, decades of fighting fanatically, enduring ridicule, and suffering as an isolated and marginalized member of his community. He did not live to see the Quakers make significant progress on the issue of slavery, but the writing was on the wall, and those words were Lay's.[25]

2

Lydia Maria Child

Not All White Suffragists

Sometimes, history can be hard for us to take. People in the early nineteenth century had beliefs about race and gender that make us cringe today. Almost anything we would identify as early-twenty-first-century progressive values barely existed at the time, especially among white people.

Moreover, as our values change, our heroes from the past also change in our estimation. In the mid-twentieth century, Andrew Jackson was a hero to American liberals because, for them, he represented the growth of white male democracy. Today, most liberals and leftists rightfully see Jackson as a slaveholder who committed genocide against the Native tribes of the South. Values change, as they should.[1]

In the late twentieth century, many progressives looked at white female suffrage activists as heroes. That's harder today as further research has uncovered more about their racial attitudes. Many leading suffragists such as Susan B. Anthony and Elizabeth Cady Stanton expressed outrage that Black men got the vote after the

Civil War and white women did not. Although they had allied with leading Black activists such as Frederick Douglass for the vote before the war, by the 1870s these legendary figures used stereotypes of Black men raping white women to justify their argument that white women should gain citizenship rights before Black men. It's a sad thing to learn about. Many, including suffragists of color, challenged the white women leaders. Increasingly, historians instead look to suffragists of color as positive figures.[2]

However, not all nineteenth-century white women acted this way. Some resisted the racism of their comrades. Let's look at Lydia Maria Child as an example.

Born in 1802 in Medford, Massachusetts, Lydia Maria Francis grew up in a religious family. Her older brother went to Harvard and became a Unitarian minister. Women could not minister in a sexist society, or for that matter work in any of the established professions that a man of her class could. So Francis went to a women's school and prepared to become a teacher, the best job an intelligent woman could get at that time. Her brother, seeing her potential and how ambitious and smart she was, exposed her to the best education he could, including reading the classics. She would chafe her whole life against having been denied an education because she was a woman.[3]

Francis began writing. Her first novel, *Hobomok,* came out in 1824 and took on a remarkable subject—a white woman who has a child by a Native man and attempts to raise it in white society. The suggestion of interracial sex attracted controversy, and reviewers hated it. But her work impressed a Harvard professor of literature named George Ticknor, who promoted the book and invited her to Boston, introducing her to the literary scene there. Read from the modern perspective, the book certainly entails the use of stereotypes, but for her audience, it established her as a social reformer.[4]

Solidarity between white people and Native Americans did not exist in this era. Francis's New England background was steeped in a missionary Christianity that believed Native culture had no value. Francis, going against the grain of her upbringing, thought harder about these issues than most of her contemporaries and challenged her society's basic assumptions.[5]

Francis continued to write while supporting herself through her teaching. She wrote a book of children's stories, becoming one of the first Americans to write in that genre. During this time, she also wrote a romantic novel about the American Revolution. In

1826 she founded *Juvenile Miscellany,* a children's magazine that was so successful she could live on its profits.

Francis married David Child, a radical journalist, in 1828. He was a deeply political man, a lover of freedom, and a romantic who swept Lydia off her feet. But, given his radical politics, his contentious personality, and the fact that the articles he published often sparked libel lawsuits, he could not hold down a job and support her. The now Lydia Maria Child turned full-time to writing, both fiction and nonfiction, to support them. He did not push her into motherhood, leaving them time to help each other expand the political horizons they had brought into the marriage.[6]

David ran a political newspaper that supported reform causes. After Lydia educated him on Native issues, he used his newspaper to attack Andrew Jackson's attempts to remove tribes to the area of land then known as "Indian Territory" (present-day Oklahoma). This continued into the late 1830s, when the Martin Van Buren administration removed the Cherokee from their land through the infamous Trail of Tears, one of the worst incidents in the long history of the American genocide against Native peoples.[7]

Fighting for Native rights in a white supremacist nation did not make the Childs many friends, or earn them money. David Child continued to get sued for libel and kept struggling to keep a job. Lydia started writing about the new field of housekeeping, authoring the popular book *The Frugal Housewife.* It went through thirty-three printings over the next twenty-five years.[8]

The growth of the middle class during the industrial revolution led to people rethinking much about society. This was the period when movements such as abolitionism, women's suffrage, temperance, prison reform, and the push for public education gained momentum. New religions such as Mormonism developed, as well as shorter-lived religious movements. People also formed communes and other intentional societies that engaged in experimental social behavior that often scandalized observers.[9]

In short, the upheavals of the industrial revolution made people reconsider everything they ever knew. While most northern states had slowly abolished slavery after the American Revolution, there still wasn't much of an anti-slavery movement by 1830, despite the brave efforts of people like Benjamin Lay. Child became one of the exceptions, someone who righteously pushed forward the cause of freedom.

Child and her husband got to know the radical abolitionist

William Lloyd Garrison. In Boston, he had started the first major abolitionist newspaper, *The Liberator,* in 1831. Garrison wasn't really an organizer; he was more known as a radical speaker and writer. He could not deal with disagreement, and even Frederick Douglass broke with him eventually. Nonetheless, Garrison moved the abolitionist movement forward. His uncompromising ways provided strength to a movement of radicals.[10]

A lot of us like to believe that if we lived in the past, we would have been one of the radicals. Maybe. Social views influenced people then the same way it does today. Even many other reformers of the time considered abolitionists to be crazy. For example, a mob in Alton, Illinois, murdered the abolitionist publisher Elijah Lovejoy and threw his printing press in the Mississippi River, despite being a free state. Garrison himself once had to spend the night in prison—so that the people of Boston would not lynch him for his abolitionism. Abolitionists were brave![11]

Child added a feminist twist to the movement. She believed that the status of slaves and married women had a lot in common given their shared servitude. Many anti-slavery feminists made this argument. However, while inequality did define marriage, the lives of most married white women were not anything like those of slaves.[12] For example, southern women often treated their slaves as terribly as the men did.[13] Child, like most abolitionists, didn't really know slavery on a personal level, but she very much knew the oppression women faced in their marriages, especially as hers began to fall apart. She fought for equal participation of women in the anti-slavery movement, which often upset abolitionist men. Even most abolitionists thought women's equality was too radical![14]

In 1833, Child published *An Appeal in Favor of That Class of Americans Called Africans,* a book that argued for the immediate emancipation of slaves without compensation to their masters. She was the first American woman to write a book on this subject, and she suffered significant social backlash for it. Her children's magazine shut down after outraged parents canceled their subscriptions. Even other abolitionists thought she might have gone too far, with some friends abandoning her entirely. But for Child, no idea could go too far in the fight for justice.[15]

As she explored abolitionist literature, Child discovered Benjamin Lay's writings. Largely forgotten in the decades after his death, Lay's work was rediscovered by this new generation of abolitionists. Working with her friend and fellow abolitionist Benjamin Lundy, Child reprinted Lay's autobiography as well as an engraving of him, bringing him to the attention of fellow anti-slavery activists. She channeled Lay's life and ideas into her own activism.[16]

In 1834, Child helped organize the first of a series of anti-slavery fairs in Boston, which raised funds for the movement. She became editor of the *National Anti-Slavery Standard* in 1841, one of the most important abolitionist newspapers in the country. The sheer fact that a woman edited a political newspaper was itself groundbreaking in the 1840s. She edited it for three years, often prioritizing Black voices and reprimanding other white abolitionists when they showed racial prejudice. Sadly, her husband's disastrous financial decisions put a lot of stress on the relationship, and they grew apart during these years. Because divorce was such a rarity at this time, they remained formally married, but she did legally separate their finances so she had control over her own life.[17]

Child continued to write political novels and essays, mostly based on her political beliefs. In them she shared her stance on various issues—slavery, feminism, poverty, prison reform, and Indigenous rights. She dealt with the sexual exploitation that respectable society avoided, even in reform movements. She also got involved in the growing women's rights movement. As a popular author, she wrote pioneering women's histories—such as *History of the Condition of Women,* published in 1835—providing her readers with women role models at a time when popular history did not discuss women. By the 1840s, she was a famous activist and writer for women's equality, furious over the legal and cultural norms in society that repressed women, especially in marriage.[18]

Initially, Child had committed herself to moral action in the fight against slavery. A lot of the early abolitionists believed that if they showed people the way to live, slaveholders would do the right thing. This was a naïve belief. She soon could no longer ignore the violence of the slave regime. She recoiled as pro-slavery settlers piled into Kansas in the 1850s and engaged in murderous violence against those who did not want slavery.[19] She read about how a South Carolina congressman named Preston Brooks walked onto the floor of the Senate and nearly beat to death Charles Sumner, the legendary abolitionist senator and her personal friend. Sumner had insulted slave owners and specifically Brooks's uncle, a senator from South Carolina.[20]

Southern violence horrified Child. But when John Brown launched his famous 1859 raid on the federal arsenal at Harpers

Ferry, Virginia—to steal arms for runaway slaves and start a guerrilla war in the Virginia mountains—she supported him, even when the raid failed and his allies abandoned him. She even expressed wanting to go to Virginia to nurse his injuries, as he faced trial before his eventual execution. Shortly after Brown's execution, the American Anti-Slavery Society published an exchange of letters between Child and Virginia's pro-slavery extremist governor Henry Wise, bringing even more attention to Brown's cause and the evils of the slave regime and helping to turn Brown into a martyr to many in the North.[21]

Child edited and wrote the introduction to Harriet Jacobs's slave narrative *Incidents in the Life of a Slave Girl,* in my opinion one of the most amazing books ever written in this nation's history. Published in 1860, it details her life under enslavement, including sexual harassment by her owner and the experience of being a mother in slavery, and her escape to freedom. Child's collaboration with Jacobs helped move forward Americans' understanding of slavery. At the time, there were few slave narratives by women. Jacobs is the real hero in this story, but it was Child's act of solidarity that gave the story to us. They became lifelong friends.[22]

Lydia eventually moved back in with David and they opened their home as a stop on the Underground Railroad, helping to spirit slaves to Canada after the passage of the Fugitive Slave Act of 1850. In 1860, Child published an impassioned message to the state legislature of Massachusetts. The pamphlet, *The Duty of Disobedience to the Fugitive Slave Act,* attacked the legislature for adhering to the Fugitive Slave Act and told the politicians that they should take as their motto, "Obedience to tyrants is the highest law."[23]

Child continued to write in support of Black rights during the Civil War years. In 1867 she published her last novel, *A Romance of the Republic,* which follows two mixed-race women in New Orleans who marry into white Boston society, where they are accepted. This was not a realistic portrayal of race relations in Boston, but in it Child articulated the Boston she wanted to see, as so much of her fiction did. During this time she also raised money for freed slaves, engaged in recruitment efforts for Black soldiers, and supported literacy campaigns for the freedpeople.[24]

Child not only continued the fight for Black rights after the Civil War, she also returned to the fight for the protection of Native rights, at a time when the U.S. government was committing genocide against Indigenous tribes in the West. Throughout her long literary career, she had explored alternatives to Indian removal, and her influence on this issue mattered. In 1868, she published *An Appeal for the Indians,* in which she argued for a humane policy and the end of the military campaigns against them.[25]

Child took some really brave positions that put her on a trajectory far beyond even that of a normal "reformer" in the era. She had lived near Abenaki and Penobscot people as a teenager, when her older sister moved to the Maine frontier and Lydia joined her for a while. She claimed this experience inspired her sympathy for Indigenous people and her resistance to American genocide, though she probably knew far less about these tribes than she claimed.[26]

Child articulated a universal sense of human rights that was rare for the nineteenth century and is tremendously useful today. She sharply criticized women's suffragists who turned to racism when the Fifteenth Amendment passed, granting the vote to Black men but not white women.[27] In one 1870 speech, she expressed her deep belief in Native rights, saying, "Human nature is essentially the same in all races and classes of men. My faith never wavers that men can be made just by being treated justly, honest by being dealt with honestly, and kindly by becoming objects of kindly sympathy."[28]

Child died in 1880, at the age of seventy-eight. In his eulogy, her old abolitionist comrade Wendell Phillips said, "We felt that neither fame, nor gain, nor danger, nor calumny had any weight with her."[29] That's right. Let's look back at her life: this was a women's rights activist, an abolitionist, and an activist for Native American rights. For some people, the best way to organize is using their writing skills. Child used her writing as a tool in a lifelong fight for justice.

What more can we ask of a human being than that?

3

Maggie Walker

Using the Tools of the Master

We live in a capitalist society. We also live in a racist society. These two things have deep historical connections. We cannot analyze one problem without the other. At some times in history, using capitalism for their own purposes has even helped Black Americans fight racism.

Capitalism and slavery coexisted from the beginning of European colonization of the Americas. Modern capitalism took shape in the seventeenth and eighteenth centuries, especially in the development of global markets for commodities such as sugar and cotton that required large labor forces to harvest and produce. Europeans used violence to wrest land and then labor from the Indigenous people who lived in the Americas.[1] When Indigenous people could not provide the necessary labor, owing to their sharp population decline from European violence and disease, Europeans turned to the African slave trade. All of this happened for the profit of private companies, individuals, and the state. Around the world, from the Caribbean to India to West Africa, people found their lives thrown into chaos.[2]

Between 1600 and 1850, Europeans sent between 10 and 11 million Africans to the Americas as slaves. The vast majority of them ended up in the Caribbean or Brazil, but around five hundred thousand were brought to what became the United States. There, the population of Africans and then African Americans grew rapidly. The legalized international slave trade to the U.S. ended in 1807, and although there was some illegal slave smuggling after that, the vast majority of the 4 million slaves in the U.S. at the time of the Civil War were American born.

Most American slaves lived lives driven by cotton capitalism. With the invention of the cotton gin and the expansion of the industrial revolution, American capitalism and slavery had become closely tied by 1800. New England capitalists made their fortunes as owners of the slave ships, while white southerners made their fortunes through the work of the slaves themselves, including, for the women, the work producing more slaves through childbirth.[3] As the nineteenth century progressed, new breeds of cotton that produced at prodigious rates incentivized increased planting. Masters forced slaves to work ever more intense hours to pick every boll of cotton possible. To make that happen, slaveholders beat, whipped, tortured, starved, and killed slaves.[4]

While the end of slavery in 1865 is the most significant moment of freedom in American history, that freedom became highly limited by both southern white violence and northern white capitalism. For good reason, in school we learn about the Ku Klux Klan and other groups engaging in mob violence to crush Black rights during Reconstruction. However, we also focus way too little on the role northern capitalists, fearful that their fortunes, based on a steady supply of cheap southern cotton, might end if the now-freed people did not keep working in the fields. Freed slaves had their own economic agenda: they wanted land and they wanted to produce for themselves, not grow cotton. Northern Republicans mostly believed that the freed people should continue to grow cotton on plantations, but for wages and with contracts. They had the power to enforce this too.

How northern Republicans responded to the first efforts at land redistribution for freed slaves laid the groundwork for their limited vision of economic emancipation. In early 1865 General William Tecumseh Sherman, attempting to free his forces from the burden of feeding the thousands of escaped slaves following his army as it marched across Georgia, issued Field Order No. 15. This order took abandoned plantations on the Georgia coast and divvied them up into forty-acre plots for freed slaves. Plus, he would give them a mule to work the land.

But Democrats and even many Republicans in Washington revolted. For many of them, private property was a far more important principle than Black economic emancipation. President Andrew Johnson revoked Sherman's order and forced the freed people to give up that land. By 1880, most attempts at Black economic emancipation had failed and sharecropping had risen to replace the plantation, often with slaves renting from northerners who had bought abandoned plantations.[5]

This was the world in which Maggie Walker, perhaps the leading Black organizer of the late-nineteenth-century South, came of age. She existed in a world in which some of the only tools she had to improve the lives of herself, her family, and her community were the tools of capitalism.

Can we use capitalism to organize our communities? Most readers of this book probably have, at a minimum, some skepticism about capitalism's potential to change anything for the better. Others reject capitalism entirely. I do not disagree with either of these positions. But we are not Maggie Walker and we do not live as she lived, a Black woman in the post–Civil War South. It's easy for us to say no one who embraced capitalism can be a model for us today because we don't have to live in that place and time. But we should avoid such easy talking points. If we are discussing different moments of change in this country, we must understand the range of possibilities and limitations in those historical contexts.

In short, people might not like capitalism, but we have had to live under that system for hundreds of years. How do we organize within capitalism, using the system's tools to build power for our own communities? How have Americans done this, especially the Americans who are among the country's most oppressed people?

This is where Maggie Walker's story helps us today. Walker used the tools at her disposal—the collective economic resources of Black Richmond—to build power in her community.

Maggie Mitchell was born sometime between 1864 and 1867 in Richmond, Virginia, the capital of the Confederacy. Her mother, Elizabeth, was a free woman and worked as the cook for Elizabeth Van Lew, a spy for the Union during the Civil War. Her biological father, Eccles Cuthbert, was an Irish American reporter for the *New York Herald* who had visited Richmond during the war and knew Van Lew. Cuthbert had nothing to do with his offspring, and Elizabeth married Van Lew's butler, who cared for the child as his own and gave her his last name.

After the war, Walker's mother and stepfather ended their employment with Van Lew, and the family moved to their own house. But soon after that, Walker's stepfather died and her mother had to take work as a laundress, a hard job that provided a modicum of support for many Black women through the years. Walker had to help her mother. This brutal labor could be isolating, but Black women often organized themselves to do these jobs together, building community.

In the early 1880s, Black laundresses in Atlanta even organized their own union to fight for higher wages and better conditions, just one of several similar movements of Black female laundry workers in the post–Civil War years.[6] A lot of Black organizing came out of these washing circles.[7] Walker grew up working hard, but also learned how women in her community could organize collectively and work toward better lives for all.

During Reconstruction, Black communities began developing their own institutions to support themselves. This was easier in urban areas than in rural ones, because a tiny urban middle class had already developed by that point, but for both urban and rural Black communities, the church became a central institution in their lives. For a young Walker, Richmond's First African Baptist Church served that function as a core community institution.[8]

Walker's early career path was typical for a middle-class Black woman. She became a schoolteacher after graduating from the Richmond Colored Normal School, a teacher training school, in 1883. She taught school for a few years, then married Armstead Walker, a contractor whom she knew through her church. Upon getting married, she had to stop teaching. That was state law, no matter the woman's race. Walker raised her three children and dedicated herself to building her community. In the words of the historian Elsa Barkley Brown, women like Walker subscribed to "a view of women in public life, developing community institutions, and contesting race and gender prescriptions."[9] Walker dedicated her life to building Black institutions and organizing her community to fight for justice.

After 1872, one by one, southern states engaged in what right-wing whites would call "Redemption," or the reestablishment of white supremacy. These new "heroes" of white supremacy, such as

South Carolina's Wade Hampton, were violent racists with blood on their hands for the murders of Black workers, journalists, land owners, and anyone else who dared challenge white supremacy.[10] The notorious case of *Plessy* v. *Ferguson* in 1896 gave official Supreme Court approval to the idea of "separate but equal." But Black political power still existed. In 1898, whites launched a violent coup against a biracial governing force in Wilmington, North Carolina. Mass murder is what it would take to end Black political power in the post-Reconstruction South.[11]

Thus, by the time Walker started organizing her community in the 1880s, Black women's political options in a racist and sexist society were quite limited. Laboring in the homes of hostile employers, subject to violence, susceptible to tuberculosis, facing gender discrimination from white society and often from their own husbands and fathers, working for less than men when they were able to get jobs, Black women had to fight and scrap for everything they got.[12]

The Knights of Labor, the first wide-scale labor movement in the United States, was active in Richmond in the late nineteenth century, including as a cross-racial organizing entity. But these workers who belonged to the movement, both white and Black, generally did not reject capitalism; rather, they sought to reshape the system for their own interests. That was Maggie Walker's political vision too. It would take a bit longer for anti-capitalism to play a larger role in the American labor movement.[13]

Given this context, what Walker and other post–Civil War southern Black organizers sought to do was build Black institutions within their own segregated communities. That meant funeral parlors and restaurants and barbershops. It meant churches and colleges. It also meant banks. Simply put, people needed these institutions, capitalist or not.

Like many other Black leaders of the era, Walker started her institution-building work in the Independent Order of St. Luke (IOSL), a Black secret society that transcended its origins to become a driver of Black economic self-sufficiency. The core mission of late-nineteenth-century fraternal societies was often providing burial services, particularly in poor and immigrant communities, including for freed slaves and other poor African Americans in the post–Civil War South. Walker had joined the organization at the age of fourteen and became a lifetime member.

Women had played a dominant role in the IOSL from the start.

Organized initially by a Baltimore Black woman named Mary Ann Prout in 1867 to provide burial insurance, the IOSL promoted Black self-help and independence from whites, which appealed to Walker, as did the fact that it challenged not only white supremacy but also Black male dominance. She was in the right time and place for this mission, as Richmond's free Black community was strong before the Civil War and remained strong in the postwar era, establishing the city as the center of Black economic development in the South.[14]

Walker started working as a clerk for the IOSL the same year that she married, in 1886. By the mid-1890s, she was employed as an IOSL organizer, traveling through Virginia and West Virginia to start new chapters, including for children. Walker rose within the society and took over the top leadership position of Right Grand Worthy Secretary in 1899. She expanded its operations considerably, creating a juvenile department for children's activities, an educational loan fund, and a department store for the Black community. Nationally, the order grew to eighty thousand members in over two thousand chapters in twenty-eight states. Walker encouraged Black women to be more involved in the day-to-day activities of the order nationwide. She immediately hired four women to help her run the central office in Richmond.[15]

As a leader of the growing Black community in Richmond at a time when Jim Crow was becoming institutionalized, Walker realized the necessity of building Black institutions to serve Black folks in the age of segregation. In 1902, Walker started the *St. Luke Herald,* an IOSL-based newspaper, to serve the city's Black community. The following year, in 1903, she founded the St. Luke Penny Savings Bank, serving as its president, which made her the first Black woman to charter a bank in the country. As with the Freedman's Savings Bank in Washington, DC, the idea behind the St. Luke Penny Savings Bank was to enable Black workers to save money so they could buy land or create their own businesses. Black women would not only be the customers, squirreling away the tiny bits they could save, but the bank would also provide credit to build Black businesses and create a community in an atmosphere incredibly hostile to any vestige of Black power.[16]

The role of banking was crucially important to building Black community power in the post-Reconstruction South. Before 1933, with the creation of the Federal Deposit Insurance Corporation early in President Franklin Delano Roosevelt's New Deal, the federal government did not guarantee your bank deposits. If you put your money into a financial institution, it really was an act of trust. Given the rampant corruption in American society in these years, it was perhaps an act of foolishness too. Banks had no responsibility to their customers. If you were Black, white-owned banks really did not care about you, so Black-owned banks were an opportunity to build financial power that would stay in that community. They might not care that you could save only a dollar here and fifty cents there. This was about community building. Walker understood this and worked to build that financial power. She believed that by providing financial services for the local community, not only would the Order of St. Luke succeed, but so would Black women.[17]

As the historian Shennette Garrett-Scott has written of Walker and women like her, "Financial institutions presented a means to both accommodate and challenge capitalist accumulation, sexism, and white supremacy."[18] Walker challenged as much oppression as she could. She spoke out publicly against the racism that all Black Americans faced. She also condemned the sexism from Black men that held Black women back.[19] However, Jim Crow America gave Black women some room to organize. Whites often felt less of a threat from Black women and gendered ideas about both men and women could work to Walker's advantage.[20] The boardroom and the bank became places where Black women could organize. Pooling resources in the bank allowed Black voters to pay poll taxes. Black financial power could help Black candidates for political office at times. In a place with very limited room for Black organizing, banks such as Walker's could make a huge difference. The state of Virginia conducted a surprise audit of Walker's bank in 1908, but the enterprise's financial honesty—a rare quality for any bank at that time—ensured it passed the audit and stayed open.[21]

Walker's bank grew and then merged with two other Black banks in Richmond to become the Consolidated Bank and Trust Company. Walker led the board of directors of what would eventually become the oldest Black-owned bank in the country. Despite her earnest wish for it be an institution run entirely by Black women and staffed entirely by women, she ran into a major obstacle when it came time to hire employees. Unable to find an experienced Black female cashier, she was forced by the bank's male officials to hire a man for the position. Still, in a misogynist age, the bank distinguished itself as an institution that specifically built up Black *female* power.[22]

Walker organized other Black institutions too. She helped lead the Richmond Council of Colored Women, the Virginia State Federation of Colored Women, the National Association of Wage Earners, the International Council of Women of the Darker Races, the National Training Center for Girls, and the Virginia Industrial School for Colored Girls. When the International Order of St. Luke under Walker's leadership opened a department store in Richmond, it again sought to create space for professional Black workers. For Walker and many other leaders of the post–Civil War Black community, building economic power through the middle class seemed like the most sensible way for broader community power in a white-dominated society.

Walker also tried to find places for Black women in politics, despite the limitations of Jim Crow. She worked for the Virginia Lily-Black Republican Party, which, as its name suggests, sought to organize Black voters to demand rights within the Republican Party's broad structure, rejecting the growing sentiment among white southern Republicans for an all-white party. She even ran for state superintendent of public education in 1921. After the passage of the Nineteenth Amendment, she registered Black women to vote in Richmond. She knew everyone, from Booker T. Washington to W.E.B. Du Bois, and, outside of Ida Wells, she was perhaps the most important female civil rights figure in her lifetime.[23]

Like everyone else, Walker was not perfect. As she aged, she rejected changes in fashion and sexual mores and was very hard on the young women working in her institutions for not dressing in the Victorian style that she preferred. She was hardly the only aging Black female organizer with conservative views on sexuality. For example, Lucy Parsons, the legendary widow of the Haymarket martyr Albert Parsons, spent much of her later life angry over the seemingly loosening sexual habits of other young women of the left, leading to a rift between her and Emma Goldman.[24]

Maggie Walker died in 1934. She is buried in Richmond's Evergreen Cemetery—a sad story in its own right, as segregation continued into the grave. While the fancy white cemeteries of Richmond—which feature two American presidents and multiple Confederate leaders—are maintained with the utmost of care, Evergreen Cemetery fell into complete disarray. When I visited it, most of the stones had fallen down, brush covered them up, and finding Walker's grave was not easy. Given the poverty of the Black community and the daily struggle it endures in the face of racism, it is understandable that maintaining old cemeteries is not the highest priority. The attention Richmond whites have given to its historically white cemeteries and the neglect it has shown toward the city's Black ones is a perfect example of the continued maintenance of white supremacy and the erasure of Black history that endures today. In recent years, volunteers have started doing the hard work to revitalize Evergreen Cemetery, but thousands of Black cemeteries across the country remain neglected, probably in your community as well.[25]

A much happier story is that Walker's home is now a National Park Service site. It's a rewarding visit, although you run the chance of being overwhelmed by schoolchildren since, as you can imagine, it's a popular field trip site for Richmond school groups. The Park Service, however, does a great job interpreting the life of this amazing woman.

Shortly after Walker died, her fellow Black organizer Nannie Helen Burroughs noted that she was "a woman who gave her life as a ransom for many," which well sums up Walker's contributions.[26] Like all of us, Walker lived within constraints set by time and place. She had the agency to improve her life and the lives of Black Richmond, but she also faced tremendous restrictions and challenges. Walker's method of organizing within capitalism may not appeal to many leftists today. But the history of organizing through capitalism has a significant history in the Black community, and was embraced much later by Marcus Garvey, by the Nation of Islam, by former Black Panthers, by Jesse Jackson, and by many others. Walker pioneered this.

4

Ida B. Wells

Intersectionality Pioneer

A journalist, anti-racist, and feminist activist, Ida Bell Wells can inspire us in so many ways today. Her fights against lynching, against racism, against giving up in the face of repression, and for the inclusion of Black women in the women's suffrage movement make her one of the great heroes in American history, and that she did this with the very real threat of murder hanging over her head makes her also one of the bravest.

Wells had a strong sense of justice, both as a Black American and as a woman. She saw the world through a lens that today we call "intersectionality." Coined by the critical race theory scholar Kimberlé Crenshaw in 1989, intersectionality describes how power works in interlocking ways to oppress the most marginalized in society. Although Wells never knew this term, she too used an intersectional lens, seeing her oppression as a Black American and as a female American as being linked together. Consequently, she spent her life challenging men, no matter their race, while also defying the racism of American life and politics.

Born in Holly Springs, Mississippi, in 1862, Wells entered life a slave. James Wells was the son of a white man and his female slave. He became a carpenter. After emancipation, when his former owner ordered him to vote for a Democrat, he refused and voted for the pro–civil rights Republican instead. The owner retaliated by locking up Wells's shop and stealing his tools. Wells responded by taking his family and walking away from the plantation. Wells's parents fought hard for Black political rights in Reconstruction and passed that set of values down to their daughter. That included a commitment to armed self-defense and resistance to the Ku Klux Klan.[1]

Wells's parents believed strongly in education. Freed people fought hard for education, sacrificing to pay for teachers in their communities. Only about 5 percent of slaves could read in 1865, and they knew literacy meant power.[2] Wells enrolled at Rust College in Holly Springs, at the age of sixteen. Sadly, her parents soon died of yellow fever, a mosquito-borne illness still common at the time. Though now orphans, Wells and her siblings had a strong family structure around them. Her extended family felt that her younger siblings should be farmed out to various family members or apprenticed to whites for work. Although still a young woman, Ida refused to see her family split apart. Unwilling to let her siblings down, she left college and went to work so she could provide for the family.[3]

Soon after, Wells moved with her sisters to Memphis. Thousands of freed slaves moved to Memphis after emancipation, seeking opportunities unavailable to them in rural areas and hoping to avoid the violent racism of the plantations. In response, the city's white residents went on a rampage in 1866, destroying most of the Black side of town and killing forty-six people. However, the community also had a strong tradition of Black activism, and that community would fight to keep their freedom.[4]

Wells got a job at a school in the town of Woodstock, north of Memphis. She also worked hard to get more education, taking courses at LeMoyne-Owen College in Memphis and Fisk University in Nashville. Her commute led to an experience that would change her life and turn her into a fierce fighter for justice. In 1883, she bought a first-class ticket to Woodstock on the Chesapeake & Ohio Railroad. The conductor ordered her back into the third-class car, a dirty, smoky coach where men smoked and often harassed women. She refused. A group of white passengers helped the conductor physically remove her from the train. She sued. After discovering that the C&O had bought off her African American lawyer, Wells fired him and hired a white lawyer. A local court ruled in her favor, demonstrating that not all white southerners had embraced segregation. But the Tennessee Supreme Court overturned the decision in 1887. She wrote in her diary, "O God, is there no . . . justice in this land for us?" The answer to that question was no, but rather than give up, she dedicated herself to changing that reality.[5]

Wells wrote to alert people to the South's violence, for which she nearly paid with her life. While still teaching, she began to write in the Black newspapers of Memphis. She wrote mostly under a pen name, because publicly attacking Jim Crow could get you killed. Although we typically think of lynching as a form of terror against men, plenty of women were lynched too. In 1889, Wells and a journalist named J.L. Fleming, an Arkansas reporter who fled his home to avoid a lynching, bought a newspaper they called the *Memphis Free Speech and Headlight,* and Wells proceeded to publish most of her work there. This led to the county firing Wells in 1891 for daring to criticize segregation, comparing her dilapidated classroom to the much nicer classrooms of white teachers in white schools.[6]

Also in 1889, Thomas Moss opened a grocery store in a Black neighborhood of Memphis. He called it the People's Grocery to communicate to the neighborhood that this was a Black-owned business serving Black people. This choice in branding challenged the white-owned store across the street. For three years, the store's proprietor stewed in his anger, until one day in 1892 a fight erupted. The white grocer pulled a gun. One of the employees of the People's Grocery named Calvin McDowell took it from him and fired, though he missed his target, after which the police broke it up. Three days later, a group of whites sought their revenge, marching to the store. A pitched battle broke out. Moss, McDowell, and William Stewart, another employee, were arrested. That night, a group of seventy-five whites took them from prison and lynched them. These were three of the more than four thousand African Americans lynched by white mobs in the South between 1877 and 1950.[7]

Wells was godmother to Moss's daughter. She responded to these horrific murders by exposing the lie behind lynching. In the racist imagination of most whites, the purpose of lynching was to avenge a supposed crime against a victim, and the most frequently stated reason was that a Black man had raped a white woman. Wells exposed the lie, writing about the frequency of consensual sex between Black men and white women. For example, she wrote of one case in Tunica, Mississippi, where a white man got a mob together to kill a Black man after he discovered that his daughter had a consensual sexual relationship with the man. Wells wrote of "that old threadbare lie that Negro men rape White women. If Southern men are not careful, a conclusion might be reached which will be very damaging to the moral reputation of their women." Moreover, she noted, only 30 percent of lynchings even named rape as the reason for killing the victim. Other lynchings took place for any number of stated reasons: resisting economic exploitation, trying to vote, supposedly disrespecting a white, or for no reason at all. The main purpose of this lie—and of lynching in general—was to keep Black people in their place.[8]

In protest of the white community's murderous ways after Moss's murder, Wells led a boycott of the Memphis streetcar lines. This went too far for Memphis whites, who called for Wells's lynching. The *Daily Commercial,* Memphis's leading white paper, ran an editorial urging her murder. While she was out of town in New York, a mob ransacked the offices of her newspaper. Knowing what awaited her if she returned to Memphis, she stayed in New York, took a job with the *New York Age,* and never returned to that city.[9]

Wells kept up her fight against lynching and violence from New York, where she soon published her influential pamphlet *Southern Horrors: Lynch Law in All Its Phases.* The culmination of her lynching research, it painted lynching victims as brave men standing up to degraded, vicious, uncivilized whites, reversing the narratives whites used to justify lynching. She demonstrated the lies about Black sexual assault and asserted that lynching usually happened simply because Black people dared to make money. Whites, she argued, feared Black economic progress and, similar to the logic of violence that underpinned slavery, they murdered Black people in order to maintain their dominance.[10]

Wells moved to Chicago continued her lifelong fight for justice. She formed the Ida B. Wells Club in 1894 to promote the Republican Party and Black political engagement, her own name enough to gather attention of politically aware Black Chicagoans. At this time, the Democratic Party was the party of the white South and while the Republican Party was shedding its anti-slavery and civil rights origins, most African Americans at that time voted for the "party of Lincoln" that ended slavery.[11] In 1895, she published *The Red Record,* a brilliant piece of journalism exploring lynching since the Emancipation Proclamation in 1863. She told the stories of lynched victims in often excruciating detail. She then put lynching into proper historical context, noting the mass murder of African Americans during slavery and Reconstruction. Through her journalism, Wells hoped to get northern whites to show a minimal level of care about Black rights, as they did briefly after the Civil War. She also recognized that lynching built white solidarity between the white working class and the upper classes, a populist strategy that served to deflect class-based critiques and make it nearly impossible for cross-racial alliances to form. Therefore, for Wells, lynching was a form of both racial and class propaganda effectively used by the southern white power structure to maintain itself.[12]

Wells succeeded Frederick Douglass as a leading voice of Black America, traveling and giving speeches to sympathetic audiences to raise awareness and money. Douglass suggested to his friends in England that they invite her to the country to speak. When she received a warm reception in Europe, white American newspapers responded with disgust. The press, using vicious racial stereotypes, attacked Wells for making the U.S. look bad. For example, the *New York Times* called her "a slanderous and nasty Mulatress," proving that racism was far from a southern problem.[13] Wells spent much of the 1890s and into the twentieth century on lecture tours around the North, organizing at the local level, and using her knowledge and fame to build Black resistance to injustice.[14]

Wells also called for armed self-defense, a long tradition in the Black community, as the upcoming chapter on Robert Williams will demonstrate. She stated in *The Red Record,* "A Winchester Rifle should have a place of honor in every black home." In her promotion of armed self-defense, Wells also attacked the complacency she saw in Black leadership at the time, specifically that of Booker T. Washington and his Atlanta Compromise. Washington told whites at an 1895 speech in the Georgia Capital that Black southerners would give up on civil rights and political activism and instead learn to work hard within the white supremacist system. Whites lauded him as the reasonable voice of Black America. Wells had no time for Washington's politics of compromise. People were *dying.* She had barely escaped the rope herself. She would shoot back if necessary.[15]

In 1895, Wells married Ferdinand Barnett, a civil rights attorney and journalist. They had four children together, and he already had two from a previous marriage. It was a full house, though the two activist parents continued with their work. Balancing organizing and parenting remains very difficult today, and so it was for Wells, who found herself doing most of the parenting while trying to maintain her struggle for justice. One way she did that was to create the first Black kindergarten in Chicago, for her own children and so many others who would have otherwise lacked basic early education.[16]

This was the era of women's clubs, a movement committed to political organizing that featured mainly middle-class women. They believed they had a duty to bring their moral power as women into politics to create reform, responding to the extreme inequality and political corruption of the Gilded Age. It led to Jane Addams and then her many followers opening settlement houses to provide immigrants social spaces in impoverished immigrant neighborhoods. It led Florence Kelley to become a national leader in the fight against child labor. It led other women to fight against alcohol abuse, for women's education, against sex work, and many other issues.[17]

Although white women started the club movement, Black women such as Wells quickly built on the idea. She became not only the movement's leader in Chicago, but arguably the most important Black club leader nationally, along with women such as Josephine St. Pierre Ruffin and Mary Church Terrell. Wells organized Jane Addams on racial issues, and they became friends and partners in broad-based justice movements in Chicago. They also both helped cofound the National Association for the Advancement of Colored People in 1905.[18] In addition, Wells cofounded the National Association of Colored Women's Clubs and opened the Negro Fellowship League, her own settlement house that provided social services for the Black community in Chicago, which occupied much of her time in the early 1910s.[19]

Too often, we think of racism as a southern problem. It's true that, as Wells could tell you, racism *was* a southern thing. But the racist views of southerners were shared by plenty of northerners as well. She took on fights against attempts to segregate schools in the North and against anti-Black violence. Much of her work consisted of convincing Black leaders in their communities to combat this violence instead of cowering in front of it. In 1909, a group of whites lynched a Black man named William James in Cairo, Illinois. Wells led a successful fight to activate the community after the city sheriff was fired for doing nothing to prosecute those involved. Her organizing to ensure the sheriff was not reinstated was one of the biggest wins in her career.[20]

Wells had a multifaceted analysis of oppression. She firmly believed that while Black women faced greater oppression than women of other races, all women faced patriarchal oppression and thus needed to unite to fight for their rights. Recognizing that Black men often ruled their wives as patriarchs and were the sources of injustice in their own homes, she became a strong and passionate activist for women's suffrage as the movement most suited for organizing Black women along both gendered and racial lines. At the same time, she understood the obstacles she faced and even showed interest in encouraging Black Americans to move to Africa, a land she believed was not touched by Anglo-Saxon domination.[21]

Many white suffragists wanted their movement to have nothing to do with Black women. The women's suffrage and anti-slavery movements had evolved together in the two decades before the Civil War, but when Black men were granted the right to vote in 1870 with the ratification of the Fifteenth Amendment, many anti-slavery women became angry that ex-slaves would get the vote before they did. Their speeches asked how Black men, whom they increasingly defined as uneducated, savage, and sexually predatory, could have the franchise instead of them. Moreover, as the suffrage movement spread tentatively to the South during the late nineteenth century, southern white suffragists became particularly touchy about being associated with extending the franchise to Black people, feeling it could discredit the already radical notion of women voting.[22]

Consequently, many white suffragists preferred to act as if Ida Wells did not exist. She did not let them.

Wells did have white allies. In 1913, Illinois granted women a partial right to vote. They could vote only for certain offices, but among them was for presidential electors. Many states passed women's suffrage before the ratification of the Nineteenth Amendment in 1920, most of them in the 1910s but a few western states did so in the nineteenth century. In response to this new law, Wells and Belle Squire, a white woman famous for refusing to pay taxes if she could not vote, created the Alpha Suffrage Club, a Black women's suffrage organization. The need for an alternative organization to fight for women in politics was clear, given that the National American Woman Suffrage Association (NAWSA) refused to extend membership to Black women. Again, the radicalism of many white women stopped at the color line. But the suffrage movement, which also included Native, Asian, and Latina women, was far more diverse than most people realize, and these activists forced white suffragists to respond to charges of racism.[23]

Another important event in 1913 was the giant women's suffrage parade organized by NAWSA in Washington, DC. Before the parade, NAWSA leaders told Wells she and her comrades were unwelcome. Finding this unacceptable, she and sixty-five members of the Alpha Suffrage Club traveled to Washington anyway. NAWSA then offered to situate the Black delegation at the very end of the parade. Wells would not accept this either, so initially, she remained in the crowd during part of the parade. But when the Illinois delegation marched by, she simply hopped out of the crowd and marched with them, desegregating the march, going arm in arm with Squire and another white ally, Virginia Brooks. This would be recognized as one of the iconic moments of her amazing life.[24]

By demanding equality, Wells challenged the power structure. During World War I, a time of repression for the country's radicals, the federal government called her a "race agitator" and put her under surveillance. She knew she was being surveilled but kept on working anyway. When whites in East St. Louis, Illinois, started a deadly race riot in 1917, Wells traveled there to report on it for the *Chicago Defender,* the most important Black-owned newspaper in the country. She investigated the causes of the 1919 Chicago Race Riot, publicizing the racism that had murdered twenty-three Black Chicagoans. Just a few months after that conflict, she returned to the South. In her first visit there since she had fled the region in 1892, she reported on the horrors of the Elaine massacre in Arkansas, after state and federal armed forces cracked down on sharecroppers' organizing for better work conditions. At least two hundred and perhaps up to five hundred sharecroppers were murdered.[25]

In 1924, Wells ran for the presidency of the National Association of Colored Women, one of the nation's leading organizations for Black political organizing, but lost to Mary McLeod Bethune, another legend of the Black freedom struggle. Wells later got more involved in electoral politics as well, working to form a Black women's political club to support candidates and running as an independent for a state senate seat in 1930, largely as a challenge to the Republican Party, which had turned its back on Black voters. She also advocated for better prison conditions for Illinois's Black prisoners.[26]

Wells died in 1931, in Chicago. In 1970, her daughter Alfreda M. Duster published Wells's incomplete autobiography, *Crusade for Justice* (which Duster also edited), in my view one of the greatest books about the freedom struggle ever written.

Wells did not live to see most of the change she demanded. Southern senators still used the filibuster to stop anti-lynching legislation. In fact, the United States did not have anti-lynching legislation until 2022, when Joe Biden signed the first bill on the subject to pass Congress![27] Yes, she lived to see the battle won for Black women's suffrage in the North, but for decades they could not vote in the South, and racism still ran through many reform movements. If Wells woke up today, she would perhaps be both amazed at the progress we have made as a society and frustrated and angry at all the work we still need to do.

We can't necessarily expect to see immediate change—or even positive change—in our lifetimes. We can only fight like hell to try. What happens in history depends so much on forces much larger than us. At the time I am writing this, I am fifty years old. I've been around long enough to feel good about some of the positive changes I've seen in my life. But I've also seen all the horrible things about our world only get worse. By no means can I say that when I die, the world will be a better place than when I entered it. But what I can say is that by keeping the story of Ida Wells front and center in my mind, knowing she laid the groundwork for so much radical and transformational change in America, I can shut out that despair and get to work myself.

Others drew more concrete lessons from Ida B. Wells's life. The reparations movement, which calls for restitution to Black Americans for the sins of slavery and racism, takes inspiration from her ideas about accountability. Moreover, today's intersectionality activists find Wells so powerful because she had an early understanding of interlocking oppressions and the need to address all of them to defeat any of them. She advocated for action. She loathed indifference, including in the Black community. She demanded accountability, including from herself, and wanted people to fight for justice.[28]

5

Eugene Debs

The American Path to Socialism

Sometimes, an organizer and activist becomes such a legend that we lose the person behind the myth. Myth tells us stories that might inspire us, but then we find out they are false. Myths get in the way of the deeper understanding we need to learn from their real lives for our real lives. The complexity of the truth helps us much more than myths, even if we find out someone wasn't a hero, but rather a flawed person like you and me.

Eugene Debs is one of those legends.

No one represents the long-term growth of an organizer through the rapid changes of American history like Debs. For many, including U.S. senator Bernie Sanders, he is a hero, one of the most inspiring Americans to ever live. Debs embodied the best about American life: he embraced being an American even as he tried to reshape the nation for justice. Few have dealt with more state repression than Debs, yet he continued to believe in what America could be until the day he died.

This chapter highlights a different side of Debs. It focuses on his earlier years, his rise toward socialism, and his path toward becoming the legend we know him as today. We will eventually get to the actions that made him famous—the Pullman strike and boycott, his presidential campaigns for the Socialist Party, and his imprisonment for speaking out against U.S. involvement in World War I—but we will understand these events far better by moving the frame of reference to Debs's early years. It provides a less heroic but more human view of Debs than you may usually be presented with.

Debs grew up in Terre Haute, Indiana. He dropped out of school in 1869, at fourteen years old, to work on the railroads. As skilled workers, railroad workers took great pride in their jobs, and for good reason: railroad work was incredibly dangerous and terrible accidents were the norm, long after European countries had made conditions safer for the workers. The unregulated version of capitalism then dominant in the United States impeded any government action to enforce safety on the railways.[1]

In 1875, Debs joined the Brotherhood of Locomotive Firemen and soon got a job in the union office. He became an important union leader within a few years. From the very beginning of his career, Debs engaged in active organizing, and not only of rail workers. When he wasn't organizing rail workers on the road, he was organizing other workers at home in Terre Haute.[2]

At this time, Debs was not radicalized—and neither was the American working class he was part of. He believed in individual responsibility and men taking control of their own lives. Skilled railroad workers felt it was each man's duty to stand up to an employer and demand a fair shake, but to do so squarely within the still-new system of industrial capitalism. Debs sometimes even questioned whether his fellow unionists weren't at fault when they got hurt on the job. He spoke against the Great Railroad Strike of 1877, saying, "A strike at the present time signifies anarchy and revolution"—and did not mean that as a good thing.[3] Yep, Debs himself lacked class consciousness in these early years. In fact, it would take him *twenty years* to become the man we lionize today.

Debs, like so many unionists of the late nineteenth century, believed that labor and capital should naturally cooperate. Capitalism would work for all hardworking Americans—or, at least, white men—in this framework. An American democratic system would ensure the wealth generated by capitalism would be spread reasonably evenly, allowing white men to control their own lives. Debs did not think workers had any kind of specific class-based interest.[4]

This vision ran up against the lies of capitalism. Debs's life and work help illustrate how much of the working class changed over these decades and moved toward a clear understanding of capitalism, eventually believing only socialism could tame it. Capitalism would not spread wealth, Debs learned. Instead, a few very rich men such as John D. Rockefeller and J.P. Morgan hogged up all the resources and left American worker mired in poverty.

Workers wanted to believe in capitalism. So they looked for simple ideas that would solve the inequities of the system.

Some of these ideas were utopian, such as Edward Bellamy's *Looking Backward,* one of the best-selling books of the nineteenth century.[5] Bellamy envisioned a peaceful voluntary societal transformation that would fix every problem without political conflict or violent revolution. Other ideas reflected the white supremacy at the heart of the American experience—such as the notion that Chinese immigrants undermined white labor because they would work for lower wages.[6] Still others focused on a magic bullet: the reformer Henry George, for example, created a brief movement revolving around his "single tax," which proposed taxing land to dismantle monopolies and redistributing the revenue it generated.[7]

Meanwhile, many thousands of workers began to follow the Knights of Labor, an organization devoted to the principle of the eight-hour day, which represented a promising real solution to inequality.[8] Distrust of the railroads, the nation's most powerful industry after the Civil War, fueled workers' interest in organizing. The railroads were run by corrupt plutocrats, men who constantly sought to undermine each other, bribe government officials, steal money from their own company coffers, and plunge the nation into depression through their greed and theft. They became the face of the newly unequal America.[9]

But Debs did not the support the Knights of Labor, even when the organization launched a successful strike against the railroads owned by Jay Gould in 1885. He wrote to Brotherhood members that they should "faithfully serve" their employers. He did not approve of the class-based language the Knights used. He also condemned, in the harshest possible language, the anarchists involved in the Chicago Haymarket bombing in 1886.[10]

The transformative moment for Debs came in 1888, after a group of railroad brotherhoods engaged in a strike that ended disastrously. What he found was no sense of solidarity and only division among workers, even among fellow members of the same union, and the reality that plenty of other workers, even members of other unions, would take those jobs if workers struck. The strike collapsed, a total defeat.[11]

This changed Debs. He started moving toward a Knights-like organizing model, talking about class and solidarity. He hoped the railroad brotherhoods would follow his lead and work together as workers with a common interest. They did not. He argued for breaking down the castes within the working class that placed the skilled rail workers at the top. He realized railroad workers could never build solidarity thinking of themselves as elite workers. When they didn't listen, he decided to leave the brotherhoods and chart his own path.

In 1893, Debs started the American Railway Union (ARU). He believed in an industrial union that represented all workers on the railroad, skilled and unskilled, as the key to improving their conditions.[12] Debs believed in democratic unionism. He would not tell workers what to support. Unfortunately, one of the first things many American workers wanted when they had a voice was to keep the workplace white. The ARU decided to refuse Black workers from joining the union. This was their demand, expressed democratically. Democratic unionism, then and now, is no guarantee for progressive policies. Solidarity might have extended across a large swath of the white working class, but it hit a brick wall on the issue of race. Debs did not necessarily support these positions, but he did not push back against them either. Plus, he personally loved to tell racist jokes. Racism was ingrained in white working-class culture and arguably remains so today.[13]

The ARU quickly found its legs. In March 1894, workers voted to go on strike against the Great Northern Railway, owned by the powerful capitalist James J. Hill. After eighteen days of shutting down one of the biggest railroads in the country, not only did the workers win, but they got back wages for the time they were on strike. Workers poured into the union and within a year boasted 150,000 members. Debs provided critical leadership by avoiding making backroom deals with Hill and preaching his new doctrine of worker unity. A new force in American unionism had arrived.[14]

In 1894, the workers at the Pullman Sleeping Car Company went on strike. George Pullman ran his company town, located south of Chicago, like a medieval fiefdom, completely controlling the lives of his employees. William Carwardine, pastor of the Pullman Methodist Church, wrote of the company's total domination,

"It is a civilized relic of European serfdom," and, of Pullman, "He is the King and he demands to the full measure of his capacity all that belongs to the insignia of royalty."[15] The workers struck after Pullman lowered their wages while declining to lower the rent in his company housing.

The ARU did not represent the Pullman strikers, but Debs believed that workers had to stand up for each other. He raised money for the workers, sent organizers, and organized supplies. He did not think it was a good idea for the ARU to boycott Pullman cars, but the ARU rank and file disagreed, and in a democratic union, the membership made the decisions. So, acting in solidarity with fellow railroad laborers, the ARU refused to move any Pullman cars, declaring an official boycott beginning on June 26. Generating its own momentum, the boycott became a larger protest against the railroads.[16] By June 29, 150,000 workers were on strike, and the American train system, vital to the nation's economy, ground to a halt. American labor leaders saw it as a battle against not just Pullman but all their corporate enemies. The Chicago Federation of Labor president said, "We all feel that in fighting any battle against the Pullman company we are aiming at the very head and front of monopoly and plutocracy."[17]

President Grover Cleveland, no friend of labor, had an ace up his sleeve. He had named Richard Olney, general counsel for the Chicago, Milwaukee, and St. Paul Railway, to be his attorney general. Normally, the attorney general cuts ties with their private legal work after they have been appointed. Not Olney! He kept representing the railroads. He hated the union and ordered federal attorneys to issue injunctions against the ARU, making it illegal for them to continue boycotting.

The ARU refused to obey. Cleveland and Olney used the military to serve as the rail companies' personal strikebreaking forces. Up until the intervention of thousands of troops, the Pullman strike had been largely nonviolent. On July 7, soldiers fired into a crowd, killing at least four strikers and wounding around twenty. The same day, the military arrested Debs and other ARU leaders. Facing unsurmountable state repression, the strike fell apart. After thirteen strikers were killed and fifty-seven were wounded, the Pullman plant reopened. Debs served six months in prison for violating an injunction.[18]

In truth, Debs himself had to be organized too, because no one just becomes an activist. Ideas are developed in conversation with others. In the case of Debs, it was Milwaukee's Victor Berger, one of the first socialists elected to Congress in the United States, who pushed him in a new direction. According to Debs, Berger "delivered the first impassioned message of Socialism I had ever heard." Berger lent Debs his copy of Marx's *Das Kapital*—Debs had plenty of time to read it while in prison. He later claimed he came out of prison a socialist.[19]

Debs declared himself a socialist in 1895, but remained a deeply American figure, still focused on the need for the individual to prosper in society. He avoided most sectarian socialist politics and preferred his personal independence. This became core to his personal identity and his ability to appeal to wider numbers of people than most leftist leaders, presenting his ideas in terms of traditional American values rather than as leftist jargon.[20]

However, now that he was a socialist, it wasn't as though there was a clear path of what to do next. Should socialists try to influence American elections? Should they prioritize organizing workers? American socialists would be divided on tactics for decades, and they remain divided today. When Debs founded Social Democracy of America in 1897, the party itself was deeply divided. The next year, the political side of the organization split off to create the Social Democratic Party of the United States and started running candidates for office. Debs was its main speaker and most famous leader.[21]

Debs ran for president for the first time in 1900. He only received only 0.8 percent of the vote, but winning was not the primary goal. He wanted to spread the gospel of socialism. Debs tapped into many Americans' desire for a transformation of American capitalism. In 1901, various socialist parties came together to form the Socialist Party of America. In 1904, Debs showed real promise in creating a viable party, as 3 percent of Americans voted for him to be president.

In 1905, Debs showed up at the founding convention of the Industrial Workers of the World, unlike many socialists who opposed the new union. (We will explore this union in depth in the next few chapters.) Debs and IWW leader Big Bill Haywood were once close. But the IWW did not believe in electoral politics and Debs did. The Socialist Party's executive committee evicted Haywood in 1912 over his disdain for voting and the IWW's use of sabotage in its actions. Debs supported the move. (Let this be a reminder that today's left infighting has roots going back a long time. People disagree. It's okay.)[22]

Debs also served as associate editor for a newspaper. *Appeal to Reason,* founded in 1895, became perhaps the most influential newspaper in the country in terms of rallying support for oppressed workers. For example, when the state of Idaho arrested Haywood, another labor leader named Charles Moyer, and rank and file worker George Pettibone and falsely accused them of assassinating former governor Frank Steunenberg in 1905, Debs helped raise awareness that the case could result in a state-sponsored lynching. Remembering how he was railroaded into prison after the Pullman episode, Debs became a great defender of working-class activists against state oppression.[23]

In the early twentieth century, Debs, along with a few others—Haywood, Emma Goldman, Elizabeth Gurley Flynn—became a premier voice for radicalism with a national following. He was a great organizer because he was a great public speaker. He learned from Christian preachers how to talk to the public, but he also learned that too many public speakers and activists focus on gaining personal followers, attracted by the stage and the bright lights. This is still the case today in our culture of celebrity, where a figure becomes a national celebrity for a single brave act or organizing victory. Debs did not get suckered in by fame. He knew that was no path to success. He told audiences not to follow him, arguing that he could not lead anyone out of capitalism. The people had to find their own way, together, collectively.

Debs's most famous moment came in 1912 when he ran for president again. In this unique election, with the Republican Party divided between the incumbent William Howard Taft and his predecessor, Theodore Roosevelt (now running as candidate of the new Progressive Party), and the Democratic Party, running New Jersey governor Woodrow Wilson, Debs provided a viable fourth option. Socialism was on the upswing in America. All four candidates ran on various campaigns of change. The subject of America's inequalities had finally reached the political mainstream. Debs's platform included providing unemployment insurance to Americans, a pioneering idea that would become law twenty-six years later.[24] That fall, Debs won a full 6 percent of the vote, by far the most a socialist has ever won nationally. He even came in second in Florida as a popular alternative in that Democratic

Party–dominated conservative state. The future of Debs's socialist movement seemed ripe.[25]

Despite Debs's personal focus on electoral politics, he felt real change would happen only with labor unions at the core of political activity. After the ARU's demise, Debs never again spent as much time as he had once had in labor organizing. But he still had a specific kind of union in mind—the industrial unionism of his ARU, where workers banded together across an industry to maximize power, or even across multiple industries. This is the same approach that the IWW tried to take. It would not succeed until the 1930s, after Debs had died. But he recognized that the craft unionism of the brotherhoods and the American Federation of Labor (AFL), formed in 1886 as a coalition of craft unions, would never lead the working class to real power. Growing up in the railroad brotherhoods, where infighting, jurisdictional disputes, and an unwillingness to engage in larger political change limited real worker power, Debs knew that the nation needed a new model of organizing, and he routinely lambasted what he considered the "corrupt boss" unionism of the AFL.[26]

Debs traveled the nation, preaching the gospel of socialism. He inspired and moved people to make change for themselves. He also grew as a person, rethinking his earlier racial politics and denouncing racist movies like *Birth of a Nation.* He refused to speak before segregated audiences while touring the South. Debs spoke out more strongly against racism than nearly any white political figure of the era.[27]

When the U.S. entered World War I in 1917, many people opposed the country's involvement. The government responded with draconian laws that effectively made protest illegal in the United States. The Espionage Act of 1917 effectively made it illegal to oppose the draft in a public setting; the Sedition Act of 1918 went even further, making public speaking against the war illegal. After the war, Congress repealed the Sedition Act, but the Espionage Act remains on the books today and has been used to prosecute Chelsea Manning and Edward Snowden, among others in the recent past.[28]

On June 16, 1918, Debs gave a speech in Canton, Ohio, to about a thousand supporters. In it, he stated his opposition to the war, which he claimed pitted two sets of capitalist nations forcing their working classes to kill each other. He urged the United States to remain neutral in the war and for people to save their lives by resisting the draft. Debs was arrested on sedition charges on June 30 in Cleveland.

Debs's arrest sparked outrage on the left. He had not really said anything controversial, unless one couldn't tolerate any disagreement with the war. But that was the type of oppression the left faced in 1918. This was the era where employers used the war as an excuse to crush radical labor. The famous lawyer of the people Clarence Darrow represented Debs in his sedition trial. But even he could do little in the face of overwhelming anti-radical sentiment. Debs spoke to the jury for two hours in his own defense, providing an incredibly passionate speech. He spoke to the general public as much as to the jury. But the jury found him guilty of violating the Espionage Act, whereupon he received three concurrent ten-year sentences.

Debs ran for president from prison in 1920. He received over nine hundred thousand votes, about 3.4 percent of the electorate. It was a smaller portion than he had won in 1912, but that's still a lot of voters, especially given the toxic political atmosphere of the moment. By this point, the public began souring on the Red Scare, and public denunciations of Debs turned into sympathy for his plight. Woodrow Wilson thought about pardoning Debs in 1919 but, convinced by his red-baiting attorney general, A. Mitchell Palmer, he declined.[29]

Despite being a conservative Republican, President Warren Harding commuted Debs's sentence in 1921 and released him from prison. In fact, Harding invited Debs to the White House. But prison had destroyed Debs's already frail health. He never did recover from his time there. He mostly remained at home in these years, too sick to keep working for socialism. He died in 1926 at the age of seventy, his health completely ruined by a nation too scared of dissension to allow this great orator and fighter for the public good to speak the truth in a war that benefited the capitalists much more than it did ordinary people.

Eugene Debs is unquestionably one of the great organizers in American history. But he wasn't born that way. He had to learn, screw up, have new experiences. It took him more than half his life to figure it out. If it took Debs that long to figure it out, it might take us that long too.

6

Clara Lemlich

A Revolutionary Life

Sometimes leaders come out of dire poverty. These are the circumstances from which Clara Lemlich, the great textile factory organizer, emerged. Lemlich would be a leader in the movement for justice for decades. Her greatest contribution to organizing came when she was young, but throughout her life she stayed loyal to her principles and the fight for freedom.

By the late nineteenth century, sweatshops were almost everywhere in New York City. The city became the center of immigration in the United States. By far the largest city in the U.S., it was where most immigrants coming from Europe disembarked. After 1880, the point of origin for the majority of immigrants shifted from western and northern Europe to southern and eastern Europe. The nation rapidly expanded in diversity, as huge Italian, Jewish, and Polish populations joined the masses of Irish, English, French, and German folks who had emigrated earlier in American history.[1]

Many of these new immigrants found both economic opportunity and massive discrimination in the United States. Most came for a good reason—to escape deep poverty, political persecution, or religious discrimination. But unlike the stories Americans often tell about immigrants, past and present, many did not intend to stay. They hoped to accrue significant wealth and return to their home countries. For members of some ethnic groups, over half did return. But for Jewish immigrants, it was a different story. There were many reasons large-scale Jewish immigration happened in these years, but the most common was that Russian leaders used Jewish people as a scapegoat for their own failures and encouraged murderous pogroms against them. Very few of these immigrants returned home.[2]

Many Jewish immigrants crowded into New York City's Lower East Side and took whatever job they could. A large number found their way into the city's growing sweatshops. At first, sweatshops were frequently run out of people's homes. As many as fifteen people, usually extended families, would squeeze into a tiny New York City apartment at night to sleep; then, in the day, they moved the furniture into a corner and stitched clothing on contract to middlemen who serviced department stores. They were paid almost nothing and labored as much as sixteen hours a day for a poverty wage that was based upon how much they produced.[3]

In the early 1900s, work began to move into larger sweatshops outside the home. Renting buildings in New York and surrounding cities, contractors made deals with department stores to produce clothing for very cheap. The department stores made a deal with a contractor for a specific price, and it was up to the contractor to produce the amount of goods required. Anything between the actual cost and what the department store paid was the profit, so it was in the interests of the sweatshop contractors to squeeze the workers as hard as possible.

Born in 1886 in what is today Ukraine, Clara Lemlich's childhood was representative of a whole generation of Russian Jews fleeing anti-Semitism and entering the new American working class. Her family emigrated to New York City in 1903. Many of these immigrants, including young Clara, already had socialist leanings. The Jewish Bund was a movement of secular Jews who had left the ghettos and shtetls of eastern Europe to find jobs in industrial factories and exposure to modern ideas, especially socialism in its wide variety of forms. Lemlich's family was not involved in this movement, but it impacted the world in which they lived. In fact, Lemlich's family was horrified by the activist she became and, throughout her adulthood, they largely shunned her for it.[4]

From the time she was a child, Lemlich stood up to anyone who got in her way. Her parents, who spoke Yiddish at home and worried about her becoming secular, banned the Russian language in their home. In defiance, she went out of her way to become fluent in Russian and learn as much as she could about Russian culture. Against her father's wishes, she built a little library, which she hid from him; he found and destroyed it, but she just kept buying books.[5]

New York's Lower East Side became the center of Jewish American life. At one point, it was the most densely populated neighborhood in the world. Immigrants crowded into these apartments. Two weeks after arriving in the neighborhood, Clara Lemlich landed her first factory job at the Gotham shirtwaist factory. She worked a sixty-six-hour week, which consisted of eleven hours a day for six days, with only Sunday off. For all this work, she earned $3 a week. Employers hired young girls instead of experienced Jewish male tailors because they thought that girls could be exploited without facing any resistance—under the assumption that they were less likely to unionize and more willing to accept meager pay. They were soon proven wrong.[6]

Many Jewish immigrants already had a well-developed political consciousness and thus added much to American political life. Owing to their collective socialist leanings, a large number of Jewish workers refused to accept terrible conditions. They wanted to organize. Although they had left Russia to escape the murderous oppression they faced, they did not see the United States as a new promised land. Rather, they saw it as a capitalist nation that, even if they faced oppression, still might offer a better life than what they had before.

Lemlich, among these workers, began organizing alongside other young women, such as Pauline Newman and Rose Schneiderman, to form a union. They would get fired for their organizing, but then go to a new shop and agitate those workers to join the union. Soon enough, Lemlich was on the executive board of the International Ladies Garment Workers Union (ILGWU) Local 25. Despite being a union with "Ladies" in its title, the union's leadership was made of men—and those men expected to stay in charge. Angry about the unwillingness of the male union leaders to take their needs seriously, Lemlich and other women began challenging them. In one shop, she simply walked in on a union meeting of men, told them that without women on their side they would lose the strike they were planning, and demanded they help her organize![7]

Just because workers want to be organized doesn't mean they are, in fact, being organized. The men of the ILGWU leadership were not only misrepresentative of the union's body, but they were also deeply out of touch with the working conditions of the shop floors. This left the perfect opening for Lemlich and Newman to tap into the very real discontent these workers felt.

On November 22, 1909, union leadership held a meeting at Cooper Union in Manhattan. The leaders of the national labor movement were there, including American Federation of Labor president Samuel Gompers. For Gompers, angry immigrant women were a problem, not an opportunity. A Jewish immigrant himself from England, Gompers believed that the American labor movement's mission was, in his eyes, the advancement and protection of skilled white men whose relatively elite jobs were under siege from employers, women, and masses of nonwhite immigrants. Unsurprisingly, when thousands of Jewish and Italian women from New York sweatshops attended the union meeting with the intent to strike, Gompers and ILG leaders urged the women against it. They waxed poetic about solidarity, but they also preached patience. In short, they were killing time.

Finally, Lemlich had enough. She demanded to speak. The crowd made way. She gave an impassioned speech in Yiddish, saying in part, "I have listened to all the speakers, and I have no further patience for talk. I am a working girl, one of those striking against intolerable conditions. I am tired of listening to speakers who talk in generalities. What we are here for is to decide whether or not to strike. I make a motion that we go out in a general strike." Now this is what the workers wanted to hear! Reflecting the largely Jewish nature of the workforce, they modified an ancient Jewish oath to Israel as their pledge to strike, saying, "If I turn traitor to the cause I now pledge, may this hand wither from the arm I now raise." The strike was on.[8]

Out of the 32,000 total shirtwaist workers in New York, 20,000 went on strike. The media would soon call this the "Uprising of the 20,000" and the name stuck. Lemlich gave speech after speech, leading rallies, convincing scared workers to walk off the job. The sweatshop owners saw Lemlich as an enemy to be stopped. The owners paid sex workers to instigate fights with strikers on the picket lines. Even if the strikers didn't take the bait, the cops could use the ruckus as an excuse to use excessive force. Lemlich herself was a victim of this tactic: a cop beat her up and broke her ribs. She spent time in the hospital recovering from her injuries, but it did not break her spirit.

The New York media were fascinated by these strikers. In an *Evening Journal* article, Lemlich shared her story with a clear message. This wasn't just about wages and hours. It was about the sexual harassment the sweatshop workers faced on the job every day. She told readers that the bosses "swear at us and sometimes they do worse—they call us names that are not pretty to hear." Lemlich was ahead of her time. She confronted workplace sexual harassment in an era decades before the term was invented. She also defended the women from the demeaning stories in the papers about them being frivolous or silly. When they attacked the workers for spending money on new clothing, Lemlich noted, "We like new hats as well as any other young women. Why shouldn't we?" Thus, the strikers also demanded dressing rooms in the factories to preserve their hard-won clothing and to have privacy from prying male bosses.[9]

Lemlich and her fellow workers tapped into the growing feminist movement. Even rich women were interested in the plight of these brave young women. Some of them came out to help. One of them was Anne Morgan, the daughter of the archcapitalist J.P. Morgan; another was the extraordinarily rich suffragist Alva Belmont. The brutality these rich women saw opened their eyes. The workers won some minor victories by waging the Uprising of the 20,000. Those included a fifty-two-hour workweek, four paid holidays per year, the end of workers having to buy their own work materials, and a general agreement to negotiate pay rates with workers. But the owners still controlled the conditions of work, including issues of workplace safety.

In the aftermath, Lemlich continued speaking out, even though she was blacklisted from the garment factories and had to use false names to get what was still dreadful work. Two years after the Uprising of the 20,000, Lemlich was now a full-time union organizer in New York. Issues of workplace safety remained a big concern for textile workers. In 1910, a fire broke out at a textile factory across the Hudson River in Newark, New Jersey. Twenty-five garment workers died that day and organizers like Lemlich agitated around safety at work. Then, on March 25, 1911, the Triangle Shirtwaist

Factory caught on fire. As a direct result of the factory's terrible and unsafe working conditions, which included several locked doors to the stairwells and exists, 146 workers died that day. Some burned, others jumped to their death from the ninth floor of the building in front of horrified onlookers. The owners of the factory had been the most anti-union of all the New York shirtwaist manufacturers. Lemlich had worked at the factory for a while herself. Upon hearing about the fire, she thought her cousin had died and went searching for her. The aftermath of Triangle led to fire and safety reforms but did not lead to workers' rights. Those still required the workers' struggle.[10]

As part of being young activist women at this time, Lemlich and many of her fellow grassroots activists in the sweatshops also became major supporters of women's suffrage. It's hard to imagine a world in which women could not vote, let alone one where women could be opposed to suffrage, but even many women did not support the idea, believing politics was a man's game that would sully women. Even great leftist organizers such as Mother Jones opposed women's suffrage. The male leadership of the ILGWU did as well.

But Lemlich and other working-class women organizers knew that they could not truly change their lives if they could not fully participate in political processes. As Lemlich stated, "The manufacturer has a vote; the bosses have votes; the foremen have votes, the inspectors have votes. The working girl has no vote. When she asks to have a building in which she must work made clean and safe, the officials do not have to listen. When she asks not to work such long hours, they do not have to listen."[11]

Lemlich and her comrades Schneiderman and Newman also felt alienated from both the women's suffrage and Socialist Party movements. The upper-class suffragists were not comfortable with the language of class struggle used by Lemlich.[12] Meanwhile, the Socialist Party largely thought suffrage was a bourgeois issue and did not like making alliances with wealthy women.[13] So Lemlich and her supporters started their own organization.

The Wage Earners' Suffrage League formed in 1911. Lemlich was hired as the chief organizer, her first opportunity for steady work since the strike and her subsequent blacklisting. She also served as its vice president. The Suffrage League would last only a year—many such organizations fall apart quickly—but Lemlich and her friends made suffrage a specifically working-class issue, a big achievement. The league organized in New York's immigrant neighborhoods and at the sweatshops where they worked. They specifically raised a suffragist consciousness in the sweatshops, distributing one pamphlet that read, "Why are you paid less than a man? Why do you work in a firetrap? Why are your hours so long? Because you are a woman and have no vote. Votes make the law. Votes enforce the law. The law controls conditions. Women who want better conditions must vote."

When the state of New York refused to pass a women's suffrage bill in 1912, the Suffrage League held a rally at Cooper Union in New York, with Lemlich, Schneiderman, and other organizers giving speeches noting that the same rich men who refused to protect women from dying in workplace fires refused to give them the vote. Organizing in this sexist and classist society was not easy. Union men threw tomatoes at Lemlich when she organized women workers around the suffrage issue in front of their factories. Then, Mary Beard, the wealthy historian who funded the Suffrage League, fired Lemlich a year later, leading the working-class organizer to become quite bitter about the patronizing attitude of wealthy suffragists who were supposedly allies. The league disappeared.[14]

When the New York state senate held hearings about the recent agitation of these working women, one senator noted that he wanted men to relieve women of the burdens of working. When Lemlich testified, she tore into him with enormous ferocity, not only noting that women were forced to work because of poverty wages but also asking him what he was doing about the many men who got women pregnant and then left them to fend for themselves and their babies. She concluded that women were integral members of the workforce, and they would fight for themselves to get recalcitrant senators like him to pass the laws they needed to survive.[15]

In 1913, Lemlich married a printer and fellow socialist named Joe Shavelson. The family moved into a small home in Brooklyn, leaving the Lower East Side where she had become a famed organizer. Many of her old allies such as Schneiderman and Newman remained involved in increasingly mainstream reform politics. Lemlich simultaneously moved in two different directions that isolated her from them. First, she spent a great deal of time raising her three children. Second, she became a devout member of the Communist Party in the aftermath of the Soviet Union's establishment in 1917. Although the radicalism of the Lower East Side working class a decade earlier did not have to attach itself to a party, after

1917, the choice to become a communist was a deeply important one that often split established political alliances. But Lemlich did not look back. For her, communism was the future.[16]

Lemlich was not an orthodox communist any more than she was orthodoxly anything else. She was a fiery organizer and that did not change. What did change was her stance within the home. She loved her husband and her children, but also chafed at the contradictions of having a radical political outlook and choosing a traditional marriage that kept her home. Naturally, she refused to choose and carved a new path altogether, turning to another form of women's activism—housewife organizing. For a working-class man of the time, Shavelson was reasonably supportive of his wife, but it definitely caused tensions in the marriage. For Lemlich, this was worth it.

While the Communist Party generally thought housewife organizing was a bourgeois distraction from a working-class revolution, Lemlich and her allies recognized the power of one abiding principle: anyone can get organized. Housewives already had a history of consumer boycotts, so Lemlich started by organizing them on the issue of consumer prices, but eventually expanded to the issues of housing and education. She once again took to the street corners and workplaces, except this time it was Brownsville, Brooklyn, instead of Manhattan's Lower East Side.

The 1920s were a hard time for working people. While the '20s in our popular imagination were a period of wealth only interrupted by the Great Depression, in fact, for the working class it was a time of downward mobility. Unions made progress through the 1910s but then got crushed by concerted corporate campaigns through the 1920s, aided by twelve years of Republican presidents. Wages stagnated or declined in many jobs, and purchasing power declined with it. The answer for radicals like Lemlich was to adapt the union organizing strategies of their youth to the consumer needs of their adult years.[17]

It did not take long for Lemlich to become a political leader in her new community. She was actively involved in the battles between tenants and landlords in New York in 1918, helping to lead the rent strike that began that year; by the middle of 1919, four thousand households were refusing to pay rent until landlords rolled back rent increases. These women were committed; some even poured boiling water on those engaged in evictions.[18]

Lemlich created the United Council of Working Class Housewives to build her vision of leftist female organizing. It became the major organ of women's organizing with the New York left in the 1930s. In 1935, working with both Jewish and Black women, it led a boycott against four thousand butcher shops that shut them down and won significant concessions. It was the biggest organizing struggle Lemlich led since her days in the textile sweatshops and she knew how to win attention for the cause. She worked to expand the boycott to other cities, leading to a response from national political leaders. By the end of the summer, the boycotts had driven down the price of meat. This built a new cadre of activists who took these lessons and applied them to local struggles in their own cities around the nation. By the late 1930s, housewife organizing was a major activist force in America, owed in great part to Lemlich's efforts.[19]

The United Council of Working Class Housewives was not officially affiliated with the Communist Party, but many of its members were also communists. Lemlich became a member at least by 1926, if not before. She remained a committed communist for the rest of her life. In 1938, the Communist Party decided to undercut feminist organizing and withdrew support from Lemlich's group. It wasn't surprising. The communists were not any more attuned to gender politics than the socialists had been. For them, it was still a distraction, at best. They ignored the fact that housewives knew more about the realities of modern consumption than anyone else. Gender ideology once again got in the way of class solidarity. But for years she remained committed to her movement. In the 1940s, she continued to organize for the United Council, which by this point had become part of the International Workers' Order.

As a mother, Lemlich passed her radicalism down to her children. Her son Irving Shavelson was at her side organizing when he was a child, and, by the time he was a teen, he was organizing children's brigades within the United Council, mobilizing pickets. Her children sometimes hated their mother using them as political props, but for Lemlich, presenting herself as a mother protecting her children from exploitation served as great political fodder, and no doubt she deeply felt that that was what she was doing.[20]

Some commenters have red-baited lifelong communists such as Lemlich for refusing to confront the crimes of Joseph Stalin in the Soviet Union. That's unfair. For people such as Lemlich, communism was the road to working-class liberation. To give that up meant betrayal of a life's work. Moreover, it's not as if this capitalist nation treated its dissenters any better in the 1950s than it had in the 1910s. When the government prosecuted Julius and Ethel Rosenberg for giving atomic secrets to the Soviets, which would end in their execution, Lemlich was one of the leaders fighting for their freedom. She raised her children to be fighters for the global revolution as well. Her son, who changed his name to Charles Velson to hide his Jewish identity and thus attract less suspicion from American workers, became a longtime longshoremen's union activist and noted Soviet spy in the 1930s and during World War II, including in the Panama Canal Zone.

Lemlich continued organizing housewives, including mobilizing them to wage a meat boycott in 1948 to protest high prices. This campaign involved 150,000 participating households, forcing cattlemen to lower prices on their beef and the Office of Price Stabilization, a government agency tasked with controlling consumer prices, to drop the price of meat by 10 percent. Again, Lemlich was a key player here.

In 1951, Lemlich traveled to the Soviet Union. The trip got her caught up in the red-baiting of the McCarthy era, and the government revoked her passport. She continued to work periodically in the garment industry until 1954, fighting a new generation of ILGWU leadership to win members a union pension.

Perhaps my favorite story about Lemlich is something from the end of her life. By the 1960s, now twice widowed, she moved to California, where her children lived. The suburbs of postwar California were a long way from the sweatshops of 1900s New York. Such was the experience of so many in that generation who saw their struggles and fights lead to real gains for the working class, even if capitalism remained as entrenched as ever. But the fire and passion for change in Lemlich's heart never faded. She spent several years in the Jewish Home for the Aged in Los Angeles at the end of her life. She was not in good health, but she continued to organize. She hectored the management of the home to support the United Farm Workers boycott on grapes, finally convincing them to join the boycott. Then, she set about helping the nursing home workers to form a union.

By the time Lemlich died in 1982, at the age of ninety-six, she had experienced a long lifetime of radicalism, success, failures, red-baiting, and the rejuvenation of leftist politics in the 1960s.

Lemlich's story has slowly become part of our shared historical knowledge, at least for lefitsts. A children's book about her and the Uprising of the 20,000 was published in 2013, for example.[21] Still, the average American has no idea who she is. We should remember her as an uncompromising voice for change, someone who maintained an intensity in her politics that made even her comrades uncomfortable, but also may inspire us to fight for change today, despite the social and personal costs. That she connected radical organizing with consumer organizing also is worth greater attention. Consumer movements often have middle-class tendencies, but it is not a requirement that consumer movements have to be led by the middle class; as Lemlich shows us, in a nation dominated by consumer capitalism, the fight for basic rights for the poor will have a consumer dimension. From the workplace to the household, Clara Lemlich is one of the great American heroes.

7

Frank Little

The Martyr

Organizing America does not always mean you win. Sometimes, it means suffering. It means standing up for your beliefs in the face of massive hostility. You might spend your whole life losing. You might get beat up. Sometimes, you pay the ultimate price.

We should not romanticize martyrdom. There's nothing good about dying a violent death. But we can learn from our martyrs, such as how to maintain bravery and principle in the face of tremendous suffering. We can also learn how to remain unswerving when we cannot compromise with evil. There can be a time and a place for compromise. But when the enemy wants to crush you completely, that is the time to stand up for justice no matter what happens. Future activists will remember you as a hero and organize using your life and martyrdom as inspiration.

This leads us to the life of Frank Little.

Born in 1879 in Oklahoma (then called Indian Territory), Little came from a Quaker family. Although he later claimed to have Cherokee blood and many histories of him have called him Native

American, this is probably untrue. The family identified as white, after all, and when Little was born, they were living in Oklahoma Territory illegally. They were evicted, but in 1889, the U.S. Congress passed a law opening up 2 million acres of Indian Territory to white settlers. The Littles joined others who lined up on the day the land opened, rushing across the border and taking the best land based on who could get there first.[1]

As with most of the white newcomers to Oklahoma, the Littles' new land did not make them rich. Frank's father died in 1899, and Frank soon followed his brother Fred out to the California mines. Fred had already started organizing his fellow workers into unions, which left a mark on his little brother. In 1903, after having worked the mines for a few years, Frank went to Bisbee, Arizona, the copper mining capital of the Southwest and a place that would later have a huge impact on both Little's life and American labor history. He got a job and joined the Western Federation of Miners.[2]

Miners labored in often brutal conditions. Dangerous work existed throughout the United States in the early twentieth century, but miners faced extreme risks. Workers breathed in poisonous dust. Mines could cave in on them. Coal was the worst, but even the hard-rock mines where Little labored could be death traps. At best, workers came out of the mines every day exhausted and filthy. It was no good way to live.[3] The isolation of the job made things even harder.

These camps were ruled by whichever capitalist could grab access to the metal. The rich believed they had the right—God-given, no less—to run their economic affairs any way they chose, no matter how much pain and suffering and death it caused. Many of the nation's most infamous and despised capitalists, such as Henry Clay Frick and Andrew Carnegie, created their wealth from mining in the eastern coal mines, as well as from the steel mills that used that coal to fuel their operations.[4]

In 1892, after a brutal miners' strike that ended with the miners blowing up a mine, after which the Idaho governor declared martial law and banned the strikers' nascent union, miners throughout the West formed the Western Federation of Miners. The WFM believed that only by unionizing all the mines—a strategy called "industrial unionism"—could workers succeed. This was still a radical idea in 1893. That they came to this idea at the same time as Eugene Debs should not surprise us. Finally, American workers realized that capitalism would not work for them. But the question of industrial versus craft unionism remained divisive for decades, dividing the working class between unions who saw the world in very different ways.[5]

The WFM's industrial unionism claimed that all miners had common interests, no matter what job they held in the mining industry. This proved attractive to workers such as Little who saw injustice in the world and wanted to revolt against it. In 1894, the WFM won a huge victory at Cripple Creek, Colorado, one of the main mine districts in the American West. Soon the new union had 28,000 members, and until 1903 it dominated the Colorado mines, operating as one of the strongest American unions of this era. But that year, the governor of Colorado crushed the WFM by declaring martial law in the town of Cripple Creek after the WFM went on strike. State violence remained employers' backstop against worker power.[6]

Little joined the WFM shortly after he arrived in the West. He soon became not only a WFM member but an organizer. This was his first major organizing experience. We do not know that many details about his daily activities. Historians rely on records—written or otherwise—to study the past, but workers often do not write down what they do every day; the same is true of other oppressed groups. So the records don't answer all the questions we would like to know about Little. Also, he did not live long enough to write his memoirs, and when he was alive, he was too busy organizing for revolutionary change to bother with thinking about his legacy. However, we do know he gained the respect of miners, and that in 1906 he spoke at the annual May Day parade in the mining town of Globe, Arizona, and thereafter became a desired speaker at union events in the region.[7]

In 1905, the Western Federation of Miners helped create the Industrial Workers of the World. The IWW gathered radicals from around the nation to form an alternative to the craft unionism of the era. Over time, it developed an ideology centered on bringing together all workers into one big union, which would then organize a general strike that would spark the workers' revolution and ultimately bring down capitalism. More concretely, the IWW called for worker activism at the point of production, creating power to set the stage for eventual revolution that would begin by workers engaging in strikes. Over the next fifteen years, it provided the most important framework American radicalism had ever seen. The WFM would not stay in the IWW for very long;

new and more conservative leadership took it back to its western roots.[8] But Little found the IWW's mission irresistible. He broke with the WFM at its 1907 convention, when he loudly proclaimed himself for IWW principles and the WFM leadership expelled him for it.[9]

Little had some learning to do. In 1907, he spoke to Mexican miners in Clifton-Morenci, Arizona. He told them that he knew what was best for them, giving them what he called "fatherly advice." Even radical unionists often treated Mexican workers as children. The Mexicans promptly evicted him from their meeting, noting they could conduct their own business and make their own decisions. Racism is not something we can just say we reject. We have to work to reject it and learn from our mistakes. It must be a lifelong struggle.[10]

In 1909, Little went to Missoula, Montana, getting involved in that city's free speech fight. This was one of several struggles across the American West in which the IWW demanded that cities protect the constitutional right of workers to publicly share their views. IWW speakers claimed that getting on a soapbox and preaching to the public about the need for revolution was protected by the First Amendment; however, then and now, the Constitution applies only if authorities permit it to be applied. The authorities frequently jailed Wobblies (as IWW members were commonly known) for speaking out in public. The IWW's strategy was to flood the prisons and force the city to take on the huge expense of holding and feeding them while the IWW continued to attract more Wobblies to the cities to show they could not be intimidated. Usually the strategy worked, though often at great physical cost to the men who were involved, as Little would soon find out. Little himself spoke out for freedom and was sentenced to jail for it. It would not be the last time.[11]

After Missoula, Little went to Spokane, Washington, where another free speech fight was taking place. He received a thirty-day sentence for daring to read the Declaration of Independence in a public place. The Spokane police routinely beat up the prisoners, used fire hoses on them in the cold northwestern winter, placed them in overcrowded prisons, withheld their food, and sprayed steam on them in what they called the "hotbox." Little was among those facing these tortures. Guards tried to force him to work on a rock pile. Little refused. So they housed him in an unheated former school building for the month he was in prison.[12]

We cannot overstate Little's bravery. He wasn't a big guy and he wasn't that strong, but he was brave. None of this broke Little's spirit. After his release, he immediately threw himself into another free speech fight, this time in Fresno, California. Over the next few years, he would help lead free speech fights in at least four other places: San Diego; Kansas City; Peoria, Illinois; and Webb City, Missouri, a mining town in the southwest part of that state. In each, he faced the same violent cops and torture in prison.[13]

Little became perhaps the IWW's most effective organizer. He would go anywhere, under any conditions, to push forward the worker struggle. This meant putting his life on the line, again and again. In 1913, he went to the Mesabi Range in Minnesota, assisting in a copper workers' strike. Company thugs kidnapped Little, took him out of town, and held him at gunpoint. Upon hearing what had happened, the striking workers engaged in a dramatic rescue effort and recovered him.[14]

In 1914, Little won a spot on the IWW's Executive Committee, a sign of the respect he had earned through his organizing. Five IWW Executive Committee members, including Little, had only one eye, including its leader Big Bill Haywood. We don't know why Little lost his eye, but many of these Wobblies had lost their eye at work.

That so many IWW members had missing eyes can help us understand why workers would listen to Little's revolutionary message. Take the example of the autoworker Charles Weaver. In 1906, Weaver had lost an eye while working in a dye factory. Despite his disability, he had to take care of himself, as the country had no social safety net for injured workers. Then, in 1913, while working in an auto plant, he lost the other eye when a crowbar struck it. He received no compensation for his blindness, meaning he had to support himself for the rest of his life, despite losing both eyes on the job. While we know nothing of Weaver's politics, one can see why some workers in a similar situation would join the IWW. All capitalism had done for them is disable them.[15]

The arrests, the beatings, the torture—none of this stopped Little's organizing. In 1916, back in Duluth, Minnesota, he and other IWW organizers were arrested for two murders they did not commit, one of a sheriff and the other of a Finnish soda pop distributor who died in a confrontation between strikers and law enforcement. The organizers won their release, but three rank-and-file workers received twenty-year prison terms, even though the verbal deal was that they would serve one year in exchange for a guilty plea. Shortly after his release, Little went to northern Michigan to assist striking iron miners fighting for decent wages and working conditions. Employers had him arrested, beaten, and tied up, and then his attackers feigned they were about to lynch him, tying a rope around his neck. They eventually let him go, but it was a premonition of what he would face the following year.[16]

When the U.S. joined World War I in 1917, the IWW leadership feared the government would use the organization's radicalism as an excuse to crack down on it. There was good reason to feel that way. President Woodrow Wilson brought organized labor into key government positions in an unprecedented way during the war, but only what he considered "respectable" labor. That meant the largely nonpolitical craft unions of the American Federation of Labor. Wilson generally supported union rights if the unions had moderate politics and he wanted to limit strikes during the war.[17] But the IWW and other radicals, the people who called for a full-fledged transformation of the American system? They deserved the iron hand of government repression, according to Wilson and his allies. Understanding this, IWW head Big Bill Haywood was reluctant to take an open stance against the war. He feared that by doing so, the government would simply destroy his union.[18]

Haywood's equivocation outraged Little. He believed in standing up for revolution, regardless of the consequences. He also knew that equivocation on the war would not stop the government from using the war as an excuse to crush radicals.. He demanded that the IWW fully denounce the war as not a war against foreign aggression, but the capitalist murder of the world's workers forced to fight it.

Most of the IWW leadership simply felt the union wasn't strong enough to resist the government on the war. Instead, leaders told workers to judge the war for themselves and make their decision based on their conscience, which betrayed Little's sharply felt sense of what was right. He told his IWW colleagues, "Either we're for this capitalistic slaughterfest or we're against it. I'm ready to face a firing squad rather than compromise. I'd rather take a firing squad."[19] There's no question that he meant it too. He may have feared dying but also knew the likelihood that he may well die in the service of the working class.

Little went back on the road to keep organizing. If he couldn't convince Haywood and his other comrades to resist the war, at least he could keep pushing workers toward revolutionary change.

He next went to Bisbee, Arizona, a town he knew from past experience was totally controlled by copper companies. The major mine there was owned by Phelps Dodge, which would later become the largest copper company in the world. Workers in Bisbee faced terrible conditions, both inside and outside the mines. The mines had enormous safety problems; worker housing was dilapidated. Miner Fred Watson recalled, "It was a pretty tough town. The conditions in the mines were intolerable. Absolutely. They never mentioned anything the miners asked for. Their demands were never mentioned."[20]

The IWW had special appeal to members of the West's mining, logging, and agricultural camps. These were workers at the very bottom of the social order, despised as they traveled around the country, often hoboing on freight trains. The union's anti-racist statements attracted Black, Mexican, and even Chinese and Japanese workers. Fighting white supremacy made the IWW an even bigger threat to the social order.

In Bisbee, many of the white miners joined an American Federation of Labor–affiliated union, while many of the Mexicans and some of the eastern Europeans joined the IWW. In May 1917, the AFL-affiliated union called a strike and the IWW agreed to join it. Within a few days, 85 percent of workers were striking. They wanted a pay raise, better working and living conditions, an end to the practice of mine blasting while workers were in the mine, a pay raise, and an end to putting union workers on a blacklist. Little helped them build these demands, organize the workers, and move the struggle forward. He even led a meeting with the governor of Arizona to urge him to mediate the conflict.[21]

The IWW gained most of its pay demands in June, as companies commonly raised the low wages to buy off workers from continuing their strike and forcing corporations from giving up power at work. Shortly after, trying to escape what he feared was a potential lynching by the copper industry's thugs. Little got in a car with some allies. The car wrecked and Little broke his ankle. He spent ten days in the hospital, limping out of Bisbee in early July. A few days later, Phelps Dodge ordered a deputized posse to round up anyone they thought was a Wobbly—which basically entailed any Mexican miner they could find—put them on a train, and drop them in the middle of the desert on the New Mexico border in the heat of summer. The infamous Bisbee Deportation, as it was known, became one of the most infamous violations of civil and labor rights in American history. Newspapers in Bisbee claimed all the strikers were pro-German and wanted to destroy the nation's war effort, an absurd claim but one that proved Little's argument that the government would not equivocate in destroying the union, regardless of which stance IWW leadership took.[22]

Little headed from Bisbee to Butte, Montana. By this time, he was a physically broken man. The years of jumping on and off moving trains to travel, all the beatings, all the torture, a serious hernia, the broken ankle took their toll. But his heart remained as strong as ever. Just before Little went to Butte, the IWW propagandist Ralph Chaplin, who in 1915 wrote the legendary labor song "Solidarity Forever," expressed concern to him about his physical state. But Little responded, "Don't worry, fellow worker, all we're going to need now is guts."[23] Well, Little had guts—no one ever questioned that.

The Anaconda Mining Company controlled Butte. It produced 10 percent of the world's copper. It also hated unions. In the late nineteenth century, Butte had perhaps the nation's strongest union culture. Some called it the "Gibraltar of Unionism." But in 1903, Anaconda had crushed the union and ran Butte with an iron hand from then on. After 1912, no one could work in the Butte mines without a "rustling card," which was effectively a permit Anaconda granted to workers on an individual basis. The company used this card to drive out anyone suspected of union organizing.[24]

Although Butte miners had been strong AFL members during their heyday, the circumstances had changed, and the post-1903 situation in Butte was precisely the kind of scenario the Industrial Workers of the World looked for: desperate yet proud workers who could be roused toward radical action. In June, a fire in the Speculator Mine killed 164 miners, the worst hard-rock mining disaster in American history. The surviving workers responded by walking out in a spontaneous strike. They formed the Metal Mine Workers' Union, demanded the end of the rustling card system, the protection of collective bargaining and free speech rights, the observance of state mining laws, the discharge of the state mine inspector, and a wage increase. This soon expanded into new demands for safety instruction for miners and the construction of manholes in the mines. By June 29, fifteen thousand men were off the job. Of course, the companies responded by blaming the

IWW. They accused the workers of being radicals and having pro-German sympathies at a time when the country was at war.[25]

Things did not go well for Little in Butte. Most of the miners were not interested in radicalism, still holding on to their older union traditions. Little tried to connect the capitalist profiteering of World War I with the capitalist profiteering that cost the lives of so many men at the Speculator. For Little, the warmongers, the capitalists, and the private detective agencies such as the Pinkertons that spied on workers' attempts to organize were all part of the same oppressive machine that could only be dismantled by revolution. This did not move many Butte workers. But that is organizing: not everyone is ready to hear your message.[26]

Little's arrival and especially his outspoken opposition to World War I threw Anaconda elites into a fury. When anti-labor spies reported that Little was calling for revolution during union meetings, the companies decided to kill him. Little's friends told him to leave town. But he would not listen to them.

Maybe he did not believe them. Maybe he did not care. Maybe he was just tired. In any case, he refused to leave Butte. On the night of August 1, 1917, six masked men came to his hotel room. They tied him up, took him to the edge of town, beat him, and hanged him from a railroad trestle. On his chest they pinned a note that read "3-7-77," a code used by the vigilantes to take credit for the murder. A few days later, Montana declared martial law against war opponents and rounded up radicals of all stripes—a massive state-sponsored violation of civil liberties. The people who murdered Little were never investigated, found, or prosecuted. They took their actions to the grave. In early 1918, Montana responded to men such as Little by passing the Montana Sedition Law, legalizing prison sentences of up to twenty years for speaking out against the government in that state.[27]

Sometimes, organizers and radicals see a heroic future in martyrdom. That was the case of the anti-slavery radical John Brown when he faced execution for trying to start a war on slavery in 1859. It was also the case of the IWW miner and songwriter Joe Hill, executed in Utah in 1915 for a crime he didn't commit. It was Hill who coined the great phrase about his own death: "Don't mourn, organize."[28]

I have no idea what Frank Little thought as he faced his martyrdom. But I am sure he would agree with Hill. On one hand, Little's death is only one of so many terrible moments in American history;

on the other, Little always kept his one good eye on the prize of worker liberation. No matter how bad things get today, we can gain inspiration from Little's dignity, vision, and struggle. Whatever we face will likely pale in comparison to his suffering. We can at least maintain the optimism for the future that never left Little's revolutionary mind.

8

Elizabeth Gurley Flynn

A Rebel Life

Throughout history, there are moments when a very young person steps into the fray and becomes a hero and leader, guiding people in search of a way forward. This phenomenon is not uncommon. In 2018, after the tragic high school shooting in Parkland, Florida, survivors such as David Hogg and Emma (now X) González became national leaders in fighting gun violence. Swedish activist Greta Thunberg became the worldwide voice of young people demanding urgent action on climate change after furiously addressing the 2018 United Nations Climate Conference. Even as far back as Joan of Arc, young people can inspire a nation to rise and fight. In American history, one such figure was Elizabeth Gurley Flynn, known as the "Rebel Girl" who rallied the masses of her time.

The daughter of socialist Irish immigrants, Elizabeth Gurley Flynn grew up in New York City learning to fight for the liberation of the working class. This was a time when socialism was emerging as a prominent response to the terror of American capitalism. It had taken American workers decades to understand that capitalism did not serve their interests. European immigrants, who brought with them the ideologies of Karl Marx and other European socialists, helped these ideas take root in American society. The Flynns, like millions of other workers, were poor and disillusioned with capitalism. They wanted an alternative. As a young girl, Flynn became a devotee of socialism. While her understanding of socialism changed over the course of her life, Flynn never abandoned the dream of a socialist world.[1]

As a young girl, Flynn began attending rallies and political actions in the socialist haven of New York's Lower East Side. Poverty and political ferment created a generation of radicals, as this book's chapter on Clara Lemlich demonstrates. At just fifteen years old, Flynn gave her first public speech, titled "What Socialism Will Do for Women." Her eloquence and conviction impressed her audience, leading her to speak more frequently, and she soon became a famed orator for radical causes of the time. People dubbed her "an East Side Joan of Arc." She dropped out of high school, thinking the fight for revolution more important. While she later regretted the decision, Flynn still managed to acquire a superb education, both in books and in life.[2]

Flynn joined the Industrial Workers of the World in 1906 and, by 1907, worked as an IWW organizer. The IWW attracted deeply dedicated and optimistic leftists, like Frank Little, who put their bodies on the line to create the revolution. Flynn traveled the country, organizing the most desperate and destitute workers for the union. As a member of the IWW, Flynn believed in syndicalism—using direct action at the point of production (i.e., the workplace) to incite change. At this stage in her life, she had a tremendously optimistic view that a working-class rebellion could lead to revolution, if only she could help activate and organize her comrades into taking power at the workplace.[3]

Flynn was a direct and forward-thinking young woman, coming of age in the early twentieth century, when women began to speak more openly about sex. Activists such as Margaret Sanger challenged laws that banished public discussions of sex and faced arrest for opening birth control clinics. The anarchist Emma Goldman enjoyed open sexual relationships and fought to make sexual freedom part of the revolution. Flynn embraced this newfound liberation in her personal life. However, she, like many women of her time, always faced a sexual double standard. The men she and Goldman were involved with had far more freedom to engage in sexual relationships without jeopardizing their respectability, a luxury not afforded to women in often puritanical leftist movements. Despite this, Flynn strongly believed that feminism should exist as part of the class struggle and always valued class analysis first and foremost. This helps explain why she never centered sexuality in her public work, though she still had to contend with the hypocrisy faced by women in her position.[4]

In 1907, Flynn met J.A. Jones, a miner and organizer in Minnesota. They married and had a son, but the marriage was short-lived. Jones, nearly two decades older than Flynn, wanted a traditional marriage while she did not. Flynn went on to have romantic relationships with other radicals, most notably the Italian anarchist Carlos Tresca. Despite the challenges, including sometimes delivering talks while pregnant, Flynn became known as the Rebel Girl as she traveled the nation, using her powerful oratory to rally workers for radical causes.[5]

In 1909, Flynn went to Spokane, Washington, to support the city's free speech fight, where Frank Little among others were making a stand for the First Amendment and radical worker action. The conflict began with a scam orchestrated by employers. Timber companies and farmers would contract with employment agencies, forcing workers to go through these agencies to secure jobs. Workers paid for the service, only to arrive at remote job sites and find that no work was available. If the job wasn't there when they arrived in the camp or farm, they were out of luck and had to return to Spokane to try again. This blatant exploitation fueled workers' anger, leading to the rise of IWW organizers in Spokane. The city's response to the IWW was brutal, with authorities resorting to mass torture of organizers, as Little experienced.[6]

When Flynn arrived in Spokane, she was nineteen years old and pregnant. In a bold act of protest, she chained herself to a lamppost, forcing the police to detach and arrest her. The city charged her with conspiracy to break the law, a far more serious charge than most workers faced. While in jail, Flynn smuggled a story to the IWW newspaper *Industrial Worker,* alleging that the Spokane police were using female prisoners to run a brothel out of the jail. Though the police tried to confiscate all copies of the story, Flynn had made her point. She was becoming a public figure and fearless organizer, well aware that her gender and pregnancy offered some protection, a lesson she had learned during her time organizing in Montana, where the police beat her husband but left her unharmed. In Spokane, the jurors ultimately found her not guilty of conspiracy—likely more out of sympathy for her gender and the fact that she was pregnant than belief that she was not a radical.[7]

Owing to her age, her pregnancy, and her bravery, the Spokane episode raised Flynn's national profile. She quickly became one of the IWW's top speakers and writers. However, it wasn't just Flynn's commitment to the workers' struggle that drew people to her. It was her sheer being, her charisma, her powerful ability to motivate others. She had a knack for explaining class struggle in plain, accessible language to workers who often struggled with English. One of the great challenges of socialism has long been that of taking often obscure theory and translating it into language that can actually organize people. IWW leader Big Bill Haywood was a master of this skill, and so was Flynn. When the socialist Max Eastman saw her speak during the Paterson, New Jersey, textile strike in 1913, he stated he felt "strongly the likeness of all human beings and their problems." The journalist Mary Heaton Vorse made a similar observation, noting that when Flynn spoke, it was as if "something beautiful and strong had swept through the people and welded them together." That kind of charisma is rare. Not all of us are natural organizers, but Flynn's example reminds us that everyone has their own gifts to contribute to the struggle for justice. You don't have to be good at everything. You just need to use your strengths to make the world a better place.[8]

Flynn became a traveling organizer, helping wherever the struggle emerged. Just hearing the Rebel Girl speak inspired countless workers. After the Lawrence, Massachusetts, textile strike of 1912 (also known as the Bread and Roses Strike), in perhaps the IWW's greatest victory, she gained ever more recognition for her work. A key part of her work in the Bread and Roses Strike was leading the fight to free her comrades Joe Ettor and Arturo Giovannitti, who were falsely accused of a murder in order to sideline them from organizing. After these trumped-up charges, Flynn and Haywood took over the IWW's organizing effort in Lawrence.

Flynn also organized the Children's Crusade with her friend Margaret Sanger, which resulted in relocating children from impoverished striking households in Lawrence to the homes of socialists in major northeastern cities. This initiative, along with a series of children's parades, proved to be such a propaganda victory that authorities responded by beating mothers at the Lawrence train station to stop another round of children from leaving. That terrible action led to federal investigation and the eventual surrender of the textile mill owners. The IWW won, the mill owners agreed to pay raises and better working conditions, and Flynn was an essential reason why it won.[9]

In 1913, Flynn's work during the silk workers' strike in Paterson, New Jersey, forged significant alliances between radical workers and upper-class liberals that lasted for the next decade and supported not only the IWW but other leftist causes. As in Lawrence, much of Flynn's primary challenge in Paterson was to get different immigrant groups, who often distrusted each other, to find a way to solidarity. She had the organizing skills to make this happen. She and other IWW organizers allowed the strikers to lead the actions while they provided advice and educated workers on solidarity and class struggle. She also organized large rallies designed to be a fun experience for workers so they would not feel demoralized. Eventually, she was arrested and jailed for supposedly inciting a riot. Although the IWW lost the silk workers' strike, and subsequently its expansion into eastern factories was largely halted, by 1914 Flynn stood alongside Eugene Debs as the most famous organizer in the United States. Her imprisonment only heightened her fame, and her wealthy liberal supporters in New York expressed their disgust over the persecution of their radical friend, drawing attention to other less-known radicals prosecuted on spurious charges.[10]

In 1914, an IWW organizer and songwriter named Joe Hill was arrested for a murder he did not commit. A grocer had been shot, and the state of Utah sentenced Hill to death. It is speculated that Hill was targeted because of his radical politics, as the prosecution had almost no evidence against him. Flynn traveled to Utah and made Hill one of the great martyrs of the American labor movement. She wrote article after article about the lack of justice in his case, his bravery in the face of repression, and his powerful songs. Although she could not save Hill from execution in 1915, this experience profoundly changed her life. Afterward, she increasingly focused on prisoner defense and civil liberties rather than direct labor organizing, providing critical solidarity work for those caught in the nation's carceral system, often on convictions based on little more than their radical beliefs.[11]

Unfortunately, Flynn's time with the IWW ended poorly, largely due to the internal conflicts of a union under constant government and police harassment. In 1916, after the miners strike in Minnesota's Mesabi Range that included the imprisonment of Frank Little, Big Bill Haywood had her expelled. That was over Flynn negotiating the deal where the rank and file leaders would plead guilty and then receive short sentences, but where they instead received twenty-year prison terms while Little and the other Wobbly organizers were freed. Haywood fired Flynn for insubordination and undermining the struggle. Flynn, in turn, accused Haywood of withholding defense funds because he disliked her. The full truth remains unclear, as federal authorities destroyed most of the IWW's archives and documents in 1923, and sadly the distrust between these two great organizers was irreparable. Flynn left the IWW the next year. Though she never again reached the prominence she had during her IWW days, she remained active in radical causes for the rest of her long career.[12]

In July 1916, someone bombed a parade organized by people who wanted the U.S. to join World War I in San Francisco, killing ten people and wounding forty others. The perpetrators have never been identified, but local authorities took advantage of the incident to arrest innocent leftists they wanted off the streets. Among those arrested were Tom Mooney and Warren Billings, who were convicted of the bombing based on false evidence. They received death sentences. Their wrongful conviction sparked a worldwide campaign among leftists for their release, with Flynn leading the charge, successfully freeing them in the late 1930s.[13]

Flynn continued organizing during World War I. She worked with the New York Bureau of Legal First Aid, the first organization to provide legal services to draft resisters. She also organized the Workers Defense Fund to raise money and support for activists imprisoned for opposing the war. She herself was arrested in 1917 for seditious conspiracy as part of a government sweep that targeted 168 IWW members, though her charges were dropped in 1919 and she spent only a weekend in prison. In fact, she spent most of her time, up until 1926, working night and day to free the nation's political prisoners.[14]

In 1920, armed robbers attacked a payroll clerk and a guard near Boston, resulting in the deaths of two company men. Suspicion quickly fell on the city's active Italian immigrant anarchist community, particularly targeting two men named Nicola Sacco and Bartolomeo Vanzetti. Both men were followers of Luigi Galleani, an Italian writer who advocated violence to overthrow the state. The year before, some of Galleani's followers had attempted to assassinate A. Mitchell Palmer, the attorney general and architect of the Red Scare crackdown on radicals during and after World War I. In any case, the judge in Sacco and Vanzetti's trial, Webster Thayer, openly bragged that he was going to send those "anarchistic bastards," as he called them, to the chair—and ended up doing so. It became an international cause to free Sacco and Vanzetti.[15]

Flynn played a critical role in the battle to free Sacco and Vanzetti through the Workers Defense Fund. She recruited and paid for a legal team to defend them and remained active in their defense strategy. Flynn realized that, although she considered herself a radical leftist, forming alliances with liberals was essential, and she committed herself to coalition building. She helped to cofound an organization called the League for Mutual Aid. In this, she worked with the American Civil Liberties Union (ACLU). They raised money for America's unjustly convicted radical prisoners. Despite her great efforts, though, Massachusetts executed the two anarchists in 1927.[16]

In 1926, Flynn collapsed from exhaustion after her work on a textile strike in Passaic, New Jersey. She was also heartbroken to discover that her comrade and lover Carlos Tresca had had an affair with her younger sister and got her pregnant. After these stressful events, Flynn mostly disappeared from politics for a decade. While on the West Coast during a speaking tour, she passed out and Marie Equi, a labor and feminist radical who lived in Portland, Oregon, took her in to take care of her. Equi and Flynn probably had a romantic relationship during these years. Scholars have also surmised that Equi probably manipulated and perhaps abused Flynn, as she controlled Flynn's life for the next decade. Finally, friends of Flynn engaged in a dramatic rescue of her from Equi's home in 1936. For the rest of her life, Flynn mostly refused to talk about this period or the relationship.[17]

In 1937, Flynn joined the Communist Party (CP). Given her fame—which was still strong despite her decade away from the struggle—the Communists believed this to be a major public relations coup. After many years with the relatively disorganized IWW, Flynn liked the discipline the CP placed on its members. She began writing a column about women for the *Daily Worker,* the CP's newspaper. However, becoming a Communist was a step too far for Flynn's former liberal allies. The ACLU ejected her from its board in 1939, thus embracing an anticommunism that broke previously friendly ties between free speech liberals and radicals. This move marked the ACLU's limits of political tolerance, and it faced scathing criticism from both liberals and leftist radicals for its red-baiting. For Flynn—at this time in a similar place as Clara Lemlich, another middle-aged woman with decades of struggle already behind her—the global success of the CP seemed to be a harbinger of a revolution that would bring freedom to the world's proletariat. Regardless of what one might think of the Soviet Union today, there is virtually nothing more pointless and counterproductive than tsk-tsking activists of nearly a century ago for fighting to see their dreams of liberation come to fruition in the most logical way they knew.[18]

Flynn became one of the leaders of the CP in the United States. After the decade in Oregon, she threw herself into the work, organizing, speaking, and writing as much as possible in favor of communism and workers' rights. During World War II, Flynn pushed for day care for the children of working women and for greater economic equality as well, in addition to encouraging workers to labor hard and win the war, aligning with the CP's position. In 1942, she ran for Congress as an independent from her New York district and garnered fifty thousand votes.[19]

After World War II, however, the government launched another attack on Flynn and other leftists for their political beliefs. A few years earlier, in 1940, Congress had passed the Smith Act, which made it a felony to advocate for the overthrow of the U.S. government. Although the nation never had anything close to a violent overthrow of its government—not until Donald Trump launched his coup attempt in 2021—the government used the Smith Act to crush leftists. While Flynn had never advocated for any specific use of violence against the government, it did not matter. She served two years in a federal women's prison in Alderson, West Virginia, during which time she turned sixty-six years old.

Flynn had the option to avoid serving her sentence—by accepting deportation to the Soviet Union—but she refused. Flynn was both a communist and a patriot who loved America and her family here. She wished to see the United States become a country dedicated to worker power; it wasn't a place she wanted to leave. As was the case for many American leftists, revolution and a love of country were not diametrically opposed. The problem was capitalism and militarism, not America itself. She decided she would rather serve her time in prison as a symbol of how America had betrayed her rather than betray the country she so loved.[20]

While in prison, Flynn worked on her autobiography. *The Rebel Girl,* published in 1955, remains an important book in the genre of American leftist memoirs. After her release, Flynn traveled to the Soviet Union, where people viewed her as an American hero, and by this point *The Rebel Girl* was translated into Russian. There, she met Soviet premier Nikita Khrushchev. The American government took away Flynn's passport in 1962, denying her the right to travel, but a federal judge overturned the government's decision the next year. She went to the USSR once again, dying there in 1964 at the age of seventy-four. She received a state funeral in Moscow, in which over 25,000 people gathered to honor this hero of the worker struggle. Her remains were then sent back to the United States for burial.[21]

Elizabeth Gurley Flynn lived a full life of radicalism. She bridged the span all the way from the early days of the IWW to the peak of the Communist Party in the Soviet Union. She survived the worst periods of the Cold War and came out on top to speak her piece about revolution. The Rebel Girl never compromised her beliefs and her principles, even at the risk of alienating other leftists, or losing liberal allies, or failing to keep herself out of prison. This unabashed modern woman embraced her sexuality, regardless of whom she was attracted to at any given time. She did the hard, often fruitless work of supporting the most despised prisoners in the United States, trying to free them from their death sentences. This is the truest form of a life radically lived, with hope for change and a determined belief that socialism can transform America. If Flynn is not a figure who can move us to action today, I don't know who in the past could.

9

Myles Horton

Organizing the South for Justice

Sometimes, change emerges from the most unexpected places. Why do so many grow up in a racist society and perpetuate its hate, while a few transcend it and dedicate their lives to fighting oppression? How can someone deeply embedded in a culture of inequality build bridges with the very people that culture harms? How can we bring together people who seem to have nothing in common? While we may not have the answers yet, the past offers guidance. Many of our most impactful organizers faced these very challenges, and their struggles can help us find a path forward.

This is the story of Myles Horton, whose work shaped both the labor and civil rights movements of the twentieth century. Born in 1905 in Savannah, Tennessee, Horton grew up poor and white in the peak of Jim Crow America. There's little reason to think that a person who grew up in these circumstances would later be one of the great fighters for justice, but Horton not only would reject the racism of his childhood, he also engaged in a lifelong struggle to create a South based on radical love and change.

Horton arrived in the world shortly after the demise of the Populist Party, a movement of poor farmers, mostly white but some Black, who organized around a platform that included corporate regulation, economic reform, and the introduction of an income tax.[1] Some rural workers became committed socialists. Horton's father joined the Workers' Alliance, a local leftist worker organization. His parents wanted to be teachers, but instead they were sharecroppers without high school educations. They pushed their son to understand that the privileged must live lives of personal sacrifice to build solidarity with the poor. Given how much Horton learned from his parents, a core tenet of his life was the belief that people did not need a formal education to do good and organize for change.[2]

Building on his parents' foiled dreams, Horton fought for an education for himself, and he ended up in New York at Union Theological Seminary. There, he became a student of Reinhold Niebuhr, one of the most influential liberal theologians in American history and later a mentor to the young Martin Luther King Jr. Like many who encountered Niebuhr, Horton found his beliefs both challenged and transformed. Niebuhr urged his students to critique capitalism and to unite the church and labor movement within a vision of socialist Christianity—exactly the message Horton longed to hear.[3]

As a southern white man, there was little precedent for the man Horton would become. He later said, "My first feeling about the wage system was that it was very unjust for somebody to have to work so hard and get so little, and for somebody else to have so much."[4] He also confronted racial discrimination as a young man. In 1928, Horton protested the segregation of YMCA college chapters and organized a desegregated luncheon.[5]

Horton was already familiar with the struggles of the southern white working class, but his education gave him a fresh perspective that galvanized his activism. In 1926, while organizing vacation Bible schools in Ozone, Tennessee, Horton found that local people were more concerned with practical needs—finding jobs, getting tested for typhoid, and restoring the deforested mountains—than religious instruction. The basic physical needs of the people struck a chord with Horton. This experience deeply affected him, and he began to consider how to organize people in a hostile environment for their collective betterment. He believed that popular education for adults was the answer.[6]

Horton then traveled, looking for models of social progress, including visiting Jane Addams's Hull House. Addams, a dedicated believer in the potential of America, told him what life was like to be a reformer in the United States—to face harassment, hate, sacrifice, but also the possibility of transformative change.[7] He visited Brookwood Labor School, an early center of working-class education sponsored by the labor movement. He also visited utopian communities, where groups of Americans chose to live separately from society to create their ideal lives. He looked for anything that would help fulfill his mission of southern transformation.[8]

Horton could have easily stayed in the North. Many left-leaning people from predominantly right-wing areas have made the choice to live in politically progressive areas—and continue to do so today. It is often easier to live in places where people share your beliefs. Moreover, there has always been plenty of work to do in the fight for racial and economic justice in cities like New York, Boston, Chicago, or virtually any other supposedly liberal northern city. In the North, you could engage in that work without facing life-threatening risks that came with organizing in the rural South. But Horton was a man of the South, and that's where he wanted to make change. So he went home.

Horton wasn't alone in his vision to bring social change to the South. One of his comrades was Don West, a teacher and pastor from north Georgia who, while still in high school, protested the racist 1915 film *The Birth of a Nation,* which helped revive the Ku Klux Klan. Horton and West decided to start their project where change was most needed. Ozone was still on Horton's mind—he wanted to help the people of southern Appalachia help themselves. In 1932, they founded what would become known as the Highlander Folk Center in Monteagle, Tennessee, on the Cumberland Plateau northwest of Chattanooga.

Grundy County was located a hundred miles southwest of Ozone, and poverty defined the county's small farmers and coal miners as it did in Ozone. Though they largely avoided political activism, the region's miners built a movement in the 1890s to resist the state's practice of leasing prisoners to mining companies for work, which undermined the labor of free workers and also exploited incarcerated people. This effort helped end convict leasing in Tennessee in 1899, and was exactly the kind of resistance Horton wanted to revive. At the peak of the Great Depression, with the county poorer than ever before, it seemed that change was possible.[9] But the whites of Grundy County also held a deep commitment to white supremacy—this was, after all, the height of Jim Crow. Challenging these racist views required tremendous sacrifice and commitment to long-term organizing in hostile conditions.

In creating Highlander, Horton and West drew inspiration from European education, much as Jane Addams did when she founded Hull House in Chicago nearly a half century before.[10] They traveled to Denmark to study the folk schools there, which aimed to empower rural people to take control of their own lives. They believed this model could be adapted to the South. Reinhold Niebuhr provided critical early support for Highlander, including leading fundraising efforts. His connections to social movements throughout the United States opened the necessary doors for Horton to get his efforts off the ground.

Almost immediately, Horton and West got involved in a local coal strike, where Horton was arrested for the first time. Shortly after Horton's arrest, the strike leader was shot in the back of the head and killed. It broke the strike and demonstrated to Horton what challenging the dominance of the coal mine operators meant in Grundy County. It also spurred local Tennessee elites to recognize the threat Horton and his Highlander Center posed. As early as 1934, they accused Highlander of being a center of communism in their conservative region. Although the county sought to keep Horton and West from teaching its children by banning the men from entering county school buildings, it did not close down their education programs.[11]

Horton taught Grundy County students, mostly adults but sometimes children, about economics, history, and their constitutional rights, which were constantly violated by the coal companies. This almost immediately paid dividends, as loggers came to Highlander asking for help in forming a union. Within a week of the workers forming the Cumberland Mountain Workers and Unemployed League, they launched their first strike. Slowly, people gained confidence that they could make a difference in improving their own lives through collective action.[12]

Highlander became a hub where organizers from outside the county and then around the South could share their knowledge and teach others, including other Highlander workers. In 1935, Dolph Vaughn, a coal miner on the blacklist for union activities, came to Highlander for classes. Though he learned a lot there, he knew more about organizing coal workers than anyone at Highlander. So he began to teach the classes himself under Horton's instruction.[13]

Soon, workers around the South turned to Highlander for support. In 1937, Horton traveled to Lumberton, North Carolina, to aid in organizing a textile strike. Despite threats of lynching, Horton remained undeterred. He did not want to lead the strike; instead, he wanted strikers to coordinate the effort themselves. He worked with them to form committees and establish democratic processes, learning that sometimes an organizer must provide guidance to people who need their experience and knowledge. He brought these valuable lessons back to Highlander.[14]

Highlander soon gained a national reputation as a stronghold for political radicalism in the region least likely to tolerate it. Highlander opened only a few years before the development of the Congress of Industrial Organizations (CIO) in 1937. The CIO was a new union federation that did not officially tolerate racism, and it aimed to organize the South. However, rank and file whites often resisted the racial integration of their unions. To overcome the racism that divided the working class meant finding ways for white and Black workers to communicate, understand each other, and build solidarity. The powers of the South recognized the CIO's intention and sought to undermine its efforts by engaging in race-baiting tactics. They made incendiary claims against CIO organizers, including that they were northern Jews intent on forcing their daughters to have sex with Black men.[15]

When the CIO sought to organize the South, it saw Horton and Highlander not only as allies, but as critical components of its strategy. In a region hostile to unions, Highlander provided a discreet organizing space, shielded from the scrutiny of company spies. By 1942, approximately 90 percent of those attending Highlander's educational programs were involved in the southern union movement.[16]

Horton welcomed CIO organizers to Highlander, facilitating connections with Black workers and welcoming Black activists fighting for civil rights. Moreover, Highlander maintained a strict policy against racial segregation. Horton and his comrades refused to replicate the system of segregation that defined the South and divided workers by race. This caused discomfort among many white southern leftists, who had to confront and overcome their own prejudices. Horton would not compromise: accept integration or go home.

Horton developed an organizing model that emphasized building on individuals' own experiences. During this period, workers faced tremendous repression throughout the South. The apparel industry had moved to the South explicitly to avoid the kind of unions that organizers like Clara Lemlich built.[17] Coal miners, performing one of the most perilous jobs in America, saw union organizers routinely murdered by companies.[18] Black workers faced even harsher oppression, working the most dangerous and difficult duties in the butcheries and steel mills of the cities, as well as the farms they sharecropped in the countryside.[19] These workers had a lot in common—if they could get beyond their histories of racial animosity, they could organize for radical change. No one would tell these workers how to act or think; they had to figure it out for themselves. Myles Horton and his colleagues at Highlander helped them do just that. Through World War II, Highlander remained dedicated to union organizing in the South.[20]

In 1935, Horton married Zilphia Johnson. Zilphia's father, an Arkansas coal mine superintendent who later bought the mine he ran, had no sympathy for organized labor. While Zilphia was at home from college in 1930, the Reverend Claude Williams came to minister at a local Presbyterian church. He supported social justice and began organizing her father's workers into the Progressive Miners' Union in 1934. Zilphia joined his effort, much to her father's outrage, and embraced leftist politics. Her father disowned her, but she had found a higher calling than being the daughter of a coal boss. She attended a workshop at Highlander, met Myles Horton, fell in love, and they married.[21]

Between 1938 and 1956, Zilphia Horton directed music and drama at Highlander, where the folk school ideal emphasized art and creative performance and building solidarity through working-class productions. Alongside Highlander allies and husband and wife duo Guy and Candie Carawan, she played a crucial role in uncovering folk songs from the South that could be repurposed for social movements. This included the old spiritual "We Shall Overcome," which became the anthem of the 1950s and '60s civil rights movement.[22] Unfortunately, in 1956, Zilphia died in a heartbreaking accident. While reaching for a glass of water, she accidentally grabbed a glass of typewriting cleaning fluid, which is poisonous, and drank it. She was only forty-five years old when she died.

To recover from Zilphia's death, Horton threw himself into his work. When the CIO started Operation Dixie in 1946, a flawed and mostly failed attempt to organize the South, Highlander played a central role, including hosting interracial gatherings for southern workers. However, despite Highlander's advice and assistance, the CIO struggled to win elections in the South. Operation Dixie failed and the South remained largely unorganized. By 1953, toward the end of the CIO organizing era and only two years before it reunited with the staid American Federation of Labor, it broke ties with Highlander.[23]

Horton found plenty of organizing to do outside of the labor movement. With the expansion of the civil rights movement underway in the early 1950s, Highlander again offered its expertise to young organizers to learn, build community, and forge solidarity. In 1953, the center began holding seminars in which both Black and white southerners could come together to discuss integration—a radical idea at that time and place. Horton and his Highlander staff began to shift their focus to a full-on assault on racial discrimination. They realized that white support for Black rights had diminished after World War II, and the anti-communist hysteria of the late 1940s meant supporting racial integration was riskier than ever. Most white workers would not show up to support Black workers, and relatively liberal white southern churches refused even to give lip service to desegregation. Meanwhile, the people most excited and energized by Highlander activities were Black organizers, whether working or middle class. After Operation Dixie's failures, Horton shifted gears in response to the new realities of the South. Highlander would become the country's single most important white-run institution supporting civil rights.[24]

In 1953, Highlander started opening what were known as "Citizenship Schools" in Black communities in South Carolina. Horton hired the great Black organizer Septima Clark, a longtime Highlander participant and later a staffer, to teach Black farmers to read. Realizing that white teachers could not be effective in these communities, Horton himself never entered these classrooms. Instead, Citizenship Schools were run by Black people, taught by Black volunteer teachers to educate Black students. This approach was consistent with Horton's belief in building power for local communities to fight their own battles, not in presenting himself as a leader of people.[25]

Including the story of Highlander and Horton in our histories should change our popular understanding of social movements. Take Rosa Parks, for example. Public memory often portrays Parks as this somewhat random woman who decided to take a stand (or a seat, more accurately) as a single isolated act of resistance to segregation. In fact, Parks had trained at Highlander before her pivotal show of defiance. Ignoring this fact obscures two important points: first, civil rights activism involved decades of planning and organization before 1955; and second, it was a direct result of collective effort rather than a spontaneous act by a single person. By not highlighting Parks's training at Highlander, we reduce the rich, collaborative history of the movement to stories of individual heroism, overlooking the extensive organizing and collective action that sustained these social changes.

Parks later said, "At Highlander, I found out for the first time in my adult life that this could be a unified society, that there was such a thing as people of different races and backgrounds meeting together in workshops and living together in peace and harmony. It was a place I was very reluctant to leave. I gained strength there to preserve in my work for freedom, not just for blacks, but all oppressed people."[26]

Of course, many white authorities in the South knew very well that figures like Rosa Parks and Martin Luther King Jr. had received training at Highlander. They labeled Highlander as communist and a site of interracial relationships, charges that were not true, although Horton and other Highlander workers had no problem with either. Since its inception, Tennessee conservatives hated Highlander and sought a reason to close it. Finally, in 1961, they were able to shut it down on a technicality: Highlander was accused of serving alcohol without a license. Highlander had allowed attendees to leave their pocket change to cover the cost of beer, which was used as a pretext to close it down, covering up the fact that the real violation was Highlander's promotion of integration and civil rights.[27]

Horton did not let the state of Tennessee bulldoze him. He told the media, "You can padlock a building. But you can't padlock an idea."[28] He relocated Highlander to the town of New Market, east of Knoxville. While local authorities hated Highlander, they had no choice but to accept its existence. Under Horton's leadership, Highlander was reorganized and, over the next several years, it continued to help train and sponsor civil rights activists. One of Highlander's biggest contributions was its influence on the Freedom Schools that the Student Nonviolent Coordinating Committee created in Mississippi in 1964. Many SNCC leaders, including a man named Bob Moses, whom you will read more about soon, had undergone at least one training at Highlander. Moses and others carried these ideas to Mississippi, where they played a key role in the Freedom Summer campaign of 1964, exposing the rest of the nation to the region's racial violence.[29]

Horton led Highlander until he retired in 1969, but he remained engaged in his life's project until his death in 1990. He was eighty-four years old. Highlander did not die with Horton, however. It shifted with the needs of Appalachia, and under the leadership of John Gaventa, and then Jim Sessions in the 1990s, it worked closely with regional environmental campaigns against coal companies strip-mining the mountains. Both Gaventa and Sessions had extensive histories leading justice campaigns against the mining industry. Beginning in the early 2000s, Highlander attended to the needs of Spanish-speaking immigrants working for the region's farms and factories. It focused on building youth-based programs and providing a critical organizing space for gay Appalachia, especially under the leadership of Suzanne Pharr, who in the 1990s had led critical organizing efforts against anti-gay ballot measures in Oregon.

The spirit of Myles Horton lives on in the mountains of East Tennessee. In fact, many local people still hate Highlander. In 2019, white supremacists burned down the main office building, which tragically included most of the center's archives. Highlander has always had the right enemies—racism, classism, and homophobia—and continues to be a beacon of training and organizing to this day. I attended an amazing program there once and encourage others to do the same if you can.

Horton once said, "When people criticize me for not having any respect for existing structures and institutions, I protest. I say I give institutions and structures and traditions all the respect that I think they deserve. That's usually mighty little, but there are things that I do respect. They have to earn that respect. They have to earn it by serving people. They don't earn it just by age or legality or tradition."[30] This is a powerful philosophy to guide our work. No matter how aged or powerful an institution may be—such as the Supreme Court, to give one important example—it does not deserve our respect if it uses its power to hurt the masses.

We should also take inspiration from Horton's theories of organizing. His folk school model incited massive change in the South and throughout the nation, bringing people together who had disagreements on the most fundamental aspects of their collective existence, especially concerning race. Finally, we can take inspiration from Horton's commitment to organizing in one's own hometown. Moving to more liberal cities as leftists from conservative areas is a personal choice. But we should keep in mind that real change often happens when we stay in challenging environments and work to foster justice and equality from within.

10

Lucy Randolph Mason

To Win These Rights

Many of the organizers discussed in this book come from a working-class background, but not all of them. The history of wealthy Americans leading fights for equality is actually quite long. Of course, far more rich people have fought to keep their wealth and oppress the poor. Some talk about the need for social and economic change but do nothing about it and oppose anything that might affect their privilege. We can't choose how we grew up. Some of us had wealthy parents, some of us didn't. Irrespective of our parents' income and what university we graduated from (if we were lucky enough or even wanted to attend college), we all can dedicate our lives to making positive change. We can transform the world by both questioning our own privilege and using that privilege for the common good.

Moving forward in a politically productive way does not mean apologizing for our past or feeling shame about it. It means taking your skills and applying them for the betterment of society through acts of solidarity. It means admitting your privilege, but then also doing something about it. It means turning pointless liberal guilt into a crusade for flattening the power structure and ensuring that, in the future, everyone has the advantages you did. It also means not letting issues of privilege get in the way of creating change. Too often today, talking about our privilege is an exercise in guilt rather than a tool to move our movements forward in a productive manner. The present and future are too important to bog down in rituals of apologies for how we grew up; the lives of people are on the line in our movements.

American history offers plenty examples of relatively wealthy people making positive change. Jane Addams is one such figure. While her early vision of political change was somewhat limited, she listened, learned, and transformed Hull House into a focal point of political activism in Chicago. She even collaborated with radical anarchist Lucy Parsons on unemployment marches and worked in solidarity with Ida B. Wells on anti-lynching efforts before becoming a mentor of Myles Horton.[1]

Eleanor Roosevelt is another example. As the niece of Theodore Roosevelt, she would become one of the most powerful women in history after marrying her distant cousin Franklin Roosevelt. As first lady, she coerced her husband to act on racial injustice and used her power to bring attention to the suffering that defined the lives of so many Americans. Frances Perkins is yet another example, as a woman who witnessed the Triangle Shirtwaist Factory fire personally and fought for labor rights for the rest of her life, becoming the first female presidential cabinet member when FDR named her secretary of labor in 1933. A lesser-known but very important case is Josephine Roche, the daughter of a rich coal capitalist who took over her father's Colorado mine and invited the United Mine Workers of America to organize her employees in 1928. She later became assistant secretary of the treasury under FDR and ended her career decades later administering the UMWA's health and safety fund.[2]

That all these examples are white women should not surprise us. As wealthy whites, they had access to economic advancement, education, and cultural capital that others did not. As women of the early twentieth century, they also lived in a deeply sexist society where women struggled to gain equality, with many professions closed off to them entirely. The long road to women's suffrage concluded in 1920 for white women everywhere and, in the northern states, for women of color, but other forms of discrimination remained in effect, especially economic discrimination, not to mention the continued denial of the vote to Black populations in the South. For some white women, the experience of sexism motivated them to fight for justice for everyone.

A largely unknown but amazing example of a wealthy white woman who became an important and nation-changing organizer is Lucy Randolph Mason. A crucial figure in the development of the modern labor movement, she not only dedicated her life to social change, but did it in the segregationist South, the most anti-worker part of the country. Born to an elite Virginia family in 1882, Mason devoted her life to improving the lives of poor southerners, both Black and white. Her family came from old Virginia stock, including prominent slaveholders, leading Confederates, and George Mason, author of the Virginia Declaration of Rights and intellectual forefather of the Bill of Rights. When she was eighteen, Mason began teaching a Sunday school class in a working-class neighborhood of Richmond, where her students shared stories with her about their harsh working and living conditions. This experience transformed Mason, and from that moment forward, she centered her life on organizing for what she saw as Christ's vision on earth—justice for all.[3]

In the early 1910s, Mason became a leader of the women's suffrage movement in Richmond, much to her father's outrage. She joined the Equal Suffrage League of Virginia and wrote articles about the suffrage fight, using a pseudonym to save her father the embarrassment of having a reformist daughter. How many of us struggle to gain acceptance for our activism in our own families?

Mason transitioned into professional reform work in 1914, when she was hired as the industrial secretary for the Richmond branch of the Young Women's Christian Association (YWCA), focusing on labor issues. She held this position until 1918, when she stepped down to take care of her ailing father. In 1923, she returned as the YWCA's general secretary, a role she held until 1932. During this time, Mason attempted to organize women factory workers, but encountered little interest among them. According to Mason, many women were ashamed of their jobs and therefore did not identify as workers.[4] This illustrates a crucial point for us today—many of us dislike our jobs, and that's completely understandable. However, workplace organizing, especially the work of forming unions, often requires a long-term commitment to those jobs. The struggle takes time and perseverance. I can absolutely understand why people quit their bad jobs. But those bad jobs cannot become union jobs without commitment from workers to stick around and organize.

We may not associate the YWCA with progressive causes today, but during Mason's time it became a space where reformist women could make a difference.[5] Mason worked hard to politicize the job by working with Richmond's Black community for economic advancement. It is likely that she and Maggie Walker, though from different generations and racial backgrounds, were aware of each other's work. Mason also lobbied Virginia legislators to end child labor, establish wages and hours standards, and mandate safer workplaces. In fact, the YWCA was a perfect place for a religious liberal to make a difference. Several years later, in 1946, when asked why she got involved in the labor movement, Mason responded, "Church people ought to do something to bring about the Kingdom of God on Earth. That's why I am in the labor movement."[6]

Very few white southerners during the Jim Crow era actively fought for and with African Americans to end discrimination. While more white people than we might assume disapproved of segregation, few acted against it. Mason chose a different path. She helped lead the opposition to a 1929 Richmond proposal to restrict Black residents to living only in certain neighborhoods. Black communities already suffered from low-quality housing, and this new ordinance would make it worse. Working with Black leaders, Mason publicly opposed the bill—the most prominent white woman in the city to do so.[7]

The early twentieth century had opened doors for young, reform-minded women. Like many leading women of the Progressive Era, Mason never married. Instead of focusing on marriage and family life, where she would likely face gender discrimination, she channeled her energy into helping the poor. Mason was part of a generation younger than founding Progressives, such as Addams, who emphasized voluntarism over state intervention. Mason—like Roosevelt and Perkins—saw the state as the ultimate guarantor of rights, and thus wanted to empower workers, both at the workplace and through the law.[8]

The connection between labor and women's rights led to some conclusions that divided the feminist movement. After the ratification of the Nineteenth Amendment, leading feminists such as Alice Paul pushed for another constitutional amendment—the Equal

Rights Amendment. But it might surprise you to learn that labor feminists such as Mason, Roosevelt, and Perkins opposed it. Ideological feminists like Alice Paul saw special protections for women as discriminatory. Paul demanded that the sexes be treated equally in all areas. At the time, the courts supported labor protections for women based only on their roles as mothers. For instance, in the 1908 *Muller v. Oregon* case, the Supreme Court upheld an Oregon law limiting women's working hours, citing their status as potential mothers. This stood in contrast to the Court's earlier decision in *Lochner v. New York* (1905), where it struck down a similar law for all workers in bakeries, ruling it unconstitutional based on the idea that if workers did not want to labor all their employment demanded, they had the right to quit but the state did not have the right to intervene in the labor markets. The Court however saw an exemption for women because they raised the next generation of Americans. Labor feminists wanted workplace protections for all workers and were not going to give up the little bit they had won for abstract rights. [9]

For labor feminists, who were acutely aware of the harsh realities faced by working women, the Equal Rights Amendment was only an irrelevant sideshow. While the push for the ERA makes sense from our modern perspective. Mason, Perkins, and Eleanor Roosevelt strongly disliked Paul, both personally and politically. Paul was outright opposed to all labor protections and later helped employers in their fight against labor rights.[10] Mason, in contrast, helped lead Virginia feminists to oppose the ERA based on their belief that women needed special protective legislation on the job.[11] What might seem politically puzzling today was often driven by the context and priorities of the time. Studying history helps us understand this.

Mason was a committed labor feminist who strongly believed in the power of unions. Despite recognizing that male union leaders were often sexist, she knew that unions created the possibility for all workers to have improved lives, especially women. She also believed that women's involvement in the labor movement would help smooth over class differences and lead to positive change with less likelihood of violence.[12]

Mason recognized that unionizing the South would be a long, hard journey. She tried to get employers around the region to sign agreements to raise labor standards based on the principle of doing the right thing, but that didn't work out the way she hoped it would; capitalists rarely do the right thing. She also lobbied Americans to buy union-label goods, which attracted the attention of the head of the American Federation of Labor, Samuel Gompers. He named Mason chair of the AFL's Women in Industry Committee during World War I, part of its National Advisory Committee on Labor. In 1931, she published a pamphlet titled *Standards for Workers in Southern Industry,* an attempt to push for regionwide standards that would match those in other parts of the nation, and which flew in the face of the cheap labor model that the South used to define itself economically.[13]

In 1932, Florence Kelley retired as head of the National Consumers League, which had formed in 1899 to fight the epidemic of child labor in American factories. Her three decades of amazing work in that position meant that her replacement had some mighty big shoes to fill. At Kelley's request, Lucy Randolph Mason took on that challenge. She had been a leading figure in the creation of the proposed 1924 Child Labor Amendment to the Constitution, banning that horrible and exploitative practice. Unfortunately, it was never ratified by the states. In fact, we could ratify it today; I recently testified before the Connecticut legislature in favor of a bill for that state to do so. When Franklin Roosevelt won the presidency in 1932, a new day for reform was born. Mason worked closely with the Roosevelt administration to fight for better labor standards nationally, and especially in the South, where the worst labor exploitation took place and where children still commonly labored in textile and glass factories.[14]

As part of her duties heading the Consumers League, Mason initially put her energy into lobbying for the National Industrial Recovery Act (NIRA), which was passed in 1933. The NIRA aimed to establish industry-wide labor standards and included enforcement measures for employers to abide by them, drawing some inspiration from the work of the Consumers League. However, the law proved unworkable, and the Supreme Court ruled the NIRA unconstitutional in 1935. Undeterred, Mason kept organizing in southern states, pressing South Carolina and Virginia to pass labor legislation.[15]

In 1934, tens of thousands of workers around the country engaged in massive strikes. Autoworkers in Toledo, longshoremen on the West Coast, Teamsters in Minneapolis, and textile workers in the South all took to the pickets to demand better conditions. Some won and some lost, but for Roosevelt and the liberal Democrats, it signified the need to unionize the country and cull the murderous violence that employers used to stop workers from forming unions. This climate of unrest led to the National Labor Relations Act in 1935, which created the framework for union elections that we use today. The Supreme Court routinely overturned progressive legislation, including a great deal of labor regulation. Roosevelt responded to the Court declaring the National Industrial Recovery Act and other legislation unconstitutional by threatening to pack the court with new justices to ensure the survival of reform initiatives. Soon after, some of the right-wing justices retired and the Court proceeded to validate new laws including the National Labor Relations Act.[16]

FDR's threats to pack the court cost him significant political capital, but it paved the way for labor allies in Congress to push through the Fair Labor Standards Act in 1938. This landmark legislation established a minimum wage, the eight-hour workday, overtime pay, and banned most child labor. Mason, with her deep understanding of southern politics, played a vital role in rounding up southern votes to get the legislation passed. At this time, she developed a close friendship with Eleanor Roosevelt, who viewed Mason as a leader in the fight for much-needed reform in the South. While the Fair Labor Standards Act had its flaws—it excluded the labor performed by Black workers in the South, especially agricultural work—such measures were sadly necessary to get southern legislators to vote for them. Despite these limitations, the act marked significant progress toward realizing the visions of Mason, Kelley, Perkins, and Eleanor Roosevelt.[17]

Mason's southern knowledge also appealed to a labor movement in the midst of transformation. In 1937, John L. Lewis, president of the United Mine Workers of America, led a group of unions out of the AFL to form the Congress of Industrial Organizations. The AFL's focus on skilled workers and its reluctance to invest in industrial organizing left many industrial workers unrepresented. Lewis, inspired by the Debs model, believed that unions need to organize all workers within an industry, not just a select few. This approach led to the establishment of unions like the United Auto Workers and United Steel Workers of America. The CIO directly challenged the AFL and it led to a civil war in the American labor movement. It also led to millions of workers joining unions.[18]

Lewis also understood that if unions failed to organize the South, employers would relocate there to undermine future union efforts.

Mason, Lewis, and Myles Horton were all aware of the history of garment workers and what happened after northerners like Clara Lemlich unionized them: the garment manufacturers moved to Tennessee, Alabama, South Carolina—non-union southern states. In these states, low wages and a high level of employer control appealed to capital, and southern politicians were happy to help capitalists keep workers down.[19]

Lewis hired Mason as the CIO's public relations representative for the South, a position she would hold until 1953. She moved to Atlanta to set up an office in the Textile Workers Organizing Committee headquarters. It's difficult to overestimate just how much the southern elite loathed the CIO. They demonized the CIO through race-baiting, anti-Semitism, and claims that unions would force racial integration. If that didn't work, southern employers and police forces resorted to violence, especially in the small textile towns that the CIO were most eager to organize. Mason went into southern towns and browbeat employers and law enforcement into refraining from taking these actions.[20]

Mason's ability to navigate the hostility of the South owed, in part, to her simply being an aging, upper-class white woman, and the daughter of one of the South's most respected and old families. She also showed no fear, although she could get frustrated. The power of employers, politicians, pastors, the media, and law enforcement against a few plucky but scared workers could be overwhelming, and the level of violence that police and employers used against workers shocked even this jaded southerner. But Mason decided she would stay on the job, no matter what, until she could change the conditions in the South. When police or employers beat up organizers, she used her connections to people in power, including President Roosevelt, to demand investigations and justice. Sometimes, she succeeded. When three CIO members were jailed in Covington, Virginia, for illegal picketing, she personally intervened, appealing to politicians she knew there to get them released. Slowly—very slowly—she got the doors of some churches opened to her: the Catholic archbishop of New Orleans agreed to work with her on opening the doors of Catholic churches to her. In 1938, she convinced the Southern Baptist Convention to pass a resolution endorsing the right to organize and engage in collective bargaining, a huge battle given the deep conservatism of that religious organization, which is today still a major part of our country's right-wing power structure.[21]

During World War II, Mason faced the challenging task of advocating for the inclusion of Black workers in southern unions. In 1943, in Mobile, Alabama, when whites nearly rioted over the hiring of Black workers in a shipyard, Mason negotiated a compromise. The company agreed to allocate an entire section of its manufacturing to Black workers, thus providing good jobs for them while allowing white workers to maintain the color line. Mason recognized that the deal reinforced segregation, but she also understood the necessity of building unions and creating opportunities for Black workers in a deeply segregated environment.[22]

In 1944, Mason took on a prominent role in CIO-PAC, the political action wing of the CIO, which aimed to capitalize on the upcoming end of World War II to push the nation toward the type of social democracy nations in western Europe would adopt after the war. Her focus remained on the South, where she organized workers, registering both white and Black workers to vote, and fought for the elimination of the poll tax and other barriers to voting. She also continued to fight southern politicians and law enforcement officers who ignored labor law and intimidated organizers, going into such states as Mississippi and Georgia to intervene, sometimes successfully. In the many magazine articles she published, she repeatedly stated that the CIO was the key to expanding real democracy across the South—economically, politically, and racially. The southern elites who hated the CIO agreed entirely, which is why they opposed it so strongly.[23]

After World War II, the CIO launched Operation Dixie, a campaign aimed at organizing the South, using Myles Horton's Highlander Center as a key organizing base. However, the initiative did not take on race as directly as Mason urged. The CIO soft-sold its commitment to racial equality to instead focus on organizing mostly white workers, even though it was the Black workers who had shown greater interest in joining unions. This alienated Black workers while failing to attract the ever-skeptical white working class, and Mason urged the CIO to embrace the potential for full emancipation through not only labor organizing but civil rights organizing. Ultimately, Operation Dixie failed. Jobs migrated to the South by the millions before eventually moving overseas in search of even cheaper labor. The inability of unions to organize the South continues to resonate today; most of the South remain the least organized states in the country.[24]

In her later years, Mason dedicated herself to fundraising for

Highlander, remaining deeply committed to the democratic civil rights unionism it championed. Her autobiography, *To Win These Rights: A Personal Story of the CIO in the South,* was published in 1952. Due to declining health, she retired in 1953 and spent her final years struggling with dementia. Mason passed away in 1959, a remarkable figure who remains too often forgotten.

Lucy Randolph Mason had the option to lead a comfortable life, enjoying her privilege and social status. Instead, she fought tooth and nail on issues of inequality that infuriated some people but inspired many others. She did not have the luxury of leading a movement to huge success. Rather, she did the hard work of boring into white supremacy and capitalist domination over American workers, fighting her entire life to tame those horrors. While we cannot control the circumstances of our birth, what is in our control is the choices we make in life. Let Mason inspire you to make the right choices.

11

Clint Jencks

El Palomino

White Americans of the past do not often make great role models for today's anti-racist struggles. Even many of the most effective organizers in our history struggled with the plague of white supremacy, sometimes overcoming it and sometimes not. Eugene Debs's initial struggle to accept Black workers is just one example.

We will never succeed to build a strong class-based movement in this nation without fighting racism. Simply put, ignoring race when organizing around class flies in the face of the lived experience of the nation's poorest workers, who are disproportionally people of color. Racism is something we have to fight inside of us. We might not be able to win that fight entirely, but we can sure use our lives to build solidarity and power in communities of color. To not do this means never defeating oppression in America. One American who understood this completely was Clinton Jencks.

Born in 1918, Jencks grew up in a white, middle-class family. From an early age, Jencks confronted people over inequality. As a child, he volunteered to give Christmas baskets to needy people in the community. On one occasion while visiting their homes, he saw eviction notices on their doors, signed by a local banker who was also the superintendent of his Sunday school. The next day, Jencks marched into the bank and confronted the man, saying he betrayed his Christian beliefs![1]

Jencks attended college at the University of Colorado. The Boulder of the 1930s was not the activist center it became in the late 1960s, but Jencks sought out organizing opportunities, joining the local Young Communist League in 1937. He became president of the university's chapter of the American Student Union, a leftist organization that demanded peace and fought the rise of global anti-Semitism. The ASU under Jencks engaged in multiracial organizing to desegregate Boulder restaurants, where segregation was not legally sanctioned but was observed in practice.[2]

Jencks graduated from college in 1939. He moved to St. Louis and got involved with the Inter-Faith Youth Council, an interracial social justice group sponsored by the YMCA. It was in St. Louis that he met his future wife and organizing partner, Virginia Derr.

Later, Jencks became national secretary of the American Youth Congress, an organization founded in 1935 to fight for the rights of young people and which had connections to the Communist Party. Eleanor Roosevelt, the first lady of the United States, supported left-wing organizations like the AYC. She cared little if there were a few communists in them and, as adviser to her husband, the president, decided to introduce AYC activists to FDR.

Now, at this moment in 1940, communist groups supported the U.S. staying out of World War II because the Soviet Union had honored its nonaggression agreement with Nazi Germany. So when Jencks got to meet Roosevelt, he started asking pointed questions about the president pushing for military preparedness. FDR was furious. Things got so heated that Eleanor stopped supporting the AYC. Jencks later felt some embarrassment about this episode of youthful exuberance and opposing resisting the Nazis. But it showed that no one could intimidate him, not even the president.[3]

When Germany invaded the Soviet Union in 1941, most leftists changed their minds about the war. When the U.S. joined World War II, Jencks, like many leftists, immediately volunteered for the fight to defeat fascism, putting his life on the line for his beliefs. Serving as a navigator in the army air force, he won the Distinguished Flying Cross and six other medals for his fighting in the Pacific. [4]

After the war, Jencks took a job working for the American Smelting and Refining Company in Denver. The plant's workers had joined the International Union of Mine, Mill, and Smelter Workers (Mine, Mill, for short) and Jencks became involved in his union. This was the descendant union of the Western Federation of Miners, where Frank Little had started his organizing career. The WFM became Mine, Mill in 1916. It left the American Federation of Labor to join the Congress of Industrial Organizations upon its formation in 1937. Jencks soon became shop steward of his section of the mill. The WFM believed in the CIO model of organizing on an industrial basis and in its ideals of progressive social change. Mine, Mill gave Jencks a sense of purpose in what would be a lifelong fight for social change. The union, he believed, would make him strong.

In his off hours, Jencks founded the Denver chapter of the American Veterans Committee, a left-wing group representing veterans' interests. The AVC sought to revive the prewar leftist movement, making demands such as national health care, racial justice, and full employment. Moreover, it provided veterans who did not want to be involved in right-wing organizations such as the American Legion a different option. It also put Jencks back in touch with the communists that he had worked with before the war.[5]

Jencks joined the Communist Party in 1946. This move took guts, regardless of what one might think of the Communist Party today. Many communists distanced themselves from the Soviet Union after the Nazi-Soviet Pact in 1939 and even repudiated Soviet ideology. The brief, if fragile, alliance between the U.S. and Soviet Union during World War II was already falling apart by 1946. In March of that year, President Harry Truman invited former British prime minister Winston Churchill to the United States, where Churchill announced the Soviets had created an "iron curtain" across eastern Europe that would define the next generation of global conflict.[6]

But on the domestic front, the CP also was a major ally of the civil rights movement, and it saw itself as the future of the worker struggle.[7] Jencks built a reputation as a ferocious attacker of racism. As AVC head in Denver, he led a fight for a fair employment commission in Colorado to fight the racism of the city's employers, and also wrote in the *Denver Post* on the evils of racism. Virginia was at his side through all of this, noted for her ability to take seemingly abstract ideological debates and remind everyone that what they should be talking about were bread-and-butter issues such as families needing to put food on the table. He also ran as a Democrat for the state legislature in 1946, though he lost. When more moderate elements took over the AVC nationally, he left the organization and committed himself to his union work.[8]

Jencks combined his hatred of racism with his belief in unionism. Left-leaning Americans today often wonder why the U.S. has a less radical working class, a less robust social safety net, and a weaker labor movement than other industrialized nations. One reason is that white workers have often chosen to prioritize their white identity over their working-class identity. In other words, they have often worked with their own employers to keep the workplace lily-white rather than express solidarity with those workers and come together to fight their employers.[9]

This was the case in the mining industry of southern New Mexico. Both whites and Mexicans commonly worked in the mines. While some IWW-led cross-racial organizing in the mines did occur in the 1910s, for the most part, the white workers had utter contempt for the Mexican miners. Moreover, these Mexican miners lived in deplorable conditions, even as late as the 1950s. Their small houses lacked plumbing and electricity. In sharp contrast, Mine, Mill's long history of interracial organizing helped build trust between workers of different backgrounds. It had spent decades building interracial solidarity between white and Mexican workers as a core principle of the union.[10]

In 1947, Mine, Mill asked Jencks to go to Grant County, New Mexico, and become the union representative for Local 890. These mostly Mexican workers demanded a full-time organizer of their own and pooled together their very limited financial resources to pay for an organizer's salary. This was a place known for enormous hostility with respect to both race and class. Some of the workers had fought in the Mexican Revolution when they were young, and their fight for decent work was a continuation of that struggle. Moreover, the mines had job classifications based on race, and Mexican miners never got promoted past basic positions that paid little. The mines also segregated the worksite, leaving Mexican workers forced to use inferior changing rooms. Basically, the mine companies used racism to divide the workforce—and the white workers happily played along.

The community's white residents, determined to keep these Mexicans as cheap labor, immediately ostracized Jencks when they discovered why the new arrival had moved there, while the Mexican workers were just as determined as their enemies to win their cause. Jencks would help them do so.

Now, Jencks did not have that much organizing experience. He was a committed leftist, but he didn't know how to organize miners in a culture he did not really know. But he did what any good organizer should do—he built connections. And he *listened*. Listening is very much a lost art in the age of social media and performing your politics. But there is no way to organize without centering listening. You have to meet people where they are at, not demand they advance to where you are.

Jencks knew he was inexperienced and out of his element. So he worked hard to build trust among the local union leaders, realizing quickly that a white man telling Mexican workers what to do would fail as an organizing strategy. Many Mexican workers resented the Anglos who dominated their life and their union, so Jencks decided to encourage local leadership to take the lead. He reduced the role of the union officers and worked with local leaders to develop their own demands and build support in the rank and file for militant action. While Mine, Mill's national leaders were divided by the battles over communism roiling the labor movement, Local 890 focused on the lived conditions of its members. These local activists by and large happily worked with the union's communists, both because they had no ideological opposition to socialism and because these radicals empowered workers to improve their own lives in the ways they themselves saw fit.

But it was when Jencks started speaking Spanish that he truly earned the workers trust. By learning the language, he had done the hard work, doing the one thing that demonstrated he really was committing himself to their cause. From then on, the workers began referring to him as "El Palomino"—slang for "the white"—for his efforts.[11]

Like most of the people we have discussed in this book, Jencks was far from perfect. As with countless flawed activists over the years, he struggled to maintain consistency in both his personal and political lives. He articulated and fought for women's rights on the job and within unions, and was personally attracted to strong labor feminists, yet he treated the women in his life quite poorly. An early marriage to a labor feminist fell apart shortly after they married. He remarried Virginia, someone with just as much commitment and organizing experience as he did, but he treated his equally talented wife as his subordinate. She did not want to move to southern

New Mexico, but he overruled her objections. In fact, even after she divorced him years later, he still struggled to treat women well in his personal life, his political rhetoric notwithstanding. Later in life, during the feminist movement of the 1970s, he came to some realization about the wrong his prior actions caused. But they are part of his story too.[12]

In 1947, Congress passed the Taft-Hartley Act over President Harry Truman's veto. This horrible law banned many of the tactics that had made labor successful over the previous fifteen years, including the sympathy strike and, by extension, the general strike. It allowed states to create "right to work" laws, where workers did not have to join a union even if their coworkers voted for one, which undermined labor's effectiveness and is a big reason why the South remains so anti-union today. It also forced union leaders to sign an affidavit that they were not communists. Of course, many of the best organizers that built the American labor movement in the 1940s were members of the Communist Party. This led to the CIO kicking out its communist-led unions. Unions were so unpopular in 1947 that even though President Harry Truman vetoed the law, Congress overrode his veto. The United States was rapidly repudiating its leftward advances of the New Deal.[13]

In southern New Mexico, Taft-Hartley gave employers an advantage over the union. The mining corporations that controlled life down there, such as Phelps Dodge and Kennecott, simply refused to sign new contracts with their unions until Mine, Mill leadership signed the anti-communist affidavit.[14]

During these challenging times, Jencks hearkened back to the IWW's approach to organizing. He would forget about the contract for the time being and organize intensively around local conditions. If the workers needed to call a strike, then he would support their wishes. He focused his organizing on members' working and living conditions. In one instance, he worked with the members to demand a full safety inspection of a mine by the U.S. Bureau of Mines, with Jencks present to ensure that the company didn't lie about the safety conditions. That led to the mine's shutdown until it was deemed safe. This was the kind of leadership that could motivate and inspire workers.[15]

Jencks empowered workers for direct action. That meant trusting them to make decisions, which would keep Local 890 going in the coming years. The forces cracking down on leftists continued to grow. In 1950, the CIO expelled Mine, Mill from the federation for its communist leadership. This was a terrible financial blow and also meant noncommunist mining unions could now steal already unionized workers. It divided the labor movement based on politics. Mine, Mill now faced raids from noncommunist CIO unions, political harassment, and dwindling funds.

The same year, Local 890 went on strike against Empire Zinc to fight against the awful treatment workers faced. Jencks had mobilized these workers. They were a disciplined force that by 1950 had spent years organizing. Mine, Mill leaders did not want the strike. They did not think they could win, so they tried to take control of the local from Jencks. He fought back, refusing to follow orders. The workers mattered more to him than his job.

The workers held fast to their position, siding with Jencks. The company reopened the mine with scab workers in June 1951. Workers kept the mine closed for a single day. But the next day, a judge issued an injunction against the workers picketing in front of the mine, which meant that continuing the strike would lead to massive fines against the union and the miners going to jail.

Such overt strikebreaking was all too typical of the way the government served as the enforcer of corporate demands—and often still does, through the evil of the injunction.

The workers' response to this injunction was the ultimate validation of Jencks's organizing. Jencks, always an advocate for women having greater involvement in unions, suggested that the miners' wives and other female supporters of the struggle take up the picketing. This caused enormous conflict for the miners. Clint and Virginia Jencks had done a lot of work to empower the miners' wives before this moment, but being on the line was dangerous and also threatened the control miners had over their wives and daughters. Who would clean and take care of the children while the women picketed? Would the women listen to their husbands now that they were empowered? On the other hand, they were private citizens, not union members on strike, and thus not subject to the injunction law.

The brilliant strategy worked to perfection. The mine owners did not know what to do when the women showed up instead of the workers. In this transformation of gender roles and labor activism from striking men to furious wives and daughters and sisters, Virginia played a critical role. She had a favorite saying—"I live, therefore I must defend others' rights to live."[16] Given the unhappiness of the marriage, her desire to spend more time as an organizer in the community made sense. As the strike went on, she became more crucial to its functioning, working long and seemingly endless hours day after day.

The miners' wives were militant. They threw ground-up chile peppers in the eyes of scabs. One day, trucks entering the mine ran over three different women trying to block the evidence. All three suffered serious injuries. Town leaders were disgusted that the Jenckses would organize Mexicans. A local store owner punched Virginia in the face, giving her a black eye. A druggist likewise assaulted Clint. He refused to fight back, as he personally rejected the use of violence. In January 1952, the company and union finally settled the strike, with the company granting not only pay raises and benefits such as vacation time, but also running water and other upgrades to worker housing. It was a big victory for Mine, Mill at a very difficult time for leftist unions. It was a far bigger victory to the rank and file miners who saw massive improvements in their lives.[17]

The transformation of gender roles that occurred in the strike came about in part from the community organizing of both Clint and Virginia. The strike, to them, was not just about the union. This was about community activism, with entire families fighting against racism as well as workplace discrimination. They felt the power of change entering their lives; their confidence grew. For the women, that sense of empowerment also led to challenging the sexism and misogyny many faced at home from their husbands and families. The revolution unleashed by Jencks's organizing did not stop at the workplace door.[18]

This strike is small in the context of our larger history. Yet we remember it today. That's because it inspired the greatest labor film ever made: *Salt of the Earth*. Released in 1954, it stars many of the union members, as well as Jencks and Virginia as fictionalized versions of themselves. The film is remarkable for its clear depiction of the workers' struggle and their fundamental demands. Opponents of the film argued that its focus on the lived experiences of workers was a false front that covered up communist propaganda. In fact, it was suppressed and barely seen for twenty years. But if capitalism requires that Mexican workers live without plumbing and have their unions crushed, well, we can make quite a moral case for communism.[19]

One movie, of course, did not make things easier for a committed leftist in this era. Empire Zinc had Jencks prosecuted for violating the court-ordered injunctions, which meant he had to do his job from jail for three months. On the day of his release, a Senate committee led by the right-wing Nevada senator Pat McCarran and dedicated to attacking leftists in unions sent him a subpoena to testify before the committee. Jencks publicly rebuked the committee for its extremist methods and its violations of free speech.[20]

This was the period of McCarthyism, one of the scariest parts of American history. Politicians found they could promote their careers by holding public hearings on supposed communist influences in America. This is how Richard Nixon got his start as a nationally famous politician. The period is named for the Wisconsin senator Joseph McCarthy, who claimed he had a list of communists in the State Department. He had no such list, making the entire thing up. He became the most powerful man in America overnight. Among his biggest supporters were a young John F. Kennedy and Robert F. Kennedy. In the House of Representatives, politicians hauled Hollywood workers to the stand forced them to "name names," i.e., rat out other communists working in the movie industry or face the blacklist. Those who did not acquiesce often did not work in the movies for the next decade or more. This was the political atmosphere Clint Jencks faced when he stood up for his civil rights.[21]

In 1953, Jencks was arrested for falsifying a "noncommunist affidavit" he had signed in 1950. Part of the Taft-Hartley Act forced union leaders to sign affidavits that they were not communists. Falsifying it was a crime. When Jencks signed that affadavit, he did not repudiate his political beliefs. Rather, he prioritized the continuation of his working with the miners over giving the government the satisfaction of kicking him out of the labor movement.[22] Committed people such as Jencks who fought for social change faced charges of communism. They had to make this hard choice. Organizing Mexican American workers for their rights on the job and better housing was not some kind of communist plot, whatever Jencks's personal beliefs. But the specter of the spread of communism was an excuse for corporate America to crack down on organizers. Anyone organizing for social change in the 1950s and 1960s faced threats of public attacks, including Martin Luther King Jr. and other figures far more moderate than the Jenckses.

Jencks's trial, which took place in El Paso, Texas, was a farce. The jury foreman was a former Phelps Dodge accountant, so this was hardly a neutral jury. The government used a paid witness named Harvey Matusow, a former communist who committed perjury on the stand on multiple occasions, lying about whether people were communists. Mine, Mill barely had the money to fund this kind of legal strategy. A media circus surrounded the trial, and it placed Jencks in even greater danger of imprisonment for his political beliefs. Jencks and his legal team fought hard, but he was convicted in 1954.[23]

Although the trial took a huge toll on Jencks's family, this story has a sort of happy ending. Shortly after Jencks's conviction, Matusow's lies fell apart. He admitted to authorities he made up his claims about communists. He then wrote a book, published in 1955, about his lies, including how he railroaded Jencks into a conviction. Jencks and his lawyers fought for a new trial. In 1956, Jencks filed an appeal to the Supreme Court over the unconstitutional nature of the case, citing the restrictions on examining the evidence against him. The Court found in Jencks's favor. In fact, the trial against Jencks became so infamous that it, along with the Supreme Court decision, inspired the passage of a law named after him. In 1957, Congress passed the Jencks Act, which requires that defendants be allowed to see the testimony of a government witness.[24]

All of this made Jencks famous, but it also made him poor. Mine, Mill was in collapse. The union suspended him during the trial and he was placed on the blacklist. Consequently, whenever he got a job, the FBI sent agents to tell his new boss about his background. However, in 1959, he won a Woodrow Wilson Foundation fellowship for graduate study in economics at the University of California, Berkeley. Seeking to embarrass the foundation, the House Un-American Activities Committee called Jencks to testify, but by this point the anti-communist wave had crested. He completed his PhD and became an economics professor at San Diego State, holding that position up until his retirement in 1988. For the rest of his life, he remained involved in leftist politics, although he played a much lower profile than in the 1940s and 1950s. Later in life, he converted to Judaism when he married a Jewish woman. He died in 2005.[25]

Clint Jencks was not a perfect man. But his organizing, in a place on the far margins of the economic mainstream and media attention, empowered workers to take control of their own lives. For Jencks, it was never about him; it was always about the workers. He transformed the lives of hundreds of people. If it wasn't for *Salt of the Earth* and the federal prosecution against him, he would be forgotten. Perhaps his example should make us reflect on the thousands of organizers working throughout the country who aren't remembered and never will be, but who fight to change the lives of people today. Maybe we can replicate what they achieved, centering the fight against racism and the fight against economic exploitation together.

12

Mike Quill

The Power of a Union

Many of the greatest American organizers have been immigrants. These individuals bring the experiences of their homes to our struggles. Emma Goldman, most of the anarchists martyred after the 1886 Haymarket bombing, Clara Lemlich—these were all people radicalized in their home countries who used that spark to transform their adopted nation. Immigrants brought socialism to the United States, and for that, we should be thankful. Letting in more immigrants today would recharge our political imagination and bring new ideas into our movements. We should support more immigration!

Mike Quill is one of those great immigrant American organizers who came here for a better life. He sought freedom in his native Ireland and then fought for a different kind of freedom in the U.S., becoming one of the great union leaders of American history. He stood up to the powerful, brought American transportation workers into the modern age, and made them a fighting force. We don't talk enough about Mike Quill today. Too often today's labor leaders seem unwilling to fight, but Quill never had that problem. We can learn a lot from him.

Born in County Kerry, Ireland, in 1905, Quill fought in the Irish Republican Army between 1919 and 1921, mostly as a dispatch rider in the struggle against the British empire. In the aftermath of the 1922 Anglo-Irish Treaty, during which Ireland suffered through a civil war, Quill decided to migrate to the United States, but the revolutionary spirit he experienced in his homeland stayed with him through his life.

Many young people in rural Ireland at that time sought better opportunities elsewhere, some in Irish cities such as Dublin, others in England, and many in the United States. Quill came to the U.S. in 1926. His uncle Patrick and his brothers Patrick and John were already living in New York City; most immigrants go where they have family who can help them get a job. Quill's uncle got him a job on the Interborough Rapid Transit Company, a private company that then ran sections of the New York subway.[1]

Transportation companies exploited their workers to a shocking degree. Twelve-hour days were common and sometimes workers had to labor eighty-four-hour weeks. Anti-union agencies specialized in busting transportation strikes. A man named James Farley, for example, became known as the "champion strikebreaker" for his effectiveness in crushing transportation union strikes. When Farley died of tuberculosis in 1913, he spent his last days hallucinating about the workers he oppressed taking their revenge on him.[2]

Brooklyn trolley workers had joined the Knights of Labor in the 1890s. The Knights had three major demands: a 25-cent raise for employees, including the part-time workers; a reduction in daily trips so that a workday never exceeded ten hours; and finally, an increase in the number of full-time workers. The Atlantic Avenue Railroad Company granted them none of the demands, and the workers went on strike in 1895. The company brought in scabs from around the nation. The New York National Guard then happily served as the personal strikebreaking force of the company. It crushed the strike and destroyed the union.[3]

This is the world of work in which Mike Quill found himself when he took that subway job. It did not take him long to start thinking about how to change these conditions. The transit companies employed many Irish immigrants, quite a few of whom had fought the British just a few years earlier. These immigrants brought the revolutionary politics of their homeland with them, forming political clubs in New York and becoming a breeding ground for organizing to make their lives better.

In April 1934, Mike Quill and five other workers met in a cafeteria with a Hungarian-born communist named Jack Weiss to form the Transport Workers Union (TWU). They drafted a constitution, writing, "We are based firmly on the principle of industrial unionism and militant struggle and against company unionism and craft unionism. We believe in one union, uniting all." A man named Tom O'Shea became TWU's first president, and Mike Quill became vice president. The union grew quickly. By the end of 1934, the TWU had 560 members and was still growing fast.[4]

These men emerged from not only the Irish Republican Army but also Ireland's union tradition. In fact, the TWU name built on the legacy of Jim Larkin and James Connolly, labor activists who had formed the Irish Transport and General Workers Union twenty years earlier.[5] By explicitly connecting the new leftism with Irish republicanism, Quill and his allies built solidarity within the workforce, giving workers a common identity to rally around. The Communist Party played an important role through this process, succeeding in organizing many recent immigrants to the United States. Quill was not a leftist in any real sense when he came to the U.S., but he liked to fight. Drawing on his Irish roots, he started making connections between the Irish struggle and that of workers globally, including himself.[6]

Quill took on the very real physical threat of being a lead organizer. Making yourself publicly known was a great way to get a beating from company thugs and then get fired from your job. But Quill enjoyed a political fight. He was young and wanted to make the world better. Quill also had a particular skill—he was an amazing public speaker. Incredibly charismatic and well versed in the Irish storytelling style, Quill alternately turned his brogue up or down to fit his audience, moving the workers with his bombastic speeches. He became the TWU's most pivotal leader because of his outstanding organizing skills, his oratory, and his mastery of political infighting.

On July 9, 1935, six squeegee workers whose job was to clean the glass of the subway trains took a stand on an equipment rule, refusing to use heavier 14-inch squeegees instead of the standard 10-inch ones. The company fired them for daring to stand up for their dignity and physical well-being. Around seventy workers walked out in solidarity. Quill and the new TWU had prepared for this and mobilized their comrades for a strike. Two days later, the workers were reinstated. Workers started joining the union in larger numbers now that it had proven what it could do.[7]

The organizing continued. On August 10, as Quill and other leaders entered union headquarters, company thugs beat them up. The New York Police Department then arrested the union leaders for "inciting a riot," an absurd charge. Workers immediately descended upon the courthouse, raising money among themselves to bail all the leaders out. The courts threw out the charges, and the incident became organizing lore in the TWU. Soon after that, Quill discovered a company spy, exposed him before a large union meeting, and told him he should go jump in front of a train. This got the workers' attention![8]

In 1935, Quill became president of the TWU, a position he held for the rest of his life. He was part of a new generation of union leaders, such as Walter Reuther in the United Auto Workers and Harry Bridges in the International Longshore and Warehouse Union, who were taking over unions and turning them into forces for massive change. Quill gets less attention today in our memory of the labor movement's fighting days than Reuther or Bridges, but he was a critical part of the transformation of the American working class in the mid-twentieth century.[9]

Over the next few years, tens of thousands of workers gained union contracts thanks to the militancy of the TWU and the new organizing framework of the New Deal. It became one of the first unions to join the CIO, leaving the more conservative AFL. It took a few years to build up the union, but by the end of 1936 it started organizing other New York transit companies. By the summer of 1937, the TWU was winning election after election thanks to its organizing and the new labor regime ushered in by the National Labor Relations Act, which created the governmental administration of union elections with employers suffering consequences if they did not comply. The TWU soon moved beyond New York and began organizing transit workers in other cities. In less than a year, it went from a tiny local of eight thousand workers to more than thirty thousand workers in New York and elsewhere. The new contracts that the union secured meant hours went down and wages went up. Workers had representation and a grievance process; sick leave and overtime pay became a real thing. By the late 1930s, the lives of transit workers had vastly improved.[10]

The Communist Party supported Quill's rise, and he also

remained close to Irish revolutionaries and socialists of many stripes. But what made Quill different from many communist-leaning unionists is that he always prioritized what his own workers needed over the needs of the Communist Party. Well into the 1940s, the Communist Party ordered communist-led unions to follow Moscow's dictates, whether on strategies to influence the labor movement or, increasingly, on foreign policy. Quill had no problem with this so long as it served his interests and the interests of the transit workers. He was also close to leading communist Earl Browder, general secretary of the Communist Party-USA at the time. Quill had no problem standing up to anticommunists either. The House Un-American Activities Committee, then chaired by the clownish right-winger Martin Dies and later notorious for its post–World War II hearings accusing Hollywood of being controlled by communists, held hearings about communist influence in the TWU. Quill railed against this fascist operation with all the force he had in that powerful voice.[11]

Quill and the TWU also had to contend with growing opposition from the Catholic Church, which did not oppose unionism per se, but very strongly opposed communism. However, for Catholics generally, things were not so simple. The prominent Catholic activist Dorothy Day, for example, used her column in the *Catholic Worker* newspaper to tell workers to join the TWU. Moreover, many Irish workers mistrusted the clergy, because the church had opposed violence in Ireland's republican movement. To build his case within the church, Quill recruited pro-union priests, scoring public relations victories when they and their parishioners supported his union.[12]

Quill wanted more than just union power. He also thought he could help the working class through electoral politics, so he ran and won election to the New York City Council in 1937. Even though he lost his reelection bid, he remained a power player in the city's politics, a role that only grew over time as the TWU became ever more powerful. Although he at first had a decent relationship with New York's powerful mayor Fiorello La Guardia, when the latter would not do what the TWU wanted, Quill would rouse his members with intense speeches and threats of strikes that would terrify La Guardia and subsequent mayors fearful of seeing the city's mass transit system shut down. Quill and his workers had power and knew how to wield it.[13]

After World War II, the political winds shifted against the

communists. Quill knew what that meant for his union. Always prioritizing his union members over ideology, Quill would not let other political commitments destroy what he had won for transport workers. As discussed in the chapter on Clint Jencks, in 1947, Congress passed the anti-communist Taft-Hartley Act. Quill realized that conservatives in Congress wanted to destroy the entire labor movement.

Quill had his own reasons, however, to break with the Communist Party. In the late 1940s, party leaders told him to oppose New York City raising its transit fares. TWU members needed those fare increases for their raises. That was the final straw for Quill. Accusing the Communists of selling out the workers, he stomped out of his relationships with the far left. It was a complicated, difficult time, and he did what he believed was necessary to save his union.[14]

He was still "Red Mike" though, at least in spirit. Quill remained on the left edge of the labor movement. He retained his leftist vision of the world, including becoming a strong supporter of racial equality, even when it cost him support with some of his fellow workers.[15] Within the labor movement, Quill demanded that unions invest in more organizing, and in 1950 he became vice president of the CIO on that platform. When the CIO rejoined the AFL in 1955, he was furious. Denouncing the AFL as standing for "racism, racketeering and raids," he was among the CIO leaders most irate about the merger. Quill wanted to fight and organize; unfortunately, too much of the labor movement did not, and over the years large parts of the movement rested on their laurels and stopped investing in new organizing. This led to disastrous results when a new round of union busting began in the U.S. in the 1970s and unions had forgotten how to organize new workers in new industries.[16]

Unlike many unions, TWU continued expanding after World War II. While its home remained New York, it brought in other CIO-based transportation unions under its umbrella. It organized airline workers after the war, becoming a real force in that growing industry, with twelve thousand workers under union contracts by 1948. Of course, it continued building its mass-transit base. The union faced a huge challenge, however, when New York took over the private subway lines in 1949. TWU had to fight for years to get the city to recognize it as the sole bargaining agent, but through Quill's commitment and the culture of solidarity in his union, they won this battle.

Quill continued to prioritize building the economic and political power of his union to provide better lives for his members, their families, and the working class as a whole. What really made Quill different was his personal style. By the 1950s, labor leaders were among the most boring guys (and they were all guys) possible. Most thought of themselves more as managers than as the rabble-rousers of the 1930s. They dressed bland, they talked bland, and they completely downplayed class conflict as they gave up on organizing to serve their members.

That was not Mike Quill. He was a loud man who used his Irish brogue to great effect. He openly challenged politicians. He frequently threatened to strike. He told his workers and the people of New York that class mattered; he represented the worker while the rich represented themselves. He kept up that fire-and-brimstone rhetoric his whole life. It endeared him to his members, while infuriating other labor leaders and New York politicians. It inspired many both inside and outside the labor movement who demanded that the movement return to its political roots. He was the undisputed leader of his union, had made friends in New York's initially hostile Catholic Church, was close to the state's Democratic Party leaders, and held an enormous amount of power and authority. Combining organizing and politics, Quill was a force of nature.

Quill also fought racism in his union, even though many members opposed that stance. In 1939, the TWU held the first desegregated union meeting in New Orleans since Reconstruction. He actively supported the civil rights movement in the 1950s. In 1960, the TWU started a fund to pay the bail of civil rights activists arrested in the South, and in 1961, Quill invited Martin Luther King Jr. to be the keynote speaker at the TWU Convention. Quill also covered the expenses for TWU members who joined the march for voting rights from Selma to Montgomery in 1965. This wasn't just lip service from Quill; he was a genuinely anti-racist union leader.[17]

The most famous moment of Quill's life came at its very end, in 1966. For years, he talked a big game about massive strikes that would shut down the city. But he really didn't want that to happen. He wanted the city to make a fair deal before his workers had to strike. That usually worked. In the late 1950s and early 1960s, Quill was close to Robert Wagner Jr., the mayor who had established collective bargaining rights for the city's workers in 1958. Wagner's father had sponsored the key labor legislation of the New Deal, and the National Labor Relations Act is colloquially known as the Wagner Act. His son brought a generally pro-labor mentality with him to the mayor's office. These were good years for the TWU. Quill and Wagner worked out good deals without strikes.[18]

When Wagner left office, however, the Republican John Lindsay took over. Lindsay's base was the city's wealthy elites. He did not like Quill's class politics, his style, or his union. This wasn't just a clash in styles, it was a low-level class war. Lindsay wanted a fight—so he got one. He rejected Quill's demands for more pay, shorter workdays, more vacation days, and better pensions.

Quill showed the new mayor who was really in charge of New York City. He led his workers off the job in the big strike that he had always threatened would happen. Think about how reliant New York is on public transportation. There were about 5 million daily subway or bus rides in the city at that time. For twelve days beginning on January 1, public transportation stopped. Children could not get to school and workers could not get to their jobs.

The city sought an injunction and a judge gladly gave one. Quill responded with a new offer that reduced some demands, but the judge was unfazed, ordering the arrest of all the strike leaders. At this point, Quill was very sick and his heart was failing, but, even knowing he was not far from death, he remained fully committed to his workers. He told the press, "The judge can drop dead in his black robes. I don't care if I rot in jail. I will not call off the strike." And he didn't. Quill was jailed but his health was so bad that he was sent to the hospital almost immediately.[19]

The two sides got more serious in working out a deal as the strike went on. Negotiations picked up after a January 10 protest at which fifteen thousand workers picketed at City Hall. Finally, in the wee hours of January 13, TWU and the city reached an agreement. Wages increased by about 25 percent and workers received an additional paid holiday, along with a wide array of other benefits. Over the next eight years, pay rose for the transit workers by an average of 9 percent a year. Quill showed up Lindsay, who had totally capitulated and would remain a weak mayor for the rest of his term.[20]

This was Quill's last great victory. He was released from the hospital on January 25, gave a big victory speech to the workers, and then died on January 28. He was sixty years old.

Shortly after the union leader's death, Martin Luther King stated:

> Mike Quill was a fighter for decent things all his life—Irish independence, labor organization, and racial equality. He spent his life ripping the chains of bondage off his fellow-man. When the totality of a man's life is consumed with enriching the lives of others, this is a man the ages will remember—this is a man who has passed on but who has not died. Negroes had desperately needed men like Mike Quill who fearlessly said what was true even when it offended. That is why Negroes shall miss Mike Quill.[21]

It was not only Black Americans who missed Mike Quill. A master organizer of his era, Quill brought enormous personality, leftist politics, and a willingness to fight to the labor movement. He was the kind of labor leader that we should want from all our unions. He might be less famous today than Eugene Debs or Big Bill Haywood or Mother Jones, because those organizers operated in a different era, when strikers faced even greater odds and employers could murder workers. Quill lived in a less violent era. But one can argue that he did as much or more for the American worker than any labor leader who ever lived.

13

Robert Williams

Organizing Through Armed Self-Defense

When we organize a protest march today, why do we often explicitly say, "This is a nonviolent protest"? Why do we feel the need to fall back on this idea of nonviolence as the guiding principle of our actions? It's as if we want to assure everyone that although we may be protesting, we aren't going to engage in any actions that will threaten law and order. With few exceptions, all our protests are nonviolent, regardless of whether or not we make such a statement. At the very worst, there may be a few anarchists looking to break a few windows. But the real violence in America comes from the police and the far right. So, again, why do we constantly define our protests in such specifically nonviolent terms?

Some of this, of course, comes from the influence of Martin Luther King and other civil rights activists. Those committed activists used nonviolence as a tactic to create great change—but they also spent months and years training themselves in the philosophy and tactics of nonviolence, lessons which we have largely forgotten today. I am most certainly not advocating violence.

Violence in social movements is usually counterproductive and disastrous. But the real history of the civil rights movement was not all about nonviolence.

In fact, there were plenty of guns in the civil rights movement—and that includes guns owned by Martin Luther King. In 1956, he applied for a concealed carry permit; one of King's advisers called his home in Montgomery "an arsenal."[1] People needed to protect themselves in the South, where white violence could happen at any time. As many rural Black people knew, the best way to save your life when attacked by racists was to have a gun.

When northern advocates of nonviolence came to the South in the 1960s, many residents looked at them as if they were insane. It was a nonsense ideology being imposed on them by outsiders. As the civil rights activist and historian Charles Cobb notes in *This Nonviolent Stuff'll Get You Killed,* even committed nonviolent activists such as Bob Moses, who we will discuss in a later chapter, simply realized that they were not going to get rid of the guns owned by Black people. Said Moses, "Self-defense is so deeply ingrained in rural southern America that we as a small group can't affect it."[2]

During the early 1960s, no one more directly personified armed self-defense than Robert Williams. Understanding his history complicates the emphasis on nonviolence present in most histories of the civil rights movement. It also demonstrates the power of armed self-defense and the appeal of radical action.

Born in 1925 in Monroe, North Carolina, Williams grew up as part of the Black working class. His father worked for the railroads as a skilled laborer. Williams came from a civil rights background: during Reconstruction, his grandfather ran a newspaper that supported Black political power. When Williams was a child, Monroe had a nasty and awful racist police chief. At the age of eleven, he witnessed the officer beat and drag a Black woman through the streets. The chief's name was Jesse Helms Sr.; his son Jesse Jr. would later become the far-right anti–civil rights senator from North Carolina.[3]

Williams went north like 1.5 million other African Americans during World War II. He ended up in Detroit and there witnessed the city's 1943 race riots, when whites killed twenty-five Black people; seventeen of them were killed by the police.[4] Williams took a job in an auto factory and joined United Auto Workers Local 600, an interracial local with communist leadership.[5] Williams did not have a particularly strong political outlook at that time, but the commitment of these leaders influenced him. He was then drafted into the marines in 1944 and served eighteen months. When he faced the white officers' racism, he talked back and refused orders, for which he got a three-month sentence in the stockade.[6]

After the war, Williams returned to North Carolina and married sixteen-year-old Mabel Robinson. With the exception of Rosa Parks and perhaps Fannie Lou Hamer, the story of the civil rights movement is told through the lives of men, but everyone knew at the time that women ran the day-to-day show and kept everything together, and the same applies to Mabel. While Robert would be the most notorious Williams, she was every bit his equal in the fight for justice that was to come.

Racism infuriated Robert and Mabel. World War II witnessed an explosion in the size of the NAACP, as a growing Black middle class joined and gave financial support to activists determined to break down the nation's racial caste system. The NAACP generally took a gradualist approach to civil rights. It used a legal strategy that slowly chipped away at desegregation, eventually leading to the *Brown v. Board of Education* decision in 1954 that ruled school segregation unconstitutional. But as a grassroots organization fighting for civil rights in small southern communities, the NAACP had limited value.[7]

In 1931, nine young Black men were falsely accused of rape and nearly lynched in Scottsboro, Alabama. The Scottsboro Boys became an international cause that the Communist Party took the lead on and that forced the NAACP to become involved, but many Black radicals were deeply disappointed by the organization's response. NAACP leadership did not want to be involved defending Black men accused of sexual crimes. Never mind that these young people were completely innocent, a fact to which one of the white "victims" later admitted.[8]

Williams was more willing to fight than the NAACP leadership, as were many World War II veterans. Shortly after Williams returned from his military service, a Black veteran named Bennie Montgomery killed his white employer, for which Montgomery was tried and executed by the State of North Carolina. When Montgomery's body was sent home to Monroe, members of the KKK, angry that they had been denied the chance to lynch Montgomery, wanted to desecrate the corpse. Williams joined other Black men in the community, armed with rifles, in guarding the funeral home that held the body. The Klan scurried away like rats. Williams learned a lot on that day in 1947.[9]

In 1948, Williams went back to Detroit to work in a Cadillac plant, and he rejoined the United Auto Workers. This time he became involved in the leftist union local and even published an article in the communist journal *Detroit Daily Worker.* General Motors fired him in 1949 for repeatedly challenging his white supervisor. This got the attention of the FBI, which noted in a report that he always complained of discrimination, whether in the military or civilian life. He then returned to Monroe and pondered how he could become a leader in the civil rights fight. Over the next few years, he moved between North and South, between various jobs, and even rejoined the marines for a short time. He was unhappy, furious about racism, and lost on how to fight it.[10]

Williams found a path forward when he joined Monroe's NAACP chapter. It did not take him long to transform that chapter into a militant force in a town where whites mostly agreed with the racial attitudes of the Helms family. In 1957, Williams led the organization in a fight to desegregate the public swimming pool, crossing a red line for whites obsessed by fears of Black sexuality. With the support of the Black community of Monroe, Williams organized active picket lines at the pools. For whites, this was race war. For Williams, it was a way to engage the community. Whereas the large majority of NAACP chapters had a notably middle-class orientation, in Williams's hands, the Monroe chapter became an organization for working-class struggle.[11]

Monroe had a large Ku Klux Klan chapter. Williams had a plan for countering that: armed self-defense. The veterans that made up large parts of this movement were simply not going to allow whites to use violence against them.[12] Word leaked that the KKK was planning to attack the vice president of the Monroe NAACP chapter, Dr. Albert Perry. He had worked with Williams to rebuild the chapter and, like Williams, he was a World War II veteran and willing to use guns to defend himself. Williams and his men put sandbags around Perry's home, and when the Klan came that night and fired into the house, they fired back. The Monroe City Council responded by banning the Klan from holding an event in the town without a special permit from authorities. For many Black residents of Monroe, Williams had launched a new volley in their freedom struggle and it came from the barrel of a gun.[13]

Williams soon opened a Monroe chapter of the National Rifle Association—this was before the NRA became the far-right extremist organization we know so well today. He announced that armed self-defense was the policy of the local NAACP. The moderate, New York–based NAACP president Roy Wilkins was furious. Finding Williams a troublemaker, Wilkins and other national leaders tried to isolate him.

In 1958, two young Black boys, ages nine and seven, were arrested in Monroe. Their "crime": kissing a white girl while playing. In fact, the girl had probably kissed them. The police threw these two young boys in jail. Such incidents often led to lynchings, even of children, as in the tragic case of Emmett Till in 1955. These little boys had the local white people salivating for a lynching. Fearing the KKK would lynch them, the city placed the boys in a reform school that more accurately should be described as a prison camp.[14]

In what became known as the "Kissing Case," Williams led the fight to save the boys and became famous in civil rights circles for his work on it. Monroe became an embarrassment to the nation and the world. With the rise of the Cold War and the Global South liberation movements creating new nations in Africa that the U.S. wanted as allies against Soviet communism, this sort of incident became important geopolitically, and was something that the Soviets were more than happy to publicize. Why would a new nation in Africa agree to unite with this superpower if it treated people of African descent so poorly? At the Eisenhower White House, letters poured in from around the nation and the world urging the president to end the case against these children.[15]

Williams found the national NAACP useless in the struggle. As with the Scottsboro Boys, its national leadership feared taking on cases that had to do with sexual relations, even something as innocent as small children kissing. So Williams worked with a communist lawyer named Conrad Lynn to create the Committee to Combat Racial Injustice, sparking a powerful local movement that not only defended these children but also channeled the discontent the local Black community felt. The committee pushed back on the ingrained deference that defined race relations in the town. Williams traveled to northern cities to give speeches about the case and, in doing so, built himself a following that soon proved invaluable.[16]

Williams paid a huge price for his activism. The FBI upped its surveillance, and his insurance company canceled his policy after he led the defense of the Perry house.

In 1959, after courts threw out a case against white men for assaulting Black women in Monroe, Williams told a group of newspaper reporters, "We must be willing to kill if necessary." Roy Wilkins was apoplectic when this story went national. In a phone call between the two men, Williams gave back to Wilkins as good as he got. Wilkins recorded the conversation, and the transcript showed a man willing to stand up to one of the most famous civil rights leaders in the country, as well as to whites. Wilkins immediately suspended Williams and moved to have him kicked out of the NAACP.[17]

Wilkins might have wanted to crush Williams politically, but many rank-and-file members of the NAACP supported his methods. They wanted to stand up for themselves too. He was hardly the only civil rights leader talking about self-defense at this time. Daisy Bates, leader of the Little Rock school desegregation effort in 1957, talked frequently about always carrying a pistol with her. She supported Williams too.[18]

Williams accepted his NAACP suspension but kept organizing in Monroe. He kept up the pressure to integrate the town's swimming pools. He and Mabel also proceeded to push a proto–Black nationalist ideology, using the outlets of both radio and his newspaper, the *Crusader Weekly Newsletter.* They made connections between the movement in the South and Black poverty in the North, placed the American struggle in context with the anti-colonial struggles happening in Asia, Latin America, and especially Africa, and gave lessons to readers on Black history. He frequently visited activists in New York and built connections between the movement he led in Monroe and the growing demands for Black Power nationwide. In doing so, he touched a large group of activists for whom the nonviolence associated with King and the fight for integration in the South had little functional appeal.[19]

In 1961, someone ran Williams's car off the road, but the police refused to investigate. Later, after a second car attack, the white man driving the other car came at him with a bat. Williams pulled a gun. As Williams later recalled of the event and his attacker, "The old man saw his way of life slipping away before his eyes."[20] Tensions rose in the days after the attacks on Williams. Random violence directed against Monroe's Black population escalated, including a firebombing campaign against the town's Black-owned businesses.

That same year saw the beginning of the Freedom Rides, the student-led movement to desegregate interstate bus transportation across the South. Williams and his comrades hosted the Freedom Riders in their homes.[21] That August, a race riot broke out in Monroe when the Freedom Riders came to town. What especially infuriated whites was an interracial group attending church together. James Forman, one of the Freedom Rider leaders, later stated he thought he would die in Monroe.[22]

Shortly after the Freedom Riders continued their journey, Williams and his allies armed themselves, barricaded the street around his home, and prepared to protect it and his family from a possible lynching. When a white couple accidently drove into the barricade, Williams had them brought to his house, for their own safety. The cops, believing Williams had taken them hostage, wanted to use this as a pretext to eliminate him. Williams, Mabel, and their children fled that day. To stay in North Carolina would have meant going to prison or even being lynched. The family left the United States and, after brief stints in Canada and Mexico, ended up in Cuba.[23]

The FBI, led by notoriously racist J. Edgar Hoover, charged Williams with unlawful interstate flight. Hoover himself signed Williams's wanted poster. Hoover thought King was a communist. If King and his doctrine of nonviolence so threatened the director, he thought someone like Williams was a revolutionary terrorist who needed elimination. Just a few years later, through the infamous COINTELPRO program, Hoover would lead the FBI in the systematic arrest and assassination of Black Panther Party leaders.[24]

Martin Luther King defended Williams's actions, noting how many times Williams had appealed to Monroe's leaders to end segregation and stop anti-Black violence. Moreover, Williams respected King. He stated in a 1959 article that King was "a great and successful leader of our race." But he also noted the realities of life in the rural South and said his only difference with King was that "I believe in flexibility in the freedom struggle."[25]

Fidel Castro welcomed the Williams family to Cuba as political exiles. Castro, basking in the glow of the brand-new revolution he led, saw them as heroes in the battle against white American racism that both Cubans and Black Americans had faced. The two already knew each other: Castro had met Williams on his 1960 trip to Harlem, and that same year, Williams made his first visit to Cuba, during which he told Cuban media about the racism in the United States, thus increasing the FBI's determination to silence him.[26]

Williams did not want to just sit around in Cuba. He wanted

to influence the struggle back home, despite being in exile. In the 1960s, the media channel for this kind of work was the radio. Williams did not believe the American media reported properly on the freedom struggle. White-owned media either opposed it outright or did not report in depth on what was happening, and much Black-owned media feared talking too much about radicalism.

Williams wanted a radio program that could transmit the real stories back to the United States, especially in the South. Castro gladly accepted Williams's proposal. *Radio Free Dixie* ran from 1962 until 1965; the program was led by Robert and Mabel Williams but benefited from plenty of help from their Cuban comrades. The Williamses also wrote their memoir, *Negroes with Guns,* while in Cuba.[27] The book is credited solely to Robert but with "input" from Mabel. More than likely, she wrote a large part of it; even more likely, she also typed it. Unfortunately, wives have long done much of the uncredited work on famous books by men.

Williams became a hero for many in the civil rights movement, especially as it moved to the left and Cuba became a prime destination for civil rights workers fleeing the racist American state. His book's influence grew as younger activists, tired of watching their comrades being slaughtered, lost interest in nonviolence. Black Power was on the rise. Black Americans in northern cities also wanted freedom and justice. Racism was not confined to the South. But it was not law that kept them in dilapidated housing and poor schools in Chicago, Oakland, and Los Angeles. It was custom. How do you fight against that? Williams became a guiding light for a new generation of Black activists undergoing new struggles. It's thus not surprising that *Negroes with Guns* was a major influence on the Black Panthers, especially its leader Huey Newton.[28]

In 1965, Williams traveled to North Vietnam to express solidarity against the racist and imperialist war the United States engaged against the attempt to unify Vietnam. That year, Robert and Mabel moved from Cuba to China, a change that didn't suit them well. Williams, who was no doctrinaire communist, hated the puritanical nature of the Cultural Revolution, which began shortly after their arrival. They longed to return home. In 1968, Williams wrote to allies at home that he would come back to the U.S. as long as there was the financial backing for a legal defense that could keep him out of jail.

By that time, many people had forgotten Williams—but not J. Edgar Hoover. Hoover still believed he was a threat equal to that of Malcolm X. But the Williamses came back anyway. Police arrested Robert at the Detroit airport and then extradited him to North Carolina, though he ended up not serving any time. He did not go to trial until 1975, with the legendary William Kunstler as his attorney, and the state immediately dismissed all the fifteen-year-old charges.

Robert and Mabel Williams lived out the rest of their lives quietly, though they remained committed leftists. Robert died in 1996; Mabel lived until 2014. Who gave the eulogy at Robert Williams's funeral? Rosa Parks—which should make you continue to rethink everything you know about nonviolence and the civil rights movement. Parks stated she "always admired Robert Williams for his courage and his commitment to freedom. The work that he did should go down in history and never be forgotten."[29]

14

Ella Baker

Give People Light and They Will Find Their Own Way

Sometimes, an activist labors her entire life to change the world. For years—decades even—she struggles to get any recognition for her work. She suffers the racism of society at large. She suffers its sexism too—from the men who are supposed to be her comrades in the struggle. She becomes a little cynical. She learns the hard way about who to trust and not to trust. For a moment, she considers dropping out and just focusing on herself. That's what a lot of people would do. But then, she resolves to take her skills, focus on the next generation, and change the world that way.

This is the story of Ella Baker, one of the most amazing people in American history. From 1930 to 1980, she fought at the forefront of radical change. Like intersectional activists today, she understood how race, gender, and class intersect in people's oppression. She knew that to take on the inequalities of capitalism, you must take on the inequalities of race at the same time. That remains true in a nation and world where the legacies of slavery, colonialism, imperialism, and incarceration define our society. Knowing Ella Baker's story can provide us inspiration in our fights against these intertwined sources of inequality.

Baker was also the organizer's organizer. She had an amazing ability to think through how to organize at the local level. At the core of Baker's organizing was something we all need to remember—to start with people where they are. In other words, you can't assume that everyone around you shares your values. Any mass movement requires real organizing. Not just talking about organizing, not just hanging out with our friends and talking about change. It requires engagement with people who might not agree with you.

The key, Baker showed, is listening. Active listening, really considering the position of others, builds empathy and solidarity. In recent years, the coal country organizer Veronica Coptis has written about how talking and listening to coal workers on the issue of climate change can help build up their organizing capacity. They don't agree with her that coal contributes to global warming, or even that global warming exists, but they do see other impacts of mining on their beloved home state and they want to organize with her around them. You build alliances around shared concerns. Whether the subject is abortion or gay rights or climate change or guns, if we want to move forward in building a better world, we have to learn to talk to people who disagree with us, find a common ground, and then provide information about a different worldview to them.[1]

Ella Baker knew this. An effective organizer doesn't accept inequalities and reactionary ideas. They attempt to move people in the right direction, shaping individuals into a fighting force for justice. And when the organizer doesn't succeed in completely transforming an individual immediately to all of their positions, they don't stomp away in frustration. They just keep working, usually out of the spotlight. For most of Baker's life, that's where she remained—building, building, and then building some more. Then it all paid off in the biggest way possible when her work changed the trajectory of American history.

Born in 1903 in Norfolk, Virginia, Baker grew up in North Carolina, after her mother fled the racial violence of that city. Baker's grandmother largely raised her, and she often told stories to young Ella about life under slavery and the need to fight for justice. As a slave, her owner whipped her severely for refusing to marry a man whom he had selected for her. After the Civil War and emancipation, she married a husband she loved and they managed to save up enough money to buy land. They became reasonably successful farmers in an era when this was quite an achievement for a Black family. Her mother was active in the Baptist church, one woman among many seeking to carve out a bigger place for women through the church. In her own fights for change, Baker took inspiration from her mother and grandmother.[2]

Baker's family did well enough that Ella could go to college. She attended Shaw University, a Black institution, in Raleigh, North Carolina. Even this early in her life, she protested the school's dress codes and its required religion courses. At this point, her concept of change centered on racial uplift, a belief that respectable behavior could elevate the entire race. This was a common belief among the Black middle class, but one that also got in the way of organizing, as it tended to have at its core a class snobbishness and an embarrassment about working-class people. W.E.B. Du Bois, who articulated the idea that the "talented tenth" of well-off Black Americans would lead the fight for equality, famously articulated these class divides.[3]

After graduation, Baker moved to New York and got a job with the *Negro National News* as a journalist. She also joined the Young Negroes Cooperative League, an early stalwart in the fight for Black economic self-sufficiency, building upon the work of the pan-Africanist Marcus Garvey. Soon the YNCL made Baker its national director. She helped turn the YNCL into a grassroots movement of Black socialists who demanded gender equality in their fight for racial justice and a fair economy. She moved to Harlem, the center of Black political and cultural radicalism—a community that his changed her life. She also got to know the Jewish socialists of Greenwich Village and started reading Karl Marx. While working at the New York Public Library's Harlem branch, Baker got involved in broader community education programs, becoming friends with other leading young Black intellectuals and activists, such as the future lawyer and freedom fighter Pauli Murray, another amazing American who would be part of the civil rights struggle over the next half century. This fertile site of political, artistic, and intellectual upheaval reshaped Baker's mind. She remained connected to her southern roots but learned much that she could then apply to the fight for broader change. The YNCL did not succeed, but it did give Baker organizing experience.[4]

During a stint in the Works Progress Administration, one of Franklin Delano Roosevelt's most important New Deal agencies, Baker continued her organizing work on two fronts—against Italy's fascist invasion of Ethiopia in 1938 and for efforts in support of the Scottsboro Boys. In Ethiopia and Alabama, Baker saw the international repression of African people by violent white supremacy.[5] Despite the NAACP's indifference to the Scottsboro Boys, to which she strongly disapproved, Baker took a job with the organization in 1940.[6]

By this time, she knew that real civil rights change would come from the bottom up, from the grassroots efforts of the Black community. So she spent as little time as possible in the national office and instead worked with the NAACP's local chapters, especially in the South, to enable them to make their own change. By this point, Baker believed strongly in direct democracy and used her powers to help the people of the South fight for their own agenda rather than push one on them. She stayed anywhere she could, with families in the poorest areas making room for her in their homes. She never made fun of anyone's accent. She did not look down on people because they did not have the education she did. Her aim was simply to organize them to take power over their own lives. As she said, "Give people light and they will find their own way."[7]

Through her years of organizing, Baker slowly built up an unprecedented network of contacts throughout the South. They knew her and trusted her. She trusted them. This placed her in a unique position to build what today we call the civil rights movement. But rather than seeing it as an isolated phenomenon, we should see the civil rights movement as the culmination of a longer Black freedom struggle. The high point of the 1950s and 1960s was possible because a generation of organizers such as Baker had spent decades preparing local people to agitate for change.[8]

In 1957, Baker entered Martin Luther King's orbit, taking a job with the Southern Christian Leadership Conference. King founded the SCLC after the world-changing victory of the Montgomery bus boycott the year before. Needing an experienced organizer, King hired Baker as the SCLC's first staffer. She continued her grassroots organizing, working with local communities in Georgia, Alabama, and Louisiana.

With the SCLC, she hoped for an organization more supportive of grassroots organizing than she had with the NAACP.[9] But Baker did not get that result. She had a strong skepticism of charismatic leadership, believing that long-term change could result only from the building of mass movements. That took hard work, and she devoted her life to achieving it. King frustrated her tremendously. She came to realize that he did not understand why they had won with the Montgomery campaign. He often expressed amazement at their success, but she knew it came from the years of local organizing that built a strong Black community in that city. She hoped King and the SCLC would see the need for mass mobilization to move forward. But for four years after the landmark 1956 victory, the organization had not developed a campaign to organize the masses. She worked to solve that problem and organized the Crusade for Citizenship, an extensive SCLC voter registration campaign, in 1958, pushing King and his allies to put major resources into the campaign's local efforts.[10]

But Baker could not get the level of attention she needed from King. She personally knew all the major leaders of the Black freedom struggle and suffered sexist treatment from most of them, from W.E.B. Du Bois to Thurgood Marshall to Martin Luther King. As a woman, her ability to influence the established leadership of the civil rights struggle had sharp limitations. So she did what she always did—went outside that leadership and focused on the grassroots, the few SCLC affiliates in the South doing organizing, especially in Birmingham, Alabama, where local leaders such as Reverend Fred Shuttlesworth were laying the groundwork for what would become one of the movement's key campaigns in 1963. She also organized a major voter registration drive in Shreveport, Louisiana.[11]

In 1960, college students revived the civil rights movement. Four students at North Carolina A&T University in Greensboro sat down at a Woolworth's lunch counter and refused to move until they were served. They returned the next day with their friends. The sit-ins worked, forcing Greensboro to desegregate its public facilities. That led to students around the South—but mostly in cities such as Nashville and Atlanta—expanding the sit-in movement to their cities. It gave the movement the shot in the arm it needed.[12]

These students were activists, not organizers. To build on their successes, they had to turn into organizers, so Ella Baker became their mentor. In 1960, the students met at Shaw University in Raleigh, North Carolina, to form a new organization, which would become known as the Student Nonviolent Coordinating Committee (SNCC). Baker organized the convention. The students were in awe of Ms. Baker, as they called her, for her extensive experience and the wise advice she shared. She also listened to them. She did not try to tell them what to do. They wanted nonhierarchical leadership, and she encouraged them to follow through on that vision.[13]

Ella Baker told SNCC to remain independent of any outside organization and to avoid "leader-centered orientation."[14] As Julian Bond, one of the leading SNCC activists, later remembered, "She didn't say, 'Don't let Martin Luther King tell you what to do,' but you got the real feeling that that's what she meant."[15]

Baker's work for SNCC did not end at the founding convention. Because she had committed herself so completely to grassroots organizing in the South, she was one of only a few national civil rights figures who knew who to contact in small towns. SNCC wanted to send organizers to Mississippi to register people to vote. This was dangerous work, as the next chapter will explore. But Baker knew exactly who to contact—Amzie Moore in Cleveland, Mississippi, a local NAACP activist she knew well and respected. In making these connections, she served as a critical bridge between two sets of democratic activists that together transformed Mississippi. As that campaign slowly grew into the kind of democratic revolution that she envisioned, empowering the impoverished sharecroppers of the region to register to vote, Baker deepened her involvement.

In Mississippi, Baker became a major influence on Fannie Lou Hamer, the grassroots activist who became the voice of the civil rights movement there, speaking out publicly about the incredible violence she had experienced at the hands of the police and demanding equal political participation for her people. Baker's focus on organizing women to be leaders greatly impressed Hamer, who, in a 1973 interview, would cite Baker as the most important Black leader in America, calling her "a beautiful human being."[16] Baker then helped SNCC organize the Mississippi Freedom Democratic Party to challenge the all-white Democratic delegation from Mississippi at the 1964 Democratic National Convention. That challenge was not successful, but it did galvanize the nation thanks to Hamer's powerful testimony of the oppression she had suffered registering people to vote. The following year, after more organizing and suffering, most notably the beatings of civil rights activists marching from Selma to Montgomery, Alabama, President Lyndon Johnson pushed for and signed the Voting Rights Act.[17]

Unlike many of the civil rights leaders of the 1950s and early

1960s, Baker did not shy away from the Black Power movement, which in part originated with the anger and disappointment felt by SNCC activists after their frustrations with the Democratic Party in 1964. She felt many of the older tactics of the movement had stopped working and that the movement needed new energy. She also did not have any particular commitment to nonviolence. She absolutely believed that people had the right to defend themselves, with arms if necessary. She remained an influential figure in SNCC through 1966. She urged SNCC's leadership to learn from Global South revolutionary leaders and created a seminar titled "Revolutionary Ethics," which provided the young leaders a solid theoretical basis for their new beliefs and helped them think through their problems. Her main criticism of the Black Power movement was that the overly masculine rhetoric of Black Power had more in common with the stale leadership of male-dominated organizations she had dealt with her entire life than the grassroots action of Mississippi.[18]

In 1967, Baker moved back to New York, where she lived in semiretirement. Of course, no organizer ever truly retires. She helped when she could, getting heavily involved in the campaign to free the radical Angela Davis from prison in 1972. She supported the anti-colonialist struggle for Puerto Rican independence from the U.S. She had long despised imperialism, but this was the first time that she organized directly against it. She spoke at rallies opposing the South African apartheid state. She also fought for women's rights. A respected senior figure, she was much beloved by the thousands of people she impacted in her life.[19]

Baker died at the age of eighty-three, in 1986. Why don't we remember Baker today like we remember King and Parks and Malcolm? One reason is that she never promoted herself as the leader she was. In fact, to call attention to herself would have betrayed what she most believed about organizing and social justice. She would have wanted us to remember the grassroots activists whom she trained.

Significant change happened because people such as Ella Baker did the hard legwork for decades, organizing before Martin Luther King ever took a job as a minister in Montgomery, Alabama. There are hundreds of people like this—though maybe not quite as prominent as Baker—who spent their whole lives leading the fight for justice and never receiving the recognition they deserved. It's well past time we recognize Ella Baker for the great leader that can inspire us toward democratic, radical change today.

15

Bob Moses

The Organizer of Mississippi

Historians tell a complex narrative about the civil rights movement. But this complexity hasn't made it into the popular narrative, which continues to tell a simple story about a small of group of deserving luminaries, with cherry-picked facts and lines of speeches taken out of context. Martin Luther King Jr.'s "I Have a Dream" speech, delivered during the March on Washington in 1963, is the most famous moment in the movement, but that speech has lost its meaning. Most mainstream narratives focus on the one line about a dream and kids playing together, which allows conservatives to make King into whatever they want him to be while eclipsing any actual beliefs King held. The Robert Williams chapter demonstrated a more complex relationship between King and guns than acknowledged in the public stories we tell about the movement—not much talk of this on Martin Luther King Day every January! We create heroes out of the handful of civil rights activists we only ever hear about—MLK, Parks, Malcolm, John Lewis. Yet it took hundreds of committed organizers to motivate tens of thousands of people to show up for events, register to vote, and fight for justice.

We need to bring complex stories to the public to discover how we got to these moments of dramatic change. What kind of grassroots organizing made the civil rights movement happen? It is in these stories where we learn the real history of civil rights. By broadening our understanding of this era, we find wisdom in the stories intentionally omitted from the mainstream, watered-down version of this radical turning point in American history.

At times when real change on the issues we care about seems distant or even impossible, we can pull from the lessons of those who came before us for guidance. Victory can be just around the corner even if you can't always see it. But to get there, you need committed organizers, a moral stance, a clear set of goals, and, most importantly, personal and organizational discipline. That last one is often a real problem in a society where individualism is the order of the day.

Like most of us, there wasn't much in Bob Moses's background to suggest he would become a legendary organizer. Born in Harlem in 1935, Moses grew up in the public housing projects. He loved books and spent his childhood in the library. He graduated from the prestigious Stuyvesant High School and then went on to Hamilton College. He played basketball while majoring in French and philosophy. He then went back home and started teaching math. Moses was an everyman, with wide-ranging interests and great tenacity.[1]

In 1958, Moses was presented with a very unusual opportunity. The Teenagers, a Black and Puerto Rican doo-wop group, toured the country. But the members, true to their name, were teenagers who still had obligations to their schooling, so their record company hired Moses to tutor Frankie Lymon, one of the band's singers, on the road. This brought Moses out of New York and enabled him to meet other Black Americans across the nation. Leaving New York also exposed him to the range of oppression that Black folks faced in other places, which at times could be even more disturbing than what he experienced at home.[2]

Once back in New York, Moses got to know Bayard Rustin, one of the most important organizers in American history. Rustin had helped organize A. Philip Randolph's March on Washington movement to desegregate the defense industry in 1941, worked during World War II to protect the property of Japanese Americans forced into the nation's concentration camps, and had engaged in personal desegregation efforts in southern bus systems as early as 1942. He was both a pacifist—he refused to fight in World War II—and a gay man, which meant he experienced additional marginalization even within his own already marginalized community. A brilliant organizer, he was everywhere in the movement for a half century. In short, he was the perfect mentor for Moses.[3]

Moses helped Rustin with the Youth Marches for Integrated Schools, two large marches in Washington organized by a coalition of northern white liberals and Black activists in support of integrating southern schools. Moses then moved to Atlanta to work in King's Southern Christian Leadership Conference. He started out stuffing fundraising packets, yet he yearned for a more integral role in the movement.[4]

In 1960, Moses joined the Student Nonviolent Coordinating Committee. He later stated about the sit-in movement that led to SNCC's formation, "Before, the Negro in the South had always looked on the defensive, cringing. This time they were taking the initiative. They were kids my age, and I knew this had something to do with my own life. It made me realize that for a long time I had been troubled by the problem of being a Negro and at the same time being an American. This was the answer."[5] In other words, it was time to take the offensive—to no longer accept the "problem" of being a Negro.

When Ella Baker gathered the students together to form SNCC, she and Moses got along immediately. He saw her as a mentor and listened closely. He found Baker's passion for local organizing especially interesting, and became perhaps her greatest student. Organizing happens generationally. One great organizer passes skills down to the next. Baker always wanted to build new leadership. They both understood that you must use your organizing skills not to promote yourself, but to find new leaders to carry the struggle forward. This is a prescient lesson for organizing today: in an era when personal branding is so prominent, we can fall into a vanity trap in which individuals become more important than the movement itself.

Moses traveled through the South building SNCC chapters on college campuses. In Mississippi, he met a man named Amzie Moore, a friend of Baker. An NAACP activist in the Mississippi Delta, Moore risked his life every day in a time and place that was radically violent. He urged Moses to put his words into action and bring committed students to Mississippi to register Black people to vote. Moses promised to do so and the next year, in 1961, SNCC launched its Mississippi Project, with Moses as its leader.[6]

Moses and two others started in the town of McComb. The work of these volunteers tapped into a tradition of activism by McComb residents. Moses and his fellow workers walked door to door, convincing people to register to vote. Most would not risk it, but some did. Almost immediately, interest spread to surrounding counties. Moses went to the tiny town of Liberty, escorting three Black residents to the county courthouse to register. There, he was arrested on made-up charges and given a ninety-day suspended sentence. He immediately resumed registering voters, for which a white sheriff beat him mercilessly. He continued organizing.[7]

The area where Moses and others were organizing, in southwest Mississippi, had a Black-majority population, which the white minority controlled through its incessant assault on Black bodies and land—lynching and property theft. When Black people stood up for any reason—social, economic, political—violence ensued. Because they dominated the legal system, white people could effectively kill a Black person for any reason without fear of punishment. According to NAACP statistics, Mississippi led the nation in lynchings between 1882 and 1968, with a horrifying 581 murders. That's the most in the nation, slightly ahead of Georgia and Texas. This was KKK country. It was also NAACP country, with active and unflinching local Black leadership.[8]

Bob Moses would soon come to realize the reality of this violence. When locals in Amite County found out that a Black man named Herbert Lee had helped Moses, the local representative in the state legislature personally shot and killed Lee. Moses demanded government protection for civil rights workers from additional white violence. The FBI and its racist chief J. Edgar Hoover refused to do anything.[9] Yet Moses kept going, despite the very real threats to his life. In fact, he faced several assassination attempts in which white people shot at the cars he and other civil rights organizers were riding in. When the Jackson-based NAACP leader R.L. Smith ran for Congress on a civil rights platform in 1962—a remarkable challenge to white supremacy at the time—Moses served as his campaign manager, building on the momentum generated by the voter registration efforts.[10]

Moses had very specific ideas about how best to organize—keep finding new leaders; train them, build them, and get them to find and train leaders of their own. He believed in hiring young organizers who were not beholden to white people economically nor had families to protect. He encouraged young activists training at Myles Horton's Highlander Folk School in Tennessee to join the struggle. They spread across the Delta, expanding the voter rights campaign into more counties.[11]

Moses did not shy away from the fear of white violence. Rather, he organized around the need to kill the fear and inferiority that a racist society had bred inside Black people. For Moses, fighting back was both a material and psychological endeavor: his organizing principle was to focus on developing new attitudes about race and justice. As he stated in 1963, "You combat your own fears about beatings, shootings, and possible mob violence; you stymie, by your mere physical presence, anxious fear of the Negro community . . . you organize, pound by pound, small bands of people . . . you create a small striking force."[12]

Moses was not a loud man. He did not have the type of charisma that so helped Eugene Debs or Mike Quill or Elizabeth Gurley Flynn. He was a quiet, bookish guy, with an amazing calm about him. People in the movement compared him to Jesus because his quiet dignity, bravery, and intellect inspired everyone around him in an almost mystical way. Once, after white supremacists destroyed a SNCC office, Moses surveyed the damage, then took a nap on a bed inside. This kind of calm impressed those who—with good reason—felt afraid under the constant threat of terror from a white supremacist state and society.[13]

Moses never liked these comparisons to Christ. He was a fighter. The Kennedy administration largely wanted the problem of civil rights to go away, but Moses and his comrades would not stop their fight. Moses stressed to anyone in power he could gain access to—congressional committees, judges, lawyers, politicians—how the "compromises" the administration tried to reach with the state's white political establishment (such as lowering the literacy test to vote to a sixth-grade education) were completely unacceptable. Through 1962 and 1963, SNCC continued organizing, but the reality of violence made their job long, hard, slow, and very dangerous.[14]

In 1964, SNCC invited white northerners to Mississippi for a gigantic voter registration drive. This became known as Freedom Summer. Today, it is often remembered as a moment of racial harmony, when good people of both races fought for justice. The reality is more complex. The decision to bring in white organizers caused a lot of dissension within SNCC. Young activists were growing more militant and distrustful of whites, even liberals. On the other hand, they needed all the help they could get with registering voters: after three years of organizing, only about 5 percent of Black adults in these counties had registered to vote. The white activist Allard Lowenstein, who in 1963 had brought some white organizers from northern college campuses to register voters for state elections that fall, immediately started planning to bring upward of a thousand students to Mississippi in the summer of 1964.

Many in SNCC opposed what became known as Freedom Summer. They worried about white organizers taking over their movement. They feared that overconfident college kids would tell experienced organizers what to do rather than listen and do the work required of them without complaining. Moses took the dissenters' concerns seriously, but ultimately won the day, in part because of the support he had from the movement's grassroots leaders such as Fannie Lou Hamer. SNCC engaged in a significant training session for the organizers to prepare them for how to operate in Mississippi. That included telling them that many of the people they came to help would resent their presence. Moses kept people focused on the task at hand, while acknowledging that it was easy to be scared, especially once the random shotgun blasts rang out in the night or someone closely followed an organizer's car on the dark roads of a Mississippi night. Moses also was candid with white recruits regarding the SNCC's ongoing debate about whether white people should be invited into the movement.[15] He wanted them to have deference and respect. They were not saviors; they were organizers in training.

One of the reasons why SNCC's advocates for Freedom Summer wanted to bring in white volunteers was their belief that the media and national politicians did not care if Black civil rights workers were killed, but that if the racists attacked some white organizers, finally someone in power would pay attention to the Mississippi struggle. On June 21, 1964, this prediction proved correct—when white northerners were in the crossfire of violence, it drew national attention. After holding a voter registration rally in Philadelphia, Mississippi, two white volunteers, Michael Schwerner and Andrew Goodman, and a local Black volunteer named James Chaney were murdered by the Ku Klux Klan. In fact, these murders were abetted by the county sheriff himself. After the ensuing uproar, J. Edgar

Hoover showed up personally to address people's demands to find the bodies, despite his open hostility to the cause they died fighting to achieve.

The murders scared the volunteers stiff. Moses had to settle them down. He had the moral authority to get them to listen. He told them that now they knew the violence SNCC volunteers and brave community members fighting for their rights experienced all the time. They knew what this commitment took. If they wanted to leave, they should go. If they wanted to stay, they understood the risks. At that fragile moment, Moses kept the movement together. Freedom Summer continued.[16]

The SNCC took its next step in challenging white supremacy later that summer. SNCC leaders decided to create the Mississippi Freedom Democratic Party (MFDP). As discussed in the Ella Baker chapter, the MFDP challenged the all-white Democratic Party at the 1964 Democratic National Convention, claiming that the mainstream Democrats in that state did not represent the people, which was of course true since they refused to let Black Mississippians vote. They wanted the Democratic National Committee to recognize the MFDP as the state's legitimate Democratic Party instead. Moses and the other SNCC leaders put the principles of Freedom Summer into action, publicizing the oppression they faced in front of national television cameras. As with Freedom Summer, creating the MFDP was controversial within the SNCC. In fact, Moses did not support the move, thinking that it would fail and drag the organizing energy away from grassroots priorities and into the cynicism of Washington politics.[17]

The MFDP challenge to the Democratic Party was a dramatic moment. Fannie Lou Hamer's testimony at the convention, in which she talked about the beatings she had suffered in the Mississippi struggle, galvanized the nation, even as President Lyndon Johnson tried to distract from her speech through a hastily planned and pointless national press conference. But in the end, the Democrats did not oust the Mississippi white supremacists. Johnson wanted to win the election, and he feared the white South would leave the party en masse if he took a firm stance. He believed that by signing the Civil Rights Act of 1964 that July, he had earned the trust of the civil rights movement, but he was wrong about that.

For Moses, the Democratic establishment's unwillingness to acquiesce to a nonviolent democratic movement was devastating. For the first time, he seriously questioned his future, the nonviolence he had embraced, and the belief that he could work within the political system for change.[18]

After three years of engaging in the hardest organizing possible, Moses was burned out. He did not give up on social change, but he understandably needed time for himself to reset and think about his future. Moses also strongly resisted the idea that a single leader could, or should, make change. He remained deeply uncomfortable with the descriptions of him as Christlike. Families in the Delta were even putting pictures of him next to their pictures of Jesus. He attempted to overcome all this by continuing to work. He visited several African nations in the fall of 1964, after which he returned with a proposal to expand the Mississippi Project, but with only Black volunteers. He came to believe that Black leadership could not develop with white people in leadership positions. However, he did not have the energy to see this vision through. It was time to move on.[19]

Late in 1964, Moses resigned from his duties. He said that his role had become "too strong, too central, so that people who did not need to began to lean on me, to use me as a crutch."[20] Once again, a key tenet of organizing is that individual organizers must eventually recede into the broader movement. Your purpose as a leader is not to establish yourself as the ultimate authority; it's to create other leaders. When the movement and the organizer become one and the same, the movement risks being enveloped by the organizer's ego and their growing desire for control. This is a common problem, one we have seen throughout the left's history. It takes a remarkable individual to see this coming and step away in time to allow the movement to grow without them. Bob Moses was such a person.

Moses tried to disappear back into grassroots initiatives, where he could do his work without adulation and praise getting in the way of the actual organizing. He stopped using his last name and instead used his middle name, going by "Bob Parris." He organized against the Vietnam War. At a large anti–Vietnam War demonstration in April 1965, Moses stated that the antiwar and civil rights struggles were essentially one and the same. He moved toward a greater critique of American militarism as well, including engaging in early anti-nuclear actions. At a protest to commemorate the twentieth anniversary of the U.S. using nuclear bombs on Japan, members of the American Nazi Party threw red paint on him and other leaders of the movement.[21] As Robert Williams and

Ella Baker did later in their lives, he adopted an increasingly global focus. This made sense. Many civil rights organizers at the time compared their struggles to the anti-colonial struggles then being waged in Asia, Africa, and Latin America. They respected global revolutionaries such as Che Guevara and Frantz Fanon, and saw the war in Vietnam as part and parcel of the same racist sins at the core of the nation's ills.

In 1966, Moses received a draft notice from the government. He refused to fight in Vietnam, so he left the country. He needed time away from the United States anyway. He first went to Canada and then lived in Tanzania from 1969 to 1976. He went back to his first love, teaching math. He believed education was a key component in creating an independent and successful post-colonial Africa. He later worked for the Tanzanian Ministry of Education. After all, organizing Black leaders for the future was Moses's goal, whether in Mississippi or Tanzania, whether as a voting organizer or as an educator.[22]

In 1977, President Jimmy Carter offered amnesty to all the people who had fled the nation to avoid the Vietnam War. Moses decided to return to the U.S., partly because the Tanzanian government, which had grown suspicious of foreign-born Black people, had denied his citizenship application.[23] He enrolled at Harvard to get his Ph.D. in philosophy. But then, after enrolling his children in the local school—a mostly Black school in the deeply segregated Boston educational system—he discovered that his daughter did not have the opportunity to learn algebra. Segregation in math education was not acceptable to a math teacher and political organizer.

Moses engaged in the next phase of his organizing career. He formed the Algebra Project in 1982, a program to help low-income Black children gain math literacy. He considered education the next stage in the civil rights struggle. Some might look at this askance—is teaching math really organizing? Sure, being a math teacher is decidedly different than leading the struggle in Mississippi, but children of color are dramatically underserved in our racist education system, including in ostensibly liberal cities such as Boston. If economic rights are going to be included in people's demands for equality, organizing to give young people the tools to gain those economic rights must be a critical part of the struggle. Moreover, Moses was not the only SNCC veteran to later focus on the math literacy of low-income Black children. In fact, the Algebra Project was later led by one of Moses's comrades from Mississippi, Dave Dennis, who grew up in a sharecropper family in Louisiana and, before becoming Moses's comrade, was involved in the political struggle through the sit-ins for desegregation.[24]

Moreover, for as much as we talk about *Brown* v. *Board of Education* as a core milestone in the civil rights movement, our schools are still tremendously segregated. *De jure* segregation may be dead, but *de facto* segregation remains the reality of America. In Rhode Island, one of the bluest states in the nation, the wealthy section of Providence, the state's capital, had front lawns festooned with "Black Lives Matter" and "This Home Believes in Science" billboards during the first Trump administration, yet many of the owners of those homes sent their children to private schools to avoid their city's majority-minority schools. Unequal education is not a phenomenon exclusive to the South or the past; it persists throughout the U.S. Bob Moses knew this and brought his expertise and organizing skills to address the issue.

Moses made these connections very clear in a book he co-wrote with another comrade from Mississippi, Charles Cobb. Published in 2001, *Radical Equations: Civil Rights from Mississippi to the Algebra Project* provided a guide for empowering young Black and Latino students to learn the skills they would need to succeed in the twenty-first-century job market. Focusing on creativity and fun in learning, Moses tried to shift educational standards away from the growing neoliberal focus on constant testing, and instead on the priority of meeting students where they were. Just as in his political organizing, he believed teaching required building hope and power in local communities. In fact, for Moses, there really wasn't any difference between the two phases of his organizing life. Math education and registering people to vote both required the same commitment, principles, and leadership building. It was a remarkable turn, and we'd be better off if both our educational and political leaders took Moses's ideas more seriously.[25]

When Moses died in 2021, at the age of eighty-six, the commemoration was similar to those for many people from the past—he was remembered with a few tributes and then mostly forgotten. He did not get the media accolades that some of his more famous colleagues have received—though he probably would have preferred it that way.

There's so much we can learn from the life of Bob Moses. There's the deep internal discipline. The focus on building new leadership. The connections between overtly political work and education. The bravery, the commitment, the sheer humanity. But what stands out to me is his humility. Moses didn't want to be famous. He wasn't in the business of change for his own sake. He put everything he had into the fight for justice.

16

Yuri Kochiyama

The Late-Life Organizer

Not everyone becomes an organizer when they are young. We often say that young people lead the charge for change, and often this is true. Young people have led many movements in American history—the civil rights and anti-Vietnam movements perhaps most notably. Young people might take more risks, often don't have children and the attendant responsibilities, and may have fewer financial obligations than their parents. Young people are the future, and on issues from transgender rights to climate change, they are the ones leading the charge today.

But sometimes people become organizers later in life. The experiences they face from oppressive forces such as racism, sexism, and capitalism transform their views on the world, and they dedicate the latter part of their lives to overthrowing a corrupt system. Life experience beats many people down, but for others, it enrages them and inspires them to make change. They have felt anger for years or even decades, but did not know how to channel that rage into activism. We are not all natural-born organizers, and sometimes we need people to help along the way and activate us to change, but each of us can become an activist at any point in life.

Yuri Kochiyama was a late-blooming activist. Her story bucks the Asian "model minority" myth—a racist construction that deprives Americans of knowing the many powerful advocates for change that have come out of Asian American communities, but also can blind Asian Americans to the history of their own community.[1] Asian Americans have faced incredible levels of racism in American history, perhaps most notably in California. From the moment white settlers came to California, they saw it as a white man's state. In the Gold Rush of 1849, white folks traveled from the east and, to their surprise, found a type of ethnic diversity unknown in the eastern United States. People from around the world had beat them to the gold diggings. There were Indigenous people who already lived there. Mexican settlers had moved north in the eighteenth century to colonize the region on Spain's behalf, and then remained there as Mexico became an independent nation. People arrived from Australia, France, Germany, Peru, Chile, Hawaii. African Americans, both enslaved and free, were there. Most of all, what shocked white folks were Chinese immigrants. The vast majority of white Californians had never encountered a Chinese person, nor could they stomach the notion that Chinese people could take their promised gold.[2]

White Californians responded with violence. They kicked Chinese and Mexican immigrants out of the gold camps. They enslaved Indigenous people and committed brutal acts of genocide. Many southerners tried to import slavery into the new territory and, until the Civil War, slavers and slavery sympathizers governed the state, even after it became a technically free state upon entering the Union in 1850. In fact, white enslavement of Native Americans continued in California for years after Black slavery ended in the South with the Civil War. Massacres of the Chinese became far too common. Finally, white American workers led the charge for the Chinese Exclusion Act in 1882, the first major national law to come out of the labor movement. At this time, employers started recruiting Japanese workers instead of Chinese workers, and once again white Californians led a racist campaign, this one forcing the end of most Japanese migration in 1907. Resentment against the Japanese continued for decades. Filipinos and Sikhs also experienced violence. For many white Americans, the mere existence of Asians in their nation was an outrage that could lead to racial violence.[3]

This is the world in which Yuri Kochiyama grew up. It took her a long time to understand her life in the context of both national and global racism. But in middle age, she figured it out and spent the rest of her life fighting for justice. In a 1997 book on Asian American feminists, the writer and activist Juliana Pegues notes of the power of young Asian American women learning about Kochiyama, saying, "Just to hear about her is a total inspiration."[4] So let's hear about her today, nearly three decades later. I hope you will be inspired too.

Yuri Kochiyama was born Mary Yuriko Nakahara in 1921. Her family lived in a Japanese American community in San Pedro, California. Her father, Seiichi Nakahara, was a fish merchant and her mother, Tsuyako Sawaguchi, had earned a college degree and taught piano. Like many Japanese Americans, the family was upwardly mobile. They lived in a mostly white neighborhood, went to good schools, and had converted to Presbyterianism. There was not much here that suggested the upbringing of a future radical. Under a different set of life circumstances, there is a very good chance that she would have lived a quiet life, and that we would not know of her.

In December 1941, when the Japanese attacked Pearl Harbor and the U.S. entered World War II, latent anti-Asian hate found a "justifiable" cause. Whites claimed that Japanese immigrants and Japanese Americans could not be trusted, that many would spy for their country and did not have loyalty to the United States. These were almost entirely lies, and the standard was not applied to other ethnic groups that also came from enemy nations during the war, such as the Germans and Italians. But racial hypocrisy was something many Americans wore on their sleeve, and the nation's horrible treatment of its own minorities was propaganda gold for the Germans and Japanese.[5]

The U.S. put Japanese Americans in concentration camps. Many often use the term "internment camps" in order to separate what the U.S. did from what Germany did in the Nazi concentration camps. And they were different. But one should not be accused of playing down the horrors of the Holocaust to note that, like the Germans, the U.S. imprisoned an entire minority group solely on the basis of their race. It's one of the great shames of this nation's history.[6]

Shortly after Pearl Harbor, the FBI visited Yuri's father. He knew the Japanese ambassador to the United States, he was proud of his Japanese heritage, and he had pictures of Japanese ships in the house. This was enough for the American government to arrest him, even though he had just been released from the hospital. Nonetheless, the government held him in detention for six weeks. During that time, his health worsened. He died the day after the government set him free.

Meanwhile, the rest of the family was rounded up like other Japanese Americans. Yuri, her mother, and her siblings were locked in horse stables at the Santa Anita racetrack in California. They remained there for several months before being shipped to a concentration camp in Jerome, Arkansas. Of all the camps, this one was the farthest distance from their home in the American West. It was hot there, unspeakably so for those not used to the humidity. Yuri and the rest of her family survived their imprisonment, but she would never forget and never forgive what the government had done to her, her family, and her people.

After her release from Jerome, she married Bill Kochiyama. He was a young Japanese American who, like so many men, got out of the prison camps by agreeing to volunteer for the U.S. military during the war. Since the government did not trust Japanese Americans, they were not allowed to fight against Japan. Instead, they went to Europe as part of the now famous 442nd combat unit. This was a brave unit of men who volunteered for many of the most dangerous missions of the war in Europe to prove their loyalty as Americans. Yuri and Bill had met while she was working at her camp in Arkansas with soldiers on leave and while he was on leave himself. They then moved to Mississippi, where she found housing for the families of Japanese American soldiers in the deeply segregated South. She faced racism there too, but again, later claimed she did not have the political education yet to understand this.[7]

After the camps closed, Kochiyama returned with her family to her hometown in California and was shocked by the hatred they faced. At the time, she believed it was postwar hysteria rather than actual racial hatred. She loved her home and struggled to recognize how deeply entrenched racism was. Looking for a new start, the Kochiyamas moved to New York. They had six children, and in the 1950s her life revolved around raising them. The government's near-murder of her father disturbed her for years, but she did not have the political insight to process it. It remained just a personal tragedy until her awakening to a revolutionary consciousness.[8]

It was only in the 1960s that Kochiyama became a legendary

activist. Struggling with racism, the death of her father, her concentration camp experience, and then the poverty of her family, she did not always have time to channel her anger into activism. But once she was activated, she was all-in. This was a time of global upheaval. Anti-colonial revolutionary movements that overthrew colonial oppressors in Asia and Africa reverberated throughout the world. So did the Cuban Revolution and the other Latin American liberation movements. Meanwhile, the civil rights movement was grabbing the headlines in the U.S.

But the civil rights movement was not just a southern phenomenon. Although northern cities did not have Jim Crow segregation, ghettoization was also a product of white supremacy and in many ways equally unjust. The need for revolution was as urgent in New York, Philadelphia, and Los Angeles as it was in Birmingham, Selma, and Montgomery.

These activists also knew they existed in a global context. The term "internal colonialism" became one that helped describe the conditions of life for people of color in the United States. Their situation wasn't that different from that of Congolese suffering from Belgian colonialism or the Vietnamese fighting against the French and then the Americans. The only difference was that marginalized Americans were living in the belly of the beast, fighting from within an imperial juggernaut.

This was the atmosphere in which Yuri Kochiyama carried out her late-life embrace of activism. She became wrapped up in the anti-colonial movements based out of New York. In fact, she probably became the single best-known Asian American ally of these movements. She later stated, "Racism has placed all ethnic peoples in similar positions of oppression, poverty and marginalization."[9]

Her transformation began in the late 1950s, when the Kochiyamas got to know anti-nuclear activists, particularly a group of women known as the Hiroshima Maidens. These were burned and scarred survivors of the American nuclear attack on Hiroshima in 1945 who toured the United States to raise awareness of nuclear weapons and raise money for their reconstructive surgery. Later, Kochiyama became one of the country's most passionate anti-nuclear organizers. The horrors suffered by the Hiroshima survivors helped Kochiyama begin to make connections between her experiences and the broader injustices of the world.[10]

In 1960, the Kochiyamas moved to Harlem. It was only a coincidence that they moved to the northern center of civil rights organizing. It took a few years for Kochiyama to get more involved than just having a passing interest for certain causes. But she eventually got to know James Peck, one of the white Freedom Riders beaten nearly to death while attempting to desegregate public transportation in the South in 1961. Peck, then an organizer with the Congress of Racial Equality, introduced her to CORE members in the city, and she started attending local civil rights protests.[11]

Soon, Kochiyama became a leader in CORE's protests against segregation in the construction of a medical center in Brooklyn that excluded Black New Yorkers from good-paying jobs. She, along with her oldest son, was almost immediately arrested for obstructing construction trucks. Shortly after these actions, the family drove west to see her family in California and, on the way, stopped in Birmingham to see the civil rights movement in action. This was shortly after the Sixteenth Street Baptist Church bombing that killed four teenage girls in September 1963. Witnessing the tragedy's aftermath in person was a profound experience that for her confirmed she was on the right path.[12]

Kochiyama, in her new political awareness, realized the magnitude of discrimination she had faced in her own life. It made her furious, thinking about the internment camps, the death of her father, her own family's poverty in New York. She became determined to end the systems of racism, colonialism, and capitalism. But, as a practical person, she also was much more comfortable with action than with toothless ideology. She applied her politics to civil rights campaigns in Harlem, especially those resisting the de facto segregation of its schools. She and her family also attended the courses on Black history that organizing groups provided the Black community in New York. Reading books such as W.E.B. Du Bois's *Souls of Black Folk* gave her the intellectual understanding of the role racism had played in her life.[13]

Then, in late 1963, Kochiyama met Malcolm X. She soon became his biggest supporter in the Asian American community, joining his Organization of Afro-American Unity (OAAU). She first met him at a protest to demand that the building trade unions open their ranks to Puerto Rican and Black workers. She approached him, introduced herself, and thanked him for his work. They became fast friends. Malcolm changed Kochiyama's life. At that time, he was moving away from the sectarianism of the Nation of Islam and toward a globalized Black nationalist ideology that also had room for the struggles of colonized people regardless of skin color. Kochiyama soon came to embrace his politics.[14]

When another group of Japanese anti-nuclear activists and survivors of the nuclear attacks on Hiroshima and Nagasaki came to New York, they met Malcolm at Kochiyama's Harlem apartment. He invited her to his OAAU Liberation School, which trained activists in the politics of nationalism and anti-colonialism. This experience expanded her understanding of how her own oppression intersected with those of Black people around the nation and world. He helped her understand the limits of integrationist politics and the need for racial nationalism, as well as to question her previous notions of nonviolence as the only way to resist racism and capitalism.[15]

Malcolm wrote to her frequently on his famed trip to Mecca to make the key pilgrimage of Islam. In fact, she was so close to Malcolm that she was in attendance for his address on February 21, 1965, when members of the Nation of Islam assassinated him. Most people hit the floor when they heard the gunshots, but she rushed the stage to protect him. She held him in her arms as he died. The picture of her holding him was published in *Life* magazine's story on the assassination. She grabbed him, felt for a heartbeat, and shouted that he was still alive. Alas, he wouldn't remain so for very long.[16]

Kochiyama would miss Malcolm terribly and, in fact, became an important mother figure for one of his daughters. But his death did not mean the end of her political engagement with his ideas. Instead, she plunged further into the world of anti-racist politics. She became a major supporter of Robert Williams and of LeRoi Jones, the legendary Black nationalist poet. In this, especially in the defense of Williams, Kochiyama channeled what she had learned from Malcolm and leaders of the nationalist movements in the developing world.[17]

The FBI began investigating Kochiyama, even calling her an agent of communist China, which was both inaccurate and racist. This was the era of COINTELPRO, the FBI program created to surveil subversive organizations and, in some cases, assassinate leftist leaders associated with the Black Panther Party and other Black Power movements. J. Edgar Hoover personally approved of this program, which completely ignored people's civil and human rights. In 1969, the FBI killed the charismatic young Chicago leader of the Black Panthers Fred Hampton, and imprisoned many others.[18] Kochiyama began corresponding with the imprisoned Panthers and gave them critical outside support during their years in prison. She also became a major ally of the Young Lords, the Puerto Rican nationalist and freedom movement in New York that took the ideas of the Black Panthers and applied them to their community.[19] By this time Kochiyama, now a veteran activist and with her history with Malcolm gaining her legitimacy in the eyes of a many young activists who otherwise could have been suspicious of a middle-aged woman from outside their community, became a critically important mentor to these young radicals.

All of this led, perhaps inevitably, to Kochiyama also becoming an important mentor to the Asian American nationalist movements of the late 1960s. At nearly fifty years old, she was now an icon in activist circles. It was at this point she started to go publicly by "Yuri," a symbol of her growing pride in her Japanese heritage.

Asian Americans for Action (AAA) formed in New York in 1969, the first pan-Asian political group in the city. This group fought against imperialism and racism, through a democratic structure that encouraged the fleshing out of ideas through long conversations and policy position statements. Kochiyama immediately plunged into AAA and worked to get the mostly young students in the group to protest the Vietnam War. By this time, although she still had only been an activist for less than a decade, she provided the critical leadership the group needed. She was a prolific organizer—a great public speaker, passionate mentor, and strong leadership builder. She produced newsletters, signs, and flyers. She even ran the AAA newspaper from her home through the early 1970s.[20]

Kochiyama also worked to promote other organizers, including Robert Williams, whose return from Cuba she covered in the AAA newspaper, an article that spread his name through the radical Asian communities in the U.S. In it, she focused on his travels in China and Vietnam and his solidarity with the anti-colonial struggle of Asians. For Kochiyama, as for Williams and many other organizers of the era, their fight for justice was wrapped up in the global anti-colonial struggle, framed by the Cold War and the appendages of imperialism.[21]

Kochiyama specifically fought against American imperialism in Asia, which included not only the war in Vietnam and its expansion into Cambodia and Laos, but also the continued American occupation of Okinawa, the Japanese archipelago that the U.S. had used as a site for its large military bases since the end of World

War II. She spoke out loudly and frequently against the U.S. for threatening the future of Chinese communism and for potentially remilitarizing Japan, after the nation disbanded the Japanese military during its post–World War II occupation. Even today, Japan engages in only extremely limited international engagement of its military forces. Kochiyama and others feared the rearmament of Japan as a major American ally to resist communist nations.[22]

One of Kochiyama's strengths was to call people into the movement, no matter where they were starting on their journey to progressivism. Rather than admonishing people for holding harmful worldviews, she used their ignorance as an opportunity for curiosity and growth. Kochiyama's legacy teaches us that to truly organize people, you have to show them the path toward a progressive future. Building connections, making people feel as if they are part of something bigger than themselves, moving forward rather than focusing on people's flaws—these are core tenets of successful organizing.

By the late 1970s, Kochiyama had circled back to her own experiences in the American concentration camps where she spent World War II. With her husband, she started Concerned Japanese Americans. Originally, it focused on fighting against American militarism and nationalism in the aftermath of the Iranian Revolution, but as that crisis faded in 1981, it moved toward fighting for reparations for Japanese Americans. Congress began exploring this issue in 1980, and the Kochiyamas joined with the East Coast Japanese Americans for Redress in late 1981, which became a broad-based organization raising money and support from large swaths of the Japanese community, not just radical leftists. The masses that attended the hearings on the issue in New York and other cities played a critical role in moving the government toward reparations. With great reluctance, President Ronald Reagan signed a bill approving reparations to Japanese Americans in 1988.[23]

Kochiyama also supported reparations for African Americans and hoped that the Japanese experience would create greater political space for that cause. But white America was more comfortable with granting a one-time payment to survivors of a specific moment in recent American memory than it was with addressing four hundred years of systemic racism against Black Americans. Reparations for slavery and Jim Crow remains an important goal of some justice communities today, but American society remains far from an honest appraisal of its disturbing history.

In her later years, Kochiyama came up against the challenges that many of us face when we age. She outlived her husband Bill and some of her children, one of whom died in a car accident. Her health began to decline in the late 1990s. But she managed to keep her voice as long as she lived. She spent these years primarily working on prisoner rights and anti-imperialist politics. She became a leader in the movement to free the Black Power activist Mumia Abu-Jamal from the prison where he has been incarcerated since 1981 for allegedly killing a police officer. She took on cases for other political prisoners as well, and also spoke out against the oppression of radical leftist groups globally, including the Shining Path in Peru.

Yuri Kochiyama combined her own experiences as an oppressed minority with an internationalist perspective that built critical connections between the American and global left. Given the amount of violence and dispossession carried out by the United States throughout the world, often unbeknownst to the American population, this specific type of activism is vitally important. But it is equally important *when* Kochiyama dedicated her life to change. It doesn't matter how old you are. You can start fighting right now for the change you want to see. Do it, whether you are eight or eighty.

17

Daniel Berrigan

The Power of Religious Example

Today, the United States is less religious than at any time in its history. The number of people claiming to be atheist or unaffiliated with any church has reached a record high. According to Pew Research polling, between 2007 and 2021, the percentage of Americans identifying as Christians fell from 78 to 63 percent, while those who identify as having no religion rose from 16 to 29 percent. This trend is especially pronounced among young Americans. Among the religiously unaffiliated, 72 percent are under the age of fifty and 35 percent under the age of thirty.[1]

The Catholic Church remains the largest single denomination in the United States, but it has seen a decline in active membership in recent years. Meanwhile, the relatively liberal mainstream Protestant denominations—such as the Lutherans, Methodists, Presbyterians, Episcopalians, and Congregationalists—have experienced significant declines as well. In contrast, far-right evangelical churches have grown and wield considerable influence over the Republican Party. According to the same Pew poll, 56 percent of evangelical Protestants are Republicans, while 54 percent of unaffiliated individuals are Democrats and only 23 percent are Republicans. This shift has notably and drastically affected American politics, contributing to the rise of the evangelical right and the increasing radicalism of the Republican Party.

The combined phenomena of declining mainstream religion and the radicalization of religious individuals on the right has had several negative implications for Americans' ability to organize for positive change. First, it has taken away a critical common space from millions of Americans. Traditionally, the church has served as a space for political organization across the spectrum, but today it's increasingly dominated by the right. The lack of common spaces to congregate has harmed social justice causes. In 2000, political scientist Robert Putnam noted in his influential book *Bowling Alone* that Americans' loss of communal spaces has undermined our civic life. The last two-plus decades have strongly demonstrated the truth of this assertion, with the generally toxic social media replacing generally beneficial physical spaces where people can come together to celebrate, play, worship, and organize.[2]

There is at least one exception to this trend: Black churches. Many of the great movements in civil rights history came from the church, and this of course includes the movement led by Martin Luther King Jr. and other leaders in the African American church. These spaces remain bastions of political engagement, including for the task of mobilizing voters. This is one reason why in states with large Black populations, Republicans have targeted early Sunday voting as part of their efforts to disfranchise Black voters, such as in Georgia in 2022.[3]

However, these Black spaces of incredible change become complicated when intersecting with the white secular left. Take, for example, Rev. William Barber, a prominent modern organizer and founder of the Moral Monday movement in North Carolina. Rev. Barber is a true inheritor of King's legacy. Some of my white organizer friends have seen Barber in person and felt inspired by his message. Yet they often find his exhortations to pray together uncomfortable and even, at times, "corny." I think they miss the point here. Barber's spiritual compassion should resonate with anyone who believes in a better life for all. But as a secular member of the white left, I struggle to address my fellow organizers' sentiments about religion. I grew up Lutheran and, like many people, eventually left the church. While people have the right to believe or not believe in a higher power, religion often poses an obstacle in the organizing of people across different belief systems. Personally, I find open displays of religion uncomfortable, but I also recognize that this discomfort is part of a larger problem we face today as a hyper-individualistic society, which gets in the way of effective organizing. I both believe in Barber's message and feel myself slightly outside it.

I want to remind leftists outside churches of the power of religious-based organizing. Religion is a dominant feature of life around the world and, regardless of personal beliefs, ignoring its influence is a mistake. Moreover, the power of organizing from a religious background can provide tremendous, overwhelming moral authority to your campaigns if it is an authentic set of beliefs.

To illustrate this point, consider the example of Daniel Berrigan.

Born in 1921 in Minnesota, Berrigan and his siblings, including his younger brother Philip, grew up in a strong Catholic and union household. His father was a union activist and instilled the values of both unionism and Catholicism in his children. However, he was also a violent man who disciplined his children harshly. He routinely beat Berrigan's mother, which created a lifetime of outrage toward injustice in the Berrigan children as they internalized the horrors of their experiences.

The Catholic Church has played a complicated role in American labor history. While it despised the Communist Party because of the latter's antagonism toward religion, the Church often supported noncommunist labor organizing efforts. In 1911, for example, the Catholic Church backed furniture strikers in Grand Rapids, Michigan, while the Dutch Reformed Church took an outright anti-union position that destroyed the strike because those workers went back to the job.[4] In the 1930s, the Catholic Church remained open to noncommunist union organizing, actively promoting acceptance of new unions such as the United Auto Workers and Steel Workers Organizing Committee.[5] This environment allowed individuals like Berrigan and his father to comfortably navigate both worlds of the union and the church, and see little reason to believe that the two did not mesh.

The Berrigans moved to Syracuse, New York, in 1926. A physically weak boy who did not learn to walk until he was four years old, Berrigan avoided the hard manual labor demanded of his brothers. He became a religious intellectual instead and announced his intention to join the Jesuits when he turned eighteen in 1939.

He received a bachelor's degree from St. Andrew-on-Hudson, a Jesuit seminary, in 1946, then taught at a Jesuit school in New Jersey until 1949, officially joining the priesthood in 1952. Berrigan taught French and theology at the Jesuit Brooklyn Preparatory School from 1954 to 1957, before returning to Syracuse to teach at Le Moyne College.

Soon after his ordination, Berrigan became known within the church for his anti-poverty work. He took his high school students into New York to meet with members of the Catholic Worker Movement, a communitarian group within Catholicism started by Dorothy Day and others in 1933. This was a courageous act at the time, as the pacifist and economic justice leanings of the organization came under attack during the Cold War, making many Catholics uneasy. However, for the young Berrigan, the Catholic Worker Movement offered a form a Catholicism that addressed the social issues of the era.[6] It was there he first met Day, who helped inspire him toward greater actions. Reflecting on her influence, Berrigan later said, "She awakened me to connections I had not thought of or been instructed in—the equation of human misery and poverty with warmaking. She had a basic hope that God created the world with enough for everyone, but there was not enough for everyone and warmaking."[7]

While Berrigan would become a great activist, inspiring people around the nation and world, he too needed to be organized by his elders. Day was that person for him. He also studied under the Catholic priest and mystic Thomas Merton, who became famous for his calls for the abolition of war. Berrigan learned much from Merton as well.[8]

In 1963, Berrigan traveled to Paris and met French Jesuits who were outraged at American and French interference in Vietnam. This was a year before the U.S. fully committed to war through congressional approval of the Gulf of Tonkin Resolution, which gave the Johnson administration its justification for military escalation. However, by 1963, the U.S. had already ensured that an election would not take place in 1956 to determine whether North Vietnam and South Vietnam would be united, as guaranteed in the 1954 treaty that ended the war with France. Fearful of the communist leader Ho Chi Minh becoming leader of a united Vietnam, the U.S. instead gave its support to the corrupt administration of Ngo Dinh Diem in the South—ironically, largely because he was a Catholic and his views seemed more aligned with the American foreign policy elite than those of a Buddhist or animist, more common religions in Vietnam.[9]

Berrigan began traveling to other global hot spots—the Soviet Union, South Africa, Hungary—gaining perspectives that were absent at home. His exposure to these international issues deepened his disgust at U.S. foreign policy in Indochina, and he became determined to take action against it. Over the course of going to Vietnam several times on fact-finding missions, Berrigan found the damage from the endless American bombing of Hanoi and other Vietnamese cities to be a moral crime. With the U.S. dropping more bombs over Vietnam than were used in the entirety of World War II, he realized that sharing a Christian message of peace was an obvious way for him to resist.

By this time, America had fully entered the Vietnam War. Berrigan and his brother Philip, also a radical anti-imperialist priest, founded the Catholic Peace Fellowship to create religious-based protests against the war. Soon, they became the leaders of something much larger. Clergy and Laymen Concerned About Vietnam (CALCAV), founded in 1965, brought major religious leaders together to oppose the war, including King, Reinhold Niebuhr, and William Sloane Coffin, with King co-chairing the organization. By 1969, the group had forty thousand members and had built ties with major politicians who opposed the war, such as Oregon's conservative but principled Republican senator Mark Hatfield and 1968 presidential candidate Eugene McCarthy.[10]

In 1967, the year King fully denounced the war, he gave a famous speech titled "Beyond Vietnam: A Time to Break Silence." Although this happened under the CALCAV's auspices, it divided the civil rights movement between those who wanted to focus on the specific conditions of Black life in America and those, like King, who thought there were larger moral questions to discuss. Organizers organize each other, and King had come under Berrigan's influence. King's incredibly brave stance would have been much more precarious without Berrigan and others leading the way toward a Christian antiwar point of view. Of course, King inspired Berrigan as well, who in turn helped with the Selma voting rights campaign in 1965.

Berrigan arrived at a simple yet profound idea: an unjust and immoral society sustained the intersecting ills of colonialization, racism, imperialism, poverty, and capitalism. This perspective aligned him with liberation theology, a larger movement within the Catholic Church at the time. Liberation theology emerged from the Latin American Catholic Church in the 1960s and 1970s, coinciding with Berrigan's activism in the U.S. In an era when the church had long supported the wealthy over peasants, a new generation of priests, influenced by the social changes of the 1960s, began to ally with liberation movements. They merged Marxist economics with church teaching, urging the poor to fight for their rights in this world and in the next. This theology would be enormously influential on the Sandinista Revolution in Nicaragua, with several priests playing leading roles in the revolutionary government, such as Ernesto and Fernando Cardenal. Eventually, Pope John Paul II and his lieutenant the future pope Benedict XVI would crush this movement from within the church. But for Berrigan, the liberation movements in Latin America gave him hope, a guiding light, and a clear mission moving forward.[11]

There were not many liberation theologians in the U.S., but Berrigan was part of a broader group of Americans known as "the Catholic left." This group included priests, nuns, and committed lay Catholics who recognized the inequality, poverty, and violence of America. They believed that the only way to reconcile these issues with their faith was through direct action.[12]

Cardinal Francis Spellman, who despised the radical Berrigans, attempted to isolate Daniel by sending him on a trip to South America. But pressure on church leaders from his allies led to his recall to the U.S. three months later. Berrigan's time in South America and the activists he met only radicalized him further. In 1966, Berrigan became campus chaplain at Cornell University. He influenced countless students at Cornell, making the university one of the beating hearts of the antiwar movement on American campuses.[13]

Moreover, Berrigan became the faculty adviser for Cornell's first student gay rights organization, the Student Homophile League. It's worth noting just how revolutionary this was in 1968: the gay rights movement was so nascent that it didn't even have a widely recognized name yet. Those brave enough to come out of the closet did so risking their life, their livelihood, and their future. They needed guidance from someone truly committed to fundamental human rights and, fortunately, Daniel Berrigan was there to help. Many staunch advocates for social justice might have fled from the gay rights issue, but not Berrigan.[14]

In 1968, Berrigan and the renowned historian Howard Zinn traveled to North Vietnam to bring home three American POWs, the first to be released in the Vietnam War. During their first day in Hanoi, they narrowly escaped an American bombing raid, which only intensified Berrigan's disdain for U.S. policy. Later that year, he appeared in the powerful antiwar documentary *In the Year of the Pig,* directed by Emile de Antonio.

At this time, Philip was encouraging Daniel to engage in more direct action. Daniel realized his brother was right and decided to join him. In May 1968, they and seven other antiwar Catholics, known as the Catonsville Nine, broke into a draft office in Catonsville, Maryland, took several hundred draft cards, and burned them in the parking lot using homemade napalm. The statement they issued read, in part:

> We destroy these draft records not only because they exploit our young men but because they represent misplaced power concentrated in the ruling class of America. . . . We confront the Catholic Church, other Christian bodies and the synagogues of America with their silence and cowardice in the face of our country's crimes.[15]

What made this action even more radical is that the draft board was housed in the local Knights of Columbus building, the fraternal organization for Catholic men and long a bastion of conservatism in the United States. Thus, the action called attention to not only the unjustness of the war, but also the out-of-touch position of the activists' own church. For Berrigan, this and other antiwar actions were not separate from his religion, but rather an integral part of his beliefs. As the writer Kurt Vonnegut stated, "For me, Father Daniel Berrigan is Jesus as a poet. If this be heresy, make the most of it."[16]

The Berrigans and their comrades framed their protest as a vigil for peace. Even as they lit the draft cards on fire with their homemade napalm, they gathered around the cards in prayer.[17] Many criticized Berrigan, including purported allies within the church and anti-Vietnam liberals, but he believed strongly that action was what mattered. Leadership toward justice could alienate people, but it was worth it. As he once stated, "A good peace movement starts out small and gets smaller."[18] Their action inspired approximately fifty similar actions by groups across the country, and the Catonsville Nine became a national story.[19] Berrigan was sentenced to three years in prison, but rather than serve the time he went into hiding. The FBI captured him in 1970 on Block Island, off the coast of Rhode Island, and he served eighteen months in prison, getting out in February 1972.

Berrigan became a prominent figure in American culture. He's the "radical priest" mentioned in Paul Simon's "Me and Julio Down by the Schoolyard." He appeared in Roland Joffé's excellent 1986 film *The Mission,* about Jesuits in South America, starring Robert De Niro, Jeremy Irons, and Liam Neeson. He became an ideal model of an activist Jesuit for a generation of Americans. He also wrote a play about his experiences as one of the Catonsville Nine, which was performed by radical theater groups several times.[20]

After the Vietnam War, Berrigan taught and continued with his activism. In 1980, he, his brother, and six others started the Plowshares movement (also known as the Plowshares Eight), an anti-nuclear Christian pacifist movement that attempted to damage weapons and military property in order to bring attention to the horrors of American militarism. Berrigan was deeply inspired by the prophet Isaiah's call to "beat swords into plowshares," and their name derived from this phrase. On September 8, 1980, the Plowshares Eight broke into the General Electric facility in King of Prussia, Pennsylvania, where the Minuteman III missile was made. They took hammers to vehicles, poured blood on materials, prayed, and other actions to simply call attention to our military-industrial complex.[21]

In the 1980s, Berrigan became a powerful advocate for another crucial social cause: the HIV/AIDS movement. Berrigan emerged as an important early representative of the Catholic community in this fight, at a time when gay people were severely stigmatized in American society. Although leaders like Harvey Milk had cracked the closet door open, most gay Americans still lived in secrecy, facing immense discrimination. Meanwhile, AIDS ravaged the gay community. For many Americans, from the Reagan administration to the churches, gay people were subjects of mockery, not empathy.[22] Berrigan was not going to stand by and let the Catholic Church remain silent about the enormous global suffering caused by HIV/AIDS. He continued in his advocacy with unwavering humanity, standing up to the homophobia that led many to ignore this crisis.[23]

Berrigan was a great man, but he was complicated too. Ideological consistency can lead people to take positions that may be controversial or make others uncomfortable. While Berrigan, unlike much of the Catholic Church, did not devote all his time and energy to the anti-abortion movement, he wholeheartedly opposed abortion. This stance was rooted not only in church doctrine, but also in his own philosophy on life. When a Planned Parenthood clinic opened in Rochester, New York, in 1991, Berrigan tried to shut it down using the same tactics of direct action and civil disobedience he used against the Vietnam War and nuclear proliferation. This might be disheartening, as it was for me when I first learned of it. For Berrigan, though, his moral compass meant supporting AIDS victims, those Nixon and Kissinger bombed in Cambodia, the Sandinistas . . . and the unborn. As he once stated, "A decent society should no more have an abortion clinic than the Pentagon."[24]

Daniel Berrigan is not the only legendary figure in the history of American organizing who opposed abortion. Civil rights leader Fannie Lou Hamer was a strong feminist but also spoke to women's groups about her opposition to abortion, which was based on both her religious beliefs and her personal experience of forced sterilization by a white doctor. She even compared it to genocide. Yet we have much to learn from both Berrigan and Hamer. Despite their views on abortion, their contributions to justice in the late twentieth century are undeniable. We must be able to reconcile positions on which we disagree while appreciating the broader scope of ideas that inspire us. Ignoring Berrigan's and Hamer's positions on reproductive choice does not mean we should ignore their legacies overall.[25]

Berrigan also maintained his anti-imperialism stance, protesting Reagan's illegal wars in Central America in the 1980s, the Gulf War in 1990–91, and Bush's war in Iraq beginning in 2003. He also opposed Israel's oppression of the Palestinians. Reflecting on his long commitment to activism, he once said, "The day I'm embalmed, that's when I'll give it up."[26] In his later life, Berrigan actively supported Occupy Wall Street and other economic populist movements. Like many of us, he felt sad over the continued existence of oppression and the slow pace of change. In 2008, he lamented in a state of near despair over the Bush wars: "This is the worst time of my long life. I have never had such meager expectations of the system."[27]

Berrigan also wrote more than fifty books, many of them on spirituality and resistance. His remarkably prolific output was yet another demonstration of his deep commitment to building resistance to evil in the world. He was able to meet only so many potential activists through his teaching, but his books could reach anyone. In 2016, he died in the Jesuit infirmary at Fordham University. He was ninety-four years old. When he passed, an entire generation of the left knew it had lost a hero and a legend.

Daniel Berrigan reminds us of the power of religion in organizing. Christianity does not have to be a right-wing force. Many religious people interpret the Bible to reinforce their own political conservatism and reaction, but historically, many have interpreted it as a moral guide for social and economic justice. Berrigan was one of the latter. So was King. So is William Barber today. Religion, regardless of personal belief, has been and is a potent organizing force. If you are religious, let it inspire you in the spirit of Daniel Berrigan. If you aren't religious, let Berrigan's spiritual righteousness inspire you anyway.

18

Barbara Gittings

The Mother of the Gay Civil Rights Movement

Many of the greatest victories for justice in recent years have come from the movement for lesbian, gay, queer, and transgender liberation. In fact, in my lifetime, I've seen wide-reaching change.

I graduated from high school in Springfield, Oregon, in 1992. At that time, a far-right group called the Oregon Citizens Alliance (OCA) in Springfield launched an anti-gay hate campaign. This was an era on the heels of the AIDS epidemic, an era of baseless fearmongering that stereotyped queer people as groomers and pedophiles. Springfield was not abjectly poor, but the town still struggled with the decline of the timber industry, which meant the loss of both work and a regional identity. That created the kind of bitterness that often swallows up deindustrialized and rural communities that used to vote blue and then spits them back out red, ready to pounce on a scapegoat as a target for their resentments.[1]

That spring, Springfield voters passed a "no special rights for gays" law. The law barred the use of public services for any group construed as pro–gay rights and mandated that gay-themed books be stripped from school libraries. My friends joined this anti-gay movement, which made me so sad and angry. I certainly did not know much about the gay community when I was eighteen. I didn't know anyone who identified as queer. What I did know was that my friends wanted to hurt others. This infuriated me. The OCA then tried to pass a statewide measure but, after an effective campaign waged by queer and straight people allied together, Oregon voters defeated it that fall. This moment moved the needle on the national gay rights movement. People were organizing for their lives.[2]

In the thirty-plus years since my hometown garnered embarrassing national headlines, mainstream acceptance of queer Americans has expanded dramatically. This did not happen instantaneously. Nor did it happen in the same way, at the same rate for everyone in the LGBTQ community. It took organizing. It required leaders to put their own lives at risk to make it happen. It still requires that new generations of queer folks and allies put their lives on the line.

There is still plenty of anti-LGBTQ hate today, as the second Trump administration shows. Transgender women, especially transgender women of color, face high rates of assault and murder, while other forms of anti-queer violence remain all too common.[3] Conservatives spew about hate drag shows. They create rabid outrage over people transforming their bodies through surgery. They pretend to care about girls' sports to demonize trans girls. They are fighting against a generational transformation in how people see sexuality, bodies, and freedom.

Our public understanding of the queer rights movement mostly focuses on struggle told through the eyes of cisgender white men. Probably one of the most famed gay historical figures is Harvey Milk. Milk certainly earned his place in the pantheon of American progressive heroes. He became the face of the gay rights community in the 1970s. He was the first openly gay man elected to public office in the United States, winning election to San Francisco's Board of Supervisors in 1977. Then, the next year, his homophobic former colleague Dan White murdered him and the city's liberal mayor, George Moscone. He became the national symbol of gay politics after his death, perhaps most memorably in a 2008 Gus Van Sant–directed biopic starring Sean Penn as Milk.[4]

Milk's story is moving but also myopic. It is a very narrow look at a queer community whose history is tremendously diverse. Queer history goes back far before Harvey Milk, including within the women's suffrage movement.[5] Trans women of color such as Marsha P. Johnson and Sylvia Rivera, both of whom were at the 1969 Stonewall riots that marked the beginning of modern queer resistance, need more attention from all of us.[6] Within the realm of organizing over the long haul of the late twentieth century, one such overlooked figure is Barbara Gittings.

Born in 1932 in Vienna, Austria, Gittings grew up in a wealthy Catholic family. In fact, she seriously contemplated becoming a nun. The priesthood and nunnery have been common routes for young Catholics uncomfortable with their sexuality, especially those who are queer. That was true of Gittings as well. Organized religion has often made life for queer Christians very difficult and continues to do so today, both in Catholicism and in evangelical Protestantism.[7]

When Gittings tried to get into the National Honor Society as a child, her teachers rejected her because of her "homosexual tendencies," though she didn't know what that meant. But she became romantically interested in girls.[8] She went to Northwestern University and majored in drama. She became close friends with another female student, and though it was a nonsexual relationship, there were rumors about them being lesbians. This sparked something in her. She didn't know what to think. She went to a psychiatrist, who told her she was a homosexual. Gittings appreciated the clarity.[9]

As the modern history of sex frames it, queer cultural acceptance before the 1960s went through a series of waves rather than an endless cycle of oppression. For example, as the historian George Chauncey has explored, drag balls were a huge draw in 1920s New York.[10] World War II permanently transformed gay life. People traveled from their homes to fight or to cities to work and met other people like them, resulting in the rise of sizable gay subcultures in New York, Los Angeles, and San Francisco. After the war, many people stayed in their newfound communities. This new generation of openly gay Americans would not take homophobia and hate lying down.[11]

Unfortunately, the late 1940s and '50s were indeed a grim time, as the government banned homosexuals from federal employment on the justification that the Soviets would lure them into sexual affairs, and then, afraid to admit their sexuality, they would be blackmailed into becoming spies for the commies. This was called the Lavender Scare, a part of the larger anti-communist Red Scare.

One major outcome of the federal government's attempt to repress homosexuality was that it gave people semiofficial permission to harass and even murder gay people without consequence. Sometimes the police even *helped* the violent homophobes. This is what Gittings and modern queer rights organizers were up against: state-sanctioned murder.[12]

Gittings felt no shame about herself, but she also did not have queer elders to guide her. She knew she liked women instead of men, but she did not know why. She read up on the existing literature, but queerness was pathologized at the time. Psychologists saw homosexuals as deviants. She rejected this entirely, knowing that she was a healthy and normal human. Disaffected, she flunked out of Northwestern, her mind more interested exploring the queer experience than her classes. She returned to Delaware, still only seventeen years old, and took night classes in Philadelphia. There, she began seeing a woman in her class, and knew that dating women was right for her.[13]

By the early 1950s, Gittings decided to be an unmistakably queer woman but, without role models to turn to, she didn't quite know how. She cross-dressed and visited gay bars in New York on the weekends, as she didn't know of any closer to home. She haunted libraries and bookstores, trying to find something to help her make sense of her place in society. She didn't find much. There were some novels, but the lesbian characters always came to a bad end. She liked one novel, *The Well of Loneliness,* and ordered her own copy. Her father found it and ordered her to burn it. She did not.[14]

Frustrated with the lack of resources for the queer community, Gittings knew she needed to organize for the society she wanted. She was involved in the very first active political organizations of the modern queer movement, working for what were then called "homophile" organizations, such as the Mattachine Society for men and the Daughters of Bilitis (DOB) for women. These early attempts at securing gay rights attempted to establish the respectability of queer people. The core organizing premise was simple: gay people were just like everyone else. From our perspective today, we might call this a repressive approach in which queer people sought to avoid drawing too much attention to themselves. They skirted overt crossdressing, discussion of trans issues, open relations with someone of the same sex, and any semblance of gender inversion. But what seems conservative to us today was quite radical for the time.[15]

Gittings soon got to know Phyllis Lyon and Del Martin, the founders of the Daughters of Bilitis. Initially founded by eight women who wanted a safer alternative than gay bars, the DOB soon transformed into a political organization. Much later, in 2008, Lyon and Martin would be the first gay couple to marry in San Francisco. Formed in San Francisco in 1955, the DOB was a lesbian group that built upon the 1951 creation of the Mattachine Society, which represented gay men. By the spring of 1953, the Mattachine Society had over one hundred local groups nationwide, with over two thousand members total. Like most other groups fighting for social change in this country in the early Cold War, it found itself riven between communist and anti-communist factions. Even in the 1950s, demands for truly radical gay liberation existed, but also were something moderates felt they had to quash. In fact, the Mattachine Society had its own anti-communist purge, replacing the communists who founded the group with political moderates.[16]

Gittings was excited to join an organization that helped situate her identity in society. Being young and brash, she told leaders of the Daughters of Bilitis that the name was terrible. As she remembered, "It was unpronounceable, and it didn't mean anything unless you knew about the stories of Bilitis, who was fictional, and she was bisexual, not fully homosexual. On all these counts I thought it was a pretty poor choice of name and I told them so. The arrogance of youth."[17]

From the beginning, Gittings would call people out on their ridiculousness, their fears, what she saw as compromising with homophobic power. This approach of speaking directly with her elders in the movement annoyed some people. But Martin and Lyon really liked her and believed in her organizing ability. In 1958, she went to New York and started a DOB chapter there, the first on the East Coast. She had to support herself, of course, and worked the mimeograph machine for an architectural firm for the next ten years.[18]

The Daughters of Bilitis attracted a lot of new members, especially through its magazine, *The Ladder.* Many of them were married to men. Married women, who would send desperate letters to the DOB detailing their urgent needs, became a major source of material support for the organization. Said one Wyoming lesbian married to a man, "Don't let *The Ladder* publication stop. It is the *best friend* we isolated folk in more remote parts of the country have. Life would be unthinkable without it."[19] But for the DOB, focusing on married women risked confirming the harmful stereotype that lesbians broke up marriages, so the organization downplayed this group as a priority.

While working in New York, Gittings met Kay Lahusen, a photographer. Born in 1930 in Cincinnati, Lahusen showed an early interest in photography, but went to Ohio State University to become a teacher instead. There, she fell in love with another woman, and they lived openly as a lesbian couple, which included moving in together after graduation. But then her girlfriend decided to leave her for a "normal life" with a man and children. In the wake of this devastation, Lahusen moved to Boston, where she worked for the *Christian Science Monitor* as a reference librarian. One of her coworkers showed her a copy of *The Ladder,* and Lahusen immediately got involved in the DOB. In 1961, she met Gittings at a picnic. They soon started dating and became a couple. In 1963, Gittings took over *The Ladder* and edited it for the next three years. Kay Tobin, Lahusen's professional name, became the magazine's photographer.[20]

The early gay liberation movement struggled against the popular psychology of the time. Psychologists insisted that homosexuality was deviant. Many queer people, even within the movement, internalized this pseudoscience as truth. Finally, Frank Kameny, another early gay rights activist, challenged the belief that homosexuality was an illness. It was not easy to get the movement to admit it, but by 1965 Kameny had convinced the Mattachine Society to affirm that homosexuality was a sexual orientation, not a deviancy.[21] Gittings first met Kameny at a landmark meeting where he and others first directly challenged a psychologist on this matter. Gittings and Kameny became fast friends, and she immediately transformed her political stance to one of an open celebration of lesbianism. Again, organizers organize each other. She needed Kameny's insights and leadership to become her own leader. It was Kameny who first called Gittings "the mother of the gay civil rights movement."[22]

The Ladder did still pander to respectability politics. In 1966, when the magazine profiled Lilli Vincenz, making her the first out lesbian to appear on the cover of a national magazine in American history, it did so in part because of her "all-American looks." Gittings stated Vincenz looked like "every mother's dream daughter."[23] This is a long way from the radical vision for queer liberation that is more widely discussed today, but it was momentous for the time.

By the mid-1960s, Gittings and Kameny led the growing gay rights movement. They organized the first gay rights parades in front of the White House in 1965. They specifically targeted President Dwight Eisenhower's Executive Order 10450 from 1953, the mandate that incited the Lavender Scare. This insidious policy was not just simply homophobic and caused greater damage than simple prejudice did. Executive Order 10450, and the witch hunt that ensued from it, deemed queer people untrustworthy, implying that they would rather betray their country than admit their sexuality to their families.[24] The Lavender Scare spread the dangerous falsehood that queer people were inherently duplicitous and deceptive. With rhetoric like this codified at the national level, gay activists faced tremendous hate from people walking by during protests. Gittings later noted, "It was risky and we were scared. Picketing was not a popular tactic at the time. And our cause seemed outlandish even to most gay people."[25] These protests built upon the Black civil rights movement. In fact, many gay rights activists came out of the civil rights movement, transferring their activism to this new political cause and once again putting their lives on the line for justice.

Gittings mostly avoided the more radical gay liberation movements that arose after the Stonewall riots in 1969. Belonging to a generation older than most of those activists, she did not much care for the counterculture. She found the new radicalism of movements such as the Gay Liberation Front shocking and didn't believe that the Soviet Union or Cuba had better answers for gay people, as some of those folks argued.[26] But she kept up the fight her way. In 1972, she and other activists found a psychologist willing to testify that homosexuality was not a disease, though, fearing exposure, he wore a wig and mask and was identified as "Dr. H. Anonymous." The next year, the American Psychological Association removed homosexuality from its official list of mental disorders. This alone was a huge victory to affirm queer dignity and humanity.[27] Gittings also helped start the National Gay and Lesbian Task Force in 1973, which became the leading lobbying organization for the gay rights movement.

As someone who tried to find her own identity through books, Gittings used her professional expertise to fight for gay-positive books in school libraries. She led a group to make gay rights central to librarian culture and created the gay caucus within the American Library Association (ALA), which was the first of its kind in any academic professional organization. Plus, she had fun. Sometimes, the struggle for political change gets in the way of what we're struggling for: the right to feel joy, fun, and pleasure. At the 1971 ALA convention in Dallas, she had a "Hug a Homosexual" booth, where she encouraged people to hug homosexuals of their shared gender. This was deeply subversive. The openly lesbian writer Isabel Miller (real name: Alma Routsong) attended the conference, and she kissed Gittings in front of the television cameras. They got the attention they wanted.[28] Today, when right-wing groups, supported by the Republican Party in many states, scour school libraries to purge books on racism or queerness that might threaten the declining status quo of white supremacy and hetero-supremacy, we can take inspiration from Gittings, who found the courage to confront homophobia at its doorstep.

In her later years, Gittings received recognition for her lifetime of activism. In 1999, PrideFest in Philadelphia honored Gittings as the "Rosa Parks of the LGBT movement."[29] She and Kay had a large collection of gay literature, especially contemporary obscure magazines and newspapers, now housed at the New York Public Library, which are key parts of the nation's archive of primary sources about the early gay movement. The couple also pushed the American Association of Retired Persons (AARP) on the insurance plans it offered, convincing the organization in 1997 to extend eligibility for reduce-price insurance plans to people in long-term gay relationships.

Like everyone else, Gittings was far from perfect. She did not get too involved in the fight for HIV-positive patients, which was mostly a male issue in the 1980s. She was indifferent to mainstream feminism and openly stated that she "couldn't care less about day care and abortion rights and the other things that women were concerned about," because her identity was as a lesbian, not a feminist.[30] She was certainly not the intersectional figure modern activists might want, but she was a radical for change on her own terms. We must remember people for the leaders they were, in their fullness, not as one-dimensional idols that do or do not suit present-day narratives. In Gittings's story there are lessons to be learned, in spite of *and* because of her misgivings.

Gittings died of breast cancer in 2007, after she and Lahusen had been together for forty-six years. She was seventy-four years old. After her death, Lahusen dedicated herself to Gittings's memory, putting together a book that included many of her pictures.

Gittings was the love of her life. As she aged, Lahusen saw even more victories for the gay rights movement than Gittings had seen. Lahusen's pioneering photographs of gay life also gained more public attention, especially after the publication of the 2019 book *Love and Resistance: Out of the Closet into the Stonewall Era,* featuring not only her photographs but those of Diana Davies, another critical documentarian of the era. Lahusen died in 2021, at the age of ninety-one.

At Gittings's funeral, the executive director of the National Gay and Lesbian Task Force, Matt Foreman, gave a eulogy. He asked the audience, "What do we owe Barbara?" He answered his own question: "Everything."[31]

That eulogy says it all. The history of queer organizing in this country is not just the story of one or two people. It's the story of thousands of activists working locally, nationally, and internationally for justice. As the parameters of queer identity expand, the need for organizers expands with it, and amazing young activists have emerged. Like any movement, the activists today build on the activists of the past. Everyone working on queer rights today builds on Gittings's work and her legacy, and that of the thousands of unnamed organizers fighting in solidarity. We need her inspiration today more than ever.

19

Richard Oakes

The Fight for Indigenous Justice

When we learn about Indigenous history, precolonial Americans are depicted as just that: history. The story of Indigeneity is left in the past, as if the remnants of our country's brutal founding are no longer ours to deal with. Many know about how Andrew Jackson and others forced the Cherokee and other southeastern tribes to leave their homes on the Trail of Tears. They may have heard of the struggles of Sitting Bull, Crazy Horse, Chief Joseph, Red Cloud, Geronimo, or other late-nineteenth-century Native leaders who led armed resistance campaigns against the United States as it sought to dominate the American West.

But what do we know about twentieth-century Indigenous American history? Not nearly enough. In fact, for most Americans, Native history might as well end with the Wounded Knee Massacre in 1890, if they even know about that horrible event. Maybe you have heard of the American Indian Movement. If you are an informed leftist, maybe you know of Leonard Peltier, the man imprisoned for life on a dubious conviction for the murder of FBI agents in 1975 and who recently had his sentence commuted by Joe Biden in the final hours of his presidency. But even for the most well-informed leftists, the stories of twentieth-century Indigenous Americans are often relegated to their periphery, if regarded at all. This lack of knowledge reflects the way settler colonialism continues to influence how history is taught and how we think about racial issues today.[1]

In mainstream modern politics, Indigenous issues are considered, at best, occasionally. For example, the fight against the Dakota Access Pipeline on the Standing Rock Reservation led to important solidarity actions, but the left, and Americans as a whole, struggle to center Indigenous issues in their daily activism.[2] Meanwhile, police kill Indigenous people at rates similar to African Americans, the poverty in Indigenous communities is among the worst in the nation, and suicide rates on reservations are the highest in the country. Yet the national conversation about reparations for Indigenous people is nearly nonexistent. This nation has simply done nothing to deal with not only its colonial past, but its continuing colonial present.[3] Without knowing the history of Indigenous resistance, from the distant past up through the present, we cannot effectively stand in solidarity with the Indigenous struggle for justice.

Richard Oakes was one of the many faces of this struggle. Oakes was born in 1942 at Akwesasne, which is the Mohawk name for the U.S. section of the Mohawk reservation in New York that stretches into Canada. Being situated across national borders meant that they had two colonial powers to deal with, not just one. However, the Mohawk managed to carve out economic opportunity. They went into ironworking, especially in New York City, where by the 1930s many of them had migrated, living in North Gowanus, Brooklyn, and building much of the New York skyline. Oakes eventually did the same, growing up between the reservation and Brooklyn. The Mohawks' expertise in ironworking led them to opportunities in bridge building and Oakes earned a living this way.[4]

In 1968, Oakes moved to San Francisco. During his move west, he stopped at reservations across the U.S. to gather stories and experiences from other Native people, which undoubtedly shaped his future as an activist. In San Francisco, he bartended in the Mission District and took courses at San Francisco State University. Oakes had arrived in the city just after a radical period of upheaval for the Indigenous community.

In the fifteen years prior to Oakes's arrival, the federal government launched another genocidal attack against the tribes. This was known as "Indian termination." The termination strategy was simple: the government dangled small cash payouts as incentive for tribal citizens in exchange for ending the federal recognition of their tribal status and the benefits that came with it. This was disastrous for the tribes who underwent it. The Klamath, who live in southern Oregon and northern California, received a pittance of money in exchange for their reservation, which included extremely valuable forests. Consequently, the timber industry got a windfall, meanwhile for the Klamath, the money dried up fast, and the tribe lost access to its sacred sites and cultural home.[5]

Indian termination, working in tandem with a government-sponsored program to get tribal members off the reservations, led to a mass relocation of Indigenous people into urban areas. By 1972, the government had moved about 100,000 people out of a total population of 764,000 people. San Francisco, Los Angeles, Albuquerque, Seattle, Minneapolis, and other cities became centers for Indigenous people looking for economic opportunities that often eluded them. They developed communities in these cities, often around cultural centers and bars, where people from different tribes would come together to drink, talk, fight, and just be people together. These Indigenous urban enclaves, including the San Francisco community of twenty thousand Indigenous residents, cultivated a newfound political culture. By 1970, San Francisco was teeming with Native bars, powwows, and neighborhoods, and became home to the San Francisco Indian Center, which hosted at least forty Native organizations.[6]

Oakes tapped into this organized world. After he moved to San Francisco, he too went to these bars where his political awareness began to incubate. Oakes developed interest in Native nationalism, part of the long-term strategy of tribes to protect their rights, heritage, culture, and law.[7]

For many people, this was the first time they had considered a unified Indigenous identity. Prior to the forced urbanization of their people, the tribes were diffuse and varied across culture, language, and tradition. Yet ironically, the U.S. government's attempt to dispossess and ghettoize Native people created an unintended outcome: a cohesive Indigenous politics that wasn't possible before. The shared experiences that came from talking to people of other tribes—stories of ethnocide, poverty, and police brutality—coalesced a Native political movement that became known as Red Power in the late 1960s. The most famous organization that emerged was the American Indian Movement, which began in Minneapolis as a fight against police brutality, among other issues that Native people faced.[8]

Oakes organized in his new community. He got to know S.I. Hayakawa, who later went on to betray his own people in the U.S. Senate and defend the internment of Japanese Americans in concentration camps during World War II. However, at this time Hayakawa was the president of San Francisco State College (today University). Oakes took classes there, they liked each other; Hayakawa took Oakes under his wing, and together they put together a pioneering American Indian Studies program in 1969. San Francisco State was a hotbed of racial student activism in the late 1960s and had just undergone enormous protests the year before, with demands to create Ethnic Studies programs. Oakes was in the first cohort of students admitted in the Native American Studies program and also was its first coordinator.[9]

While at San Francisco State, Oakes got to know Belva Cottier, a Lakota citizen who in 1964 was part of a group that briefly took over Alcatraz Island, the abandoned prison in San Francisco Bay. She told Oakes and other students that under the Fort Laramie Treaty of 1868, the Lakota could reclaim any federal land the government had abandoned. This got Oakes thinking, and he organized other Native students around this same principle. Oakes built connections with the media and leftist lawyers who would provide free legal services and found people to join him in the dramatic plan to take over Alcatraz again.[10]

The Bay Area was filled with young radicals ready to act in solidarity. The Black Panther Party, based in Oakland, was not only coordinating militant resistance to police brutality, but also providing important community-building services such as education and free meals. The Brown Berets, a Chicano power organization, had pulled off a brief occupation of another island nearby. The 1967 Summer of Love had already taken place, but the Haight was still a major center of the counterculture, attracting many white kids interested in Indigenous culture. All these movements influenced Oakes. The larger political atmosphere was ripe for a dramatic action that would garner media attention.[11]

During the night of November 20, 1969, Oakes led eighty people, including his daughter Yvonne, onto boats and headed toward

Alcatraz. Calling themselves Indians of All Tribes (IAT), they landed, set up security posts, and sent press releases via friends on the mainland. They created their own Indigenous city on Alcatraz, in hopes of building a place to memorialize, create, and carry on their way of life. They dreamt of a center for Native American Studies, a spiritual center to protect Native religious practices that would decriminalize peyote, banned as a harmful drug by the federal government, and recognize its use as a spiritual force, an ecology center, a center for traditional arts, a school to research ways to create greater economic opportunities for Native people, and a museum to display the true history of American colonization and genocide. These were ambitious plans, but it mirrored ambitious times, and Oakes, his wife Annie, and their comrades planned to transform America.[12]

For Oakes, Alcatraz itself wasn't the point. It was a long way from his Native home on Mohawk land, after all. As he stated, "Alcatraz is not an island, it's an idea." It became a site for Red Power activists to stake their claims on U.S. territory, remind the state of the broken treaties that continued to define their lives, and announce they would fight back by any means necessary.[13] But pulling off the idea was no easy task. Everything needed organization. The island had three working toilets. All the food had to come from the mainland. Initially, the Coast Guard was able to blockade the island, but then Oakes devised a distraction, starting a bonfire some distance away from the food drop-off point. It worked like a charm, and they got to eat.[14]

The work that Oakes and IAT did to build solidarity networks made the difference. They organized media and legal teams out of San Francisco. They even had a bookkeeper. Oakes took over as spokesperson for the movement, together with Dennis Turner, a Luiseño occupier. IAT on the mainland worked to gain a legal title to Alcatraz. Oakes called for a meeting with Walter Hickel, the secretary of the interior in the Nixon administration. The Interior Department had jurisdiction over Native land, and it was the department's agencies, such as the Bureau of Indian Affairs, that had exploited Native people for over a century.[15]

Oakes's demand to meet with Hickel sought more than just securing a simple land transfer. It was a challenge to the structural relations between the tribes and the federal government and the ways it treated them. Hickel first agreed, then backed out, claiming he had a pinched nerve in his neck, which few believed was credible.[16]

For the next nineteen months, IAT activists stayed on Alcatraz. Seeing the overwhelming support the California public showed the occupation, even the state's governor, Ronald Reagan, called for more federal investment in Native health care. The idea spread. People showed up from tribes all over the nation, and by Thanksgiving, three hundred people had come to the island. Oakes even built a home for his family there. He learned a lot and made a lot of mistakes. He had a hot temper and fought when he was angry. Unfortunately, he made enemies, and by January 1970 he began to fear for not only his leadership, but even potentially his life. Violence was part of the revolutionary ferment of the period, and that animosity could easily lead to conflict within the movement, as many other movements of the time discovered.[17]

But it was tragedy that ended Oakes's time on Alcatraz. On January 5, Oakes's daughter Yvonne fell down three flights of stairs and died. The old prison was not a safe place; children played, as they naturally do, and a young life ended. Oakes was devastated. He left the occupation, and it splintered without his leadership. Unfortunately, all of Oakes's organizing and charismatic leadership could not stitch up the many fractures in the movement that arose after he left. The occupation didn't work in the long run. Power struggles continued to plague leadership, the government shut off water and electricity, and in June 1971 authorities forced from the island the final fifteen people who remained.[18]

That said, Alcatraz should be considered a significant victory if the point was to create the idea. Oakes inspired Native activists across the nation. He recovered from the loss of Yvonne by throwing himself back into the struggle. He provided key support to activists who took the Alcatraz idea and engaged in their own occupations. Perhaps the most pivotal effort was at Fort Lawton, in Seattle. A decommissioned World War II–era base, Fort Lawton stood empty in 1970. As at Alcatraz, activists made the same argument for legal occupation, basing their claim on the Fort Laramie Treaty. Like San Francisco, Seattle had become an Indigenous enclave as a result of the relocation program, and subsequently became a center of activism, especially for fishing rights. The Nisqually activist Billy Frank became the leader of the movement to enforce salmon fishing treaty rights in the Puget Sound and its tributaries, leading "fish-ins" to force the arrest of himself and other activists. This would lead to the Boldt decision in 1974, in which a court mandated the enforcement of the treaties, granting unprecedented fishing access to the tribes and launching a transformation in how the law treated Native people.[19]

In 1970, the city of Seattle intended to turn Fort Lawton into a public park. Indigenous organizers had different ideas. The Fort Lawton movement had a cadre of bold Native leaders, such as Janet McCloud (Tulalip), Hank Adams (Assiniboine), Ramona Bennett (Puyallup), Bernie Whitebear (Colville), and Don Matheson (Puyallup), among others. Oakes was not involved in the planning of the occupation, but after the group made a couple of failed attempts to occupy Fort Lawton in early 1970, he came to Seattle in March and assisted in taking the fort and raising a traditional lodge to mark it as Indian land. Soon, a military patrol spotted and arrested the activists. In the fort's jail, Oakes gave a speech that roused his fellow occupiers on their great success. Another occupation in April had a similar result. Eventually, Seattle's government gave in, and the activists received twenty acres of land to create the Daybreak Star Cultural Center. The facility remains open today and has a preschool, holds powwows, and tells the story of Indigenous people in the Puget Sound area. This victory was a direct manifestation of the sentiment behind Oakes's organizing principle back at Alcatraz, which stressed nurturing the idea of Indigenous sovereignty, no matter where Native people gathered.[20]

The other major campaign for which Oakes showed his solidarity was the Pit River fight for lost lands in northeast California. In 1970, Pit River was a tiny tribe with 530 residents, led by a twenty-five-year-old classmate of Oakes's at San Francisco State named Mickey Gemmill. Their protest targeted Pacific Gas and Electric (PG&E), California's largest electric company. Pit River had never agreed to a treaty that gave up tribal lands, but the federal government recognized only a tiny plot of northeastern California land as theirs. Meanwhile, corporations were free to despoil the rest of their traditional lands. Gladly accepting Gemmill's invitation, Oakes went to Pit River to help organize a movement to regain their lands.[21]

Pit River people had already confronted the police over PG&E's domination of their land and were ready to act. Oakes held organizing meetings to develop strategy and used his media connections to ensure attention to the problems of this remote tribe. They first occupied a PG&E campground, asking to be arrested so they could take the battle into the courts, where they could get the media attention the campaign needed. Then they occupied sites in the Lassen National Forest, also on traditional Pit River land. The attention worked as planned. As this movement got attention, musicians such as Wavy Gravy came out in support and this obscure cause became part of a larger national movement.[22]

As the legal proceedings around Pit River wound on, Oakes returned to San Francisco. He was in a bar with his friends one night when a man named Tommy Pritchard approached him. The two had fought in a bar two months earlier, and Oakes had broken his nose. Pritchard wanted revenge. He took a pool cue and bashed in Oakes's head, breaking his skull. It required a six-hour brain surgery to keep him alive. Oakes spent two months in the hospital. His health never fully recovered. In the aftermath, he went back to his Mohawk home for the first time in five years and received better medical care under the Canadian health care system than he could in the United States.[23]

As soon as he could, Oakes returned to the Pit River struggle. The tribe had kept up the fight, but they needed Oakes. They initiated an occupation of more PG&E lands, this time in the town of Burney, California. In October 1970, in what became known as the Battle of the Four Corners, the unabashedly racist cops ordered the tribe to leave the occupation site. Oakes and his comrades refused. The police then attacked, badly beating the occupiers. This led to lawsuits for police brutality. After the attack, the occupiers returned and organized a roadblock to demand fees from any non-Native driver using the road. The cops responded by arresting Oakes; for his toll-charging action, he was charged with armed robbery. As in the earlier protest, the events caused a media frenzy and brought more attention to the cause. The struggle at Pit River goes on to this day as the tribe continues to refuse the pittance the government has offered for its lands.[24]

In 1971, Oakes suffered another beating, this time from an unknown assailant who attacked him at home. He and his family left for New York after that to ensure his safety. He stayed there briefly, participating in a few demonstrations on Mohawk land, but then returned to California because he lacked economic opportunities in New York, especially since his head injury made it impossible for him to get ironwork. Then, in September 1972, Oakes got into an argument with a white man over Native hunting rights. Things heated up. Much to Oakes's shock, a man named Michael Morgan, who had heard the argument, came over from a nearby home and fired a shot over Oakes's head. When the police arrived, the cop asked Morgan why he didn't kill Oakes. Morgan asked the cop if he could get away with killing a Native. The deputy nodded his head. Oakes was shocked, as were witnesses to the event. [25]

The next day, Morgan told friends he was going to kill Oakes, and four days later that's what he did. Oakes was thirty years old. Morgan later claimed that Oakes attacked him and he was acting in self-defense, but he almost certainly lied. Oakes was unarmed and Morgan carried a gun. Morgan, who faced a voluntary manslaughter charge, was acquitted by an all-white jury. The cop was right: Morgan could kill Indigenous people without consequence.

As with the murders of Martin Luther King Jr., Fred Hampton, and one of the three SNCC workers in Mississippi, this was another white person killing an activist of color. A racist nation and its racist people had taken another civil and human rights leader. Native leaders marched on Washington in the Trail of Broken Treaties in November 1972. It was a fitting way to honor Oakes, who was remembered during the event's speeches.[26]

Indigenous activism certainly did not end with Oakes's death. In fact, the Native rights movement continues in the present, with enormous struggles across the nation and a lot of work left to do. The battle over the Dakota Access Pipeline is just one example of the continued exploitation Indigenous tribes face. But the movement lost an enormously important leader in 1972, and the lack of justice for his killing remains outrageous. Oakes has been largely forgotten by the mainstream masses, but the work he did, especially at Alcatraz, contributed mightily to changing the ways that Americans think about Indigenous rights and sovereignty. And there are still people who are invested in excavating these stories, including the historian Kent Blansett, whose biography of Oakes much of this chapter draws from. In 2023, Oakes's assassination was the subject of a *San Francisco Chronicle* investigation that went in depth on the crime and the reasons why Morgan suffered no consequences.[27]

For non-Native activists who believe in allyship, Oakes's story illuminates a path to solidarity. One of the reasons for his success was his ability to build alliances across racial lines, especially in white spaces, where power is highly concentrated. Lawyers, journalists, and everyday people found the occupations he led transfixing. They wanted to help. We can be those allies today. Indigenous people live in every state in this country. Some tribes have official government recognition, others do not have that right and still fight for it. Some tribes have gained significant economic power, while others are fighting for economic stability. The first step to being an ally is to listen and learn about the struggle for sovereign Indigeneity, not just in the distant past, but in the ongoing fight for a free Indigenous future.

20

Dolores Huerta

A Living Legend

Dolores Huerta is one of the most important organizers of the late twentieth century, Huerta's story is an amazing tale of the struggle for justice, not only for California farmworkers but for people worldwide. Reading about Dolores Huerta is like reading a primer on how to organize; it's a window into the world of long-term activism and the remarkable progress that can be achieved. Few Americans have made as much positive change as Huerta.

Huerta's story also highlights the challenges organizers often face, including dealing with the egos of other leaders and the stress and insecurity that can sometimes interfere with their original goals. Huerta was not a perfect person, but who is? We can look at her accomplishments and even her failings as a lesson in understanding how to fight for justice and how to avoid pitfalls along the way.

Born in 1930 in Dawson, New Mexico, Dolores Fernández grew up in a Mexican American migrant labor family. Her father worked in the mines and in the sugar beet fields of the American West and

Great Plains, following work migration patterns that were common to New Mexicans in this era. Active in politics despite being a working man, her father served a term in the state legislature in the late 1930s. Both her parents were strong unionists. Her father was a member of the United Mine Workers of America, but Dolores had little contact with him after her parents divorced in 1933.

Huerta's mother, Alicia, moved to Stockton, California, where she became an active community member and organizer, mostly through the Catholic Church. A leader in Stockton's Mexican American community, she owned a restaurant and hotel, acquiring the hotel cheaply when its original Japanese American owners were sent to American concentration camps in World War II. Drawing from her union background, Alicia supported the United Cannery, Agricultural, Packing, and Allied Workers of America (UCAPAWA) cannery strike in 1939. UCAPAWA was a leftist union with a strong agenda focused on organizing the Mexican American communities of the Southwest.[1] In other words, Alicia was a middle-class woman with a working-class mentality.[2] Her background would have a great influence on Huerta.

In school, a teacher accused Dolores of cheating off a white student, which Dolores believed was retaliation for her, a Mexican girl, excelling as a student. At that moment, she understood how racism impacted her life, and she decided to fight against it. She went to community college at a teaching school associated with the University of the Pacific in Stockton and taught elementary school for a bit. She got married, had two children, and later divorced her husband.

In the mid-1950s, Huerta began working as an organizer. She had gotten to know Fred Ross, one of the great yet little-known organizers of mid-twentieth-century America. Ross was a white social worker who realized that the way to solve social problems was to empower local communities to fight for themselves. He knew Saul Alinsky, the legendary activist and theorist of organizing, who trained him. Ross then went into California's rural and largely Spanish-speaking towns and villages to find potential activists who would lead the fight for social change. That's where he met Huerta, an encounter that changed both his life and hers. Ross had recently recruited another young Mexican American leader, Cesar Chavez, as well. Together, they would transform America.[3]

Huerta was initially skeptical of Ross. His talk of bringing hundreds of people together for social change seemed outlandish. But he also talked about the issues that she knew affected her community, especially police violence. At this time, Huerta was a Republican and worried that Ross was a communist. She was wrong on both fronts: Ross was not a communist, and Huerta would not remain a Republican for long.

Eventually, Ross earned Huerta's trust, and he trusted her. Ross was involved in creating chapters for the Community Service Organization (CSO), established to organize the Latino population of California for the justice they demanded. Based on the Alinsky organizing model, the CSO had played a major role in the election of Edward Roybal to the Los Angeles City Council in 1949, a key moment in Latino political organizing. Ross saw Huerta as a potential leader, and together they founded the Stockton chapter of the CSO. This was Ross and Huerta applying Alinsky's methods to the field, which included organizers putting themselves in the background and building leadership in local communities. This is also when she met and married her second husband, Ventura Huerta; she would take his last name for the rest of her life despite a later divorce.[4]

Tremendously talented as both an organizer and an administrator, Huerta was one of Ross's greatest organizing finds. They registered thousands of voters, confronted the cops about police violence toward Mexican immigrants and Mexican Americans, and pressured cities to pave the streets of the Mexican neighborhoods. Huerta's work ethic amazed Ross. He encouraged her to organize people to make change for themselves rather than making herself the focus, a common error for professional organizers. Huerta learned and, over time, became a master organizer, someone who could really motivate people to take power to control of their own lives. She even tried to help a group of Catholic priests form their own union.[5]

In 1960, Ross assigned Huerta to be the CSO legislative advocate at the statehouse in Sacramento. CSO claimed it was "the first time in the history of California the Spanish-speaking community had one of their own as a full-time legislative advocate at the State Capitol working toward the solution of their problems." It was perhaps a hyperbolic statement, but regardless, Huerta was a pioneering organizer and advocate in pressing for Mexican American rights. She testified in favor of bills to extend social security to noncitizens, create disability insurance for farmworkers, and end the Bracero Program, the exploitative guest worker program for farm laborers that had existed since World War II.[6] Moreover, she became an expert at providing powerful testimony that moved legislators, a huge asset for any activist organization.[7]

As Huerta rose in the organizing world of California, she faced both racial and gendered stereotypes and resentment. The sexism often manifested in her own community, where men resented a woman leading them. Also, because Huerta was raising seven children from two previous marriages, the responsibility of taking care of her kids was a source of immense pressure. She later stated, "My biggest problem was not feeling guilty about it. I don't anymore, but then everybody used to lay these guilt trips on me, about what a bad mother I was, neglecting my children."[8] For Huerta, being both mother and organizer did not amount to performing double duty; rather, it was more like *quadruple* duty, considering the strain and toll of doing mass organizing. She always chafed against male chauvinism, which was one reason she had a poor relationship with her father, who might have been a leftist in many ways but was sexist as well—and she confronted him often about it.[9] A major piece of Huerta's legacy was her fight against sexism, one that she would continue long after the farmworker campaigns that made her famous faded. In 1964, she eventually moved to Delano, California, where Cesar and Helen Chavez lived and where the two leaders of what would become the United Farm Workers raised each other's children.

In 1960, Huerta cofounded the Agricultural Workers Association (AWA). Rather than functioning as a union, it built political power in the rural Mexican community by focusing on issues such as voter registration and better housing. But then she and Chavez, working closely together by this time, realized they needed to focus more on the labor conditions of the fields. Fieldworkers and farmworkers were among the poorest people in America. Their houses, such as they were, often were converted chicken coops. They usually had no running water or flush toilets. They got sprayed with toxic chemicals and had no recourse when they got sick. With no access to shade or cold water in the middle of a hot California summer, they would die of heat exposure. The average life expectancy for California farmworkers in the 1960s was only forty-nine.[10] The AWA sought to achieve real gains for farmworkers, including fighting for a 1960 bill in the state legislature to allow people to take the California driver's license exam in Spanish.[11]

The AWA was a good start, but farmworkers needed a more

explicitly labor-oriented organization. In 1962, Huerta and Chavez left the CSO and started the National Farm Workers Association (NFWA). She and Chavez wanted an organization that focused on workers, not bureaucracy.[12] CSO leadership opposed turning its organization into one that fought for labor rights, which was a huge mistake. Huerta and Chavez were moving away from the Alinsky model and toward a model of collective action needed for winning labor rights. Huerta threw herself into this project with all the energy she could muster and led the fight for some of the early farmworkers' victories, such as winning the expansion of Aid for Dependent Families and disability insurance for California farmworkers in 1963.[13]

Huerta and Chavez were not the only farmworker organizers in California. Filipino-led farmworkers had created the Agricultural Workers Organizing Committee (AWOC), Huerta had actually worked with AWOC briefly in 1960, but disliked the lack of attention it paid to the region's Mexican Americans. In 1965, Filipino grape farmworkers affiliated with AWOC went on strike. These workers had a long history of labor activism and pressured Chavez to embrace the idea of a labor organization, which he was initially reluctant to do. However, the financial backing that the AFL-CIO would provide for a unionization effort was crucial, and the NFWA was in desperate need of funds. Additionally, AWOC feared being overshadowed by the Chavez-and-Huerta-led movement and wanted to be involved. Huerta and Chavez led their workers in support of the strike, recognizing that their members also wanted a union. This collaboration ultimately resulted in the formation of the United Farm Workers in 1966.[14]

In those early years of collaborating with the Filipino farmworker leaders, Huerta and Chavez created a vibrant grassroots organization that for the first time garnered the nation's attention on the hard lives of West Coast farmworkers. The UFW became renowned for its grape boycott, which sought to secure workers' rights by persuading consumers nationwide to stop buying table grapes. Although Chavez was originally hesitant about organizing the grape boycott, an idea proposed by fellow CSO veteran Jim Drake, he invested its leadership in the person he trusted most: Dolores Huerta. Organizing the boycott was a monumental task, involving the coordination of a nationwide effort with volunteers. It was only someone with Huerta's commitment and training who could pull it off, and she organized the action by leveraging the expertise of other movement veterans now involved in the UFW. She also came up with the iconic "Sí Se Puede!" slogan of the UFW. Like many other things regarding the union, that slogan became associated in the public mind with Chavez, partly because Chavez indeed saw himself as the face of the union, and partly because of the pervasive sexism that sidelined women leaders in American social movements.[15]

It is important to acknowledge that any biography of an organizer or leader inevitably overlooks the contribution of many less famous individuals who were equally involved in a campaign. The role of these people spread in cities across the nation was as pivotal as Huerta's was, even if they are not as well known. The boycott was built on the CSO model, with its focus on doing organizing work in people's houses, where organizers and activists lived together. Being a part of the boycott wasn't something you did after work, it was your life. Living with other activists, you lived, breathed, and slept it. It required a significant sacrifice, but it also worked. Huerta knew what she was doing.[16]

The most famous moment of the Delano strike and grape boycott was the march from Delano to Sacramento in 1966, led predominantly by men, with Chavez at the forefront.[17] The strike continued even as the march took place, and the UFW remained concerned about non-union workers in the fields undermining their strike. Huerta stayed behind to coordinate the women on the picket lines. Her efforts were as symbolic as they were functional; many women who joined the boycott viewed Huerta as a hero, precisely because she stood up to the movement's men and provided them a role model against the sexism they faced from their supposed comrades.

Huerta also spearheaded efforts to get other unions to support the boycott. In 1968, she appealed to groups such as the Seafarers International Union and the Amalgamated Meat Cutters in New York to engage in a complete boycott of California grapes, to which they agreed, even though secondary boycotts were illegal under the Taft-Hartley Act. As a result, the grapes rotted on the docks. The unions argued that the boycott was actually legal, because the National Labor Relations Act specifically excluded farmworkers. During this period, the fact that the farmworkers existed outside the protections and restrictions of American labor law ironically worked toward the movement's advantage.

Huerta also organized consumer boycotts and massive picketing of grocery stores such as A&P in New York. While she was not the only person responsible for the workers scoring a significant victory in 1970 that ended the first boycott, she certainly deserves her share of the accolades. Her efforts were especially notable given the opposition, including Ronald Reagan, then governor of California, eating grapes on television to show his support for the growers. Overcoming the massive resistance of California's economic and political elite was an astounding victory.[18]

Huerta worked diligently to ensure other social movements supported the farmworkers' struggle. She collaborated personally with Gloria Steinem to gain backing from feminists, and later credited Steinem with opening her mind to feminism, which she then brought to a farmworkers' movement plagued by sexism.[19] Huerta became so close to many leading liberal figures that she was even on the stage with Robert F. Kennedy in Los Angeles moments before he was assassinated in 1968.

Relations with the farmers did not improve after the UFW suspended the boycott, as growers continued to resist contracts that would grant workers dignity. In 1973, the UFW restarted the grape boycott, with Huerta once again at the helm. This time, the effort led to the passage of the 1975 California Agricultural Labor Relations Act, a groundbreaking piece of legislation that allowed farmworkers to form unions and engage in collective bargaining.[20] This was an ambivalent win for Chavez, and to a lesser extent Huerta, as they had grown accustomed to running the UFW in a top-down manner rather than following the bottom-up model that a union requires to be effective. Chavez long felt he lost something by having to work within labor law, though he accepted the need for the law at the time. American labor law disciplines workers as much as it protects them and now some of his most effective tactics such as secondary boycotts were legally questionable. In fact, Chavez increasingly centralized leadership in himself, which not only undermined the UFW's effectiveness, but also placed Huerta in a very difficult position.

By the mid-1970s, Chavez was deep into the process of turning the UFW into a cult of personality. Huerta deserves some blame for not standing up to him, as she was perhaps the only person who could. Chavez had become paranoid about the independence that the boycott organizers and other union officials enjoyed. He was always uncomfortable with the potential for democratic participation in the movement, and now, believing *he* was the UFW, Chavez started looking to weed out competitors. At this time, he came under the influence of the New Age Synanon cult, which used a form of manipulation called "the Game" to get participants in a communal living environment to say the worst possible things to each other and to purge union insiders not deemed sufficiently loyal to him.

The Game was perfect for Chavez. He wanted to create a new generation of union activists fully devoted to him, and that included Huerta's children. Huerta tried to ignore what Chavez was doing, focusing on the grape boycott and the workers. However, once she witnessed the Game in action, she embraced it, speaking later about how it "took people who are broken and made them whole." She started using the Game to embarrass and turn on other UFW leaders. Chavez began firing anyone he perceived as disloyal, and Huerta defended Chavez, accusing those dismissed of betraying the entire farmworkers' movement. She even came to believe that the UFW childcare center for farmworkers' children was staffed with untrustworthy workers intent on sabotaging the union. Over the objection of the workers who relied on the childcare, she and Chavez closed the center. This was a particularly disheartening moment, one that is as integral to Huerta's legacy as it is to Chavez's. By the late 1970s, it also contributed to the UFW losing the momentum it had gained in the 1960s.[21]

In fact, since the early '70s, Huerta's status within the union had taken a serious hit. She frequently picked fights with younger volunteers, who in turn viewed her as a bully. She consistently claimed that "conspirators" were "trying to fuck her, fuck Cesar, and fuck the union." This behavior reflected the abuse she received from Chavez, who used her as a verbal punching bag when he felt the need to attack someone, or as someone to routinely praise him when he needed validation. This tension made her feel more insecure, leading her to lash out at those below her in the organization. Consequently, the UFW became a highly dysfunctional organization, and the dysfunction directly stemmed not only from Chavez but from Huerta. Some even accused her of using anti-Semitic language against Marshall Ganz and other Jewish UFW organizers she had turned against.[22]

This part of the narrative is difficult for me to share and probably for you to read. We want to view Huerta as a hero, not a flawed organizer who made mistakes under stress. We have so few living organizers left from that great period of social change in the 1960s and 1970s. However, it is crucial to discuss this aspect of history. If we are to learn from our organizers and the great movements of the past, we must be honest about their failings. Viewing historical figures as untouchable heroes does not help anyone succeed. Too often, we think of the great organizers of the past as perfect figures, incapable of causing harm. The problem with this approach is that we negatively compare ourselves to these people, as if we could never live up to their greatness. But they were flawed too—they were just regular people trying to figure it out, with huge egos and susceptible to the corruption that comes with power. Being honest about all aspects of a great organizer is not about criticizing the past, but rather understanding it to inform our actions today.

For Huerta, many of her problems were caused by Chavez himself, who treated her so badly despite her being his right-hand woman for decades. His obsession with loyalty and control meant that even those closest to him were suspect. This is not an excuse for the way Huerta lashed out at others in the UFW, but it provides some context for her actions. Moreover, both Chavez and Huerta forgot the key lesson of the CSO and a lesson people such as Myles Horton and Bob Moses always remembered: keep yourself in the background and let the people lead. When they failed to adhere to this principle, they let their own interpersonal issues get in the way of organizing the workers. This is a lesson worth remembering.

Despite her flaws, Huerta's bravery and pioneering spirit cannot be overlooked. Like nearly any woman of color organizing against injustice, Huerta personally felt the batons of the cops. In 1988, she was leading a protest in San Francisco against the campaign of George H.W. Bush when a cop named Frank Achim brutally beat her—and he did it on tape. He repeatedly hit her with his baton, including while she was down. He broke several of her ribs and she suffered internal injuries that resulted in the removal of her spleen. Huerta sued the San Francisco Police Department and won a significant settlement that she then donated to the farmworker cause. In the aftermath, she largely stepped away from her role in the UFW. She took a leave of absence to focus on women's organizing, working for Feminist Majority and advancing its mission of getting women elected to office.[23]

In her later years, Huerta's legacy only grew. By the twenty-first century, she was recognized not only as a leader and inspiration in the farmworkers' movement, but also as a feminist icon and a woman of color who championed intersectional analysis. She became particularly interested in convincing women, especially women of color, to run for office. In 2002, she established the Dolores Huerta Foundation to build grassroots leadership, support political campaigns, and organize around key issues such as building infrastructure in underserved Latino communities in California.

Huerta was showered with well-deserved accolades in the last decades of her life. Several colleges awarded her honorary doctorates, and many school districts named new schools after her. She won award after award. In 2014, Rosario Dawson played her in *Cesar Chavez,* a biopic directed by Diego Luna, and in 2017, the PBS documentary *Dolores* was released.

Was Dolores Huerta flawed? Certainly. But who among us is without flaws? Few have done more to fight for justice in America over the last century. She made a crucial contribution to one of the most iconic civil and labor rights struggles of the twentieth century, becoming an organizing legend through her work. She played an invaluable role in giving the most disempowered workers in America a voice and remains a true legend of American organizing.

Conclusion

These twenty Americans inspire me daily. They did so much good and we can learn so much from them. But maybe the biggest thing to learn from them is that they were not above us or better than us. They didn't have special powers. They didn't conjure social change out of the air.

Nope, they just did the work. They dedicated their lives to change and they worked to make it happen. There were no guarantees. They all suffered setback after setback. Some were seen as crazy people at the time. Others were red-baited and persecuted for their politics. Others faced racism or sexism or homophobia, including from other organizers and purported allies. They all had reasons to disappear, to fall into exhaustion and grief and leave the movement. Who could blame them? But they didn't take the easy way out. They just kept at it.

Nothing guarantees that our lifelong work will make a difference. Plenty of people fight their whole life and don't see the fruits of their labor. When we are talking about an existential issue like climate change, where it is just so hard to see a path forward in the era of Donald Trump, it's hard to imagine how we keep up the fight for decades. Again, I get it.

But what else are we supposed to do other than fight? Despair and hopelessness only serve to assist capitalism, fascism, racism, homophobia, and misogyny. Cynicism is the worst mindset you can have. What we face today is certainly no more daunting than what these twenty individuals faced and overcame. Take the stories of the past and use them to keep up the struggle for justice!

Here are a few tips to making positive change that I hope you picked up in the book and can take with you into the future.

First, listen.

Too often today, we don't listen. We want our own views reinforced, so we pick social groups of people similar to us. But that's not organizing. Neither is using our social media accounts. We have to move beyond our friends and the people who believe the same things we do. We have become so conditioned to demanding that our beliefs be repeated back to us that we have become intolerant ourselves. Snapping at someone when they take a political position you disagree with is not organizing them. Listening, creating common ground, and moving them toward your position through love and understanding and compassion will do far greater good. That might mean you have to swallow your own anger and your personal identity for the larger cause. Solidarity requires sacrifice.

I want to borrow from the excellent book *Contemporary Asian American Activism: Building Movements for Liberation,* edited by Robyn Magalit Rodriguez and Diane C. Fujino. They note the criticality of relationship building. Too often, they and many others argue, so-called cancel culture leads to people ending personal relationships with those they need for the fights ahead. We need to build alliances, not cut someone out for taking a position different from ours. Rather, we need to emphasize deep *listening.* Rodriguez and Fujino note that too many contemporary activists engage in a fundamentalist version of identity-based politics that actually hurts others. As they write, "Having one's complex, intersectional identities and experiences finally acknowledged has led some to demand punishment for any and every instance of written, spoken, or acted-out harm. This response is creating an atmosphere in which a charge becomes a conviction, without the benefit of any investigation or due process and without processes of restorative justice that are necessary if we are to create abolitionist futures."[1]

I could not agree more. Organizing requires understanding and embracing the deep flaws that make up human beings. It requires understanding that we will all make mistakes. It requires knowing that we can grow. It requires knowing that our past is not out future. It requires forgiveness. And it requires building *mass movements* that are inherently diverse in ideology, experience, and perspective.

Second, embrace conflict within our movements, but also have a path forward out of that conflict.

These histories demonstrate that activists never really agree on much of anything. Making change is hard. You will never reach consensus decision making on any issue of importance. Ensuring that people have their voices heard is important. But in the end, you have to have processes that allow for disagreement and the ability to move on. Bob Moses sometimes won and sometimes lost internal SNCC battles over how to run the Mississippi voter registration campaign, but he remained deeply committed to the cause no matter the outcome. The stories of radical history we read show leftist movements splitting all the time. If that happens, then it happens, as long as it is over a principled matter and activists continue to organize in the best way they know how. However, we really do have to learn how to disagree among ourselves—even disagree passionately—and accept that a democratic movement can have space for conflict.

Third, keep fighting!

I have to admit, I have little tolerance for the notions of exhaustion and grief that currently dominate both leftist and liberal spaces. Our political culture does lend itself toward this. But doomscrolling is not organizing. Reading bad news all day may make you sad. It makes me sad too. Engaging in a real struggle and losing to the forces of capitalism and racism may make you sad too. Again, I feel the same.

But so what? Look at the twenty great Americans in this book. Were they exhausted? Frank Little and Elizabeth Gurley Flynn and Ella Baker and Benjamin Lay and Richard Oakes all had the deep vision and internal fortitude to just keep going. The personal toll on the organizer can be a very real thing, but the best way to avoid that exhaustion is in fact more organizing! Get back into the struggle, build those relationships, make new friends, have new fights, work toward the future you want to see. I know you get tired. But exhaustion is another friend of the wealthy, the racist, the transphobe.

Also, one mistake we have made in the recent past is to think that when a fight is won, we can move on. The rise of the far right has shown this to be an error. For them, gay marriage can be overturned. In fact, they want to overturn all the economic, political, and social rights we won in the twentieth century. Their weird obsession with returning the nation to the horrors of the late nineteenth century means they have a reactionary vision based on their version of history, one that I disagree with. In fact, I find it abhorrent and grotesque. But somehow, we started assuming that abortion was an established right, that environmental protections were permanent, and that we would not pull what were once uncontroversial books off school library shelves to accommodate far-right paranoia. But that is exactly what has happened.

This means the fight never ends. It never will end. The only choice is to continue that fight. Every victory can be expanded upon with another victory. We can out-organize our enemies and overturn defeats. But the struggle is lifelong. You can withdraw from that struggle if you want, but if no one takes it up, we hand power back to those who want to take it from us.

Fourth, nobody's perfect.

If there's one thing you should take from this book, it is that even the heroes of our past can really screw up. They are human! Some of the things I've written about in this book are actually disturbing. Eugene Debs loved racist jokes! Dolores Huerta bullied the workers under her! Guess what? Everyone has issues, past and present. People are products of their time. So are you. Don't judge people of the past too harshly. Don't judge people of the present too harshly, either. Work with them. Take what you can take from the past and make it work for you. Work with people in the present to get them to the positions they need to take.

And again, we have to completely reject the Mount Rushmore model of leftist history. Having heroes is counterproductive. It requires us to either lie to ourselves about their flaws and failings or reject the past entirely as useless. With respect to the latter way of viewing the past, we will never organize Americans without embracing some of the things that people think is great about America. And what do we think is great about America? Can we organize around ideas of justice and liberty and tolerance instead of defining America as a racist nation filled with guns that forces the poor to suffer? That definition is true, but so is the first definition. We have to define this nation for ourselves. That means deciding what we think the core values of Americans should be, reading about people in the past who shared or influenced those values, and then create our narratives about making this country great again. Tear down Confederate statues and put up statues of Elizabeth Gurley Flynn and Richard Oakes!

As for mythmaking, when we compare ourselves to myths, we always come up short and wonder why we can't be like our heroes. The twenty stories in this book show that everyone more or less makes it up as they go along. So do we. There are models and ideas and strategies that we can employ in our work, but there's no magic formula we can use to become King or Parks or Chavez or Malcolm or Milk. Besides, they too all screwed up along the way. Let's tell the full stories of these amazing people and let them inspire us to become *fully storied* amazing people.

Fifth, imagine the future and then make it.

We can be thankful for the rise of the prison abolition movement. Many liberals fret over the slogan of "defund the police," but ideas that fight oppression often seem unbelievably radical upon their formulation. It takes organizing to change that. As Mariame Kaba notes in her book *We Do This 'Til We Free Us,* in our organizing we have to engage in "thinking through the end of the police and imagining alternatives," even as those alternatives make potential allies nervous. She asks what the nation would be like if we moved the billions we spent on policing and prison to housing, food, and education. Putting ideas into people's heads, making them think differently about the world in which they live—this is key in the development of organizational capacity.[2] Even if we don't abolish the police, reorienting our society toward better ideas and pushing back on police supremacy still can lay the groundwork for enormous change going forward.

This point about envisioning the ideal in order to enable initial change applies to every issue. Envision a perfect world, but don't expect perfection. Imagine changing the world, but don't expect to change the world in one try. Every change in our history is incremental. One election, one campaign, one law—none of these things alone is sufficient for permanent change. We need all of them, over and over again.

I don't have the answer for fixing this world. The problems we face are very real. Anyone who claims they can solve everything through their ideas or political program is a fraud and a narcissist. But what I do know is that many Americans have done the work, and you can do that work too. Americans, both past and present, can inspire us tremendously. They can keep us going. The same is true with past leaders from many other nations, from Nelson Mandela to James Connolly to Rosa Luxemburg to Salvador Allende. They struggled. They failed. They often paid a serious price, even the ultimate price. But every one of them made the world a better place by working hard at it.

You can follow their lead by keeping in mind their lives and sacrifices and wins and even failures. The only way to do that, though, is to read and know your history, and not just the superficial, heroic version of it. Real stories of the past can inspire real change in the present and the future.

I hope this book has helped you move forward in your commitment to organizing.

Notes

Introduction

1. Pramila Jayapal, *Using the Power You Have: A Brown Woman's Guide to Politics and Political Change* (The New Press, 2020); Alicia Garza, *The Purpose of Power: How We Come Together When We Fall Apart* (Random House, 2021).

2. Robert Putnam, *Bowling Alone: The Collapse and Revival of American Community* (Simon & Schuster, 2000).

1. Benjamin Lay: The First Anti-Slavery Crusader

1. Annette Gordon-Reed, *The Hemingses of Monticello: An American Family* (Norton, 2008).

2. Marcus Rediker, *The Fearless Benjamin Lay: The Quaker Dwarf Who Became the First Revolutionary Abolitionist* (Beacon Press, 2017).

3. Rediker, *The Fearless Benjamin Lay*, 11–20.

4. Brycchan Carey, *From Peace to Freedom: Quaker Rhetoric and the Birth of American Antislavery, 1657–1761* (Yale University Press, 2012), 8.

5. For a good entry point into this work, see Daniel Heimmermann, *Work, Regulation, and Identity in Provincial France: The Bordeaux Leather Trades, 1740–1815* (Palgrave Macmillan, 2014).

6. Eugene Grant, "The Fearless Benjamin Lay: Activist, Abolitionist,

Dwarf Person," in *Disability Visibility: First-Person Stories from the Twenty-First Century,* ed. Alice Wong (Vintage Books, 2020), 229–31.

7. Rediker, *The Fearless Benjamin Lay,* 20–32.

8. Perhaps the best book in terms of tracing the global reach of slavery, exploitation, and genocide at the hands of Europeans in these years is Sven Beckert, *Empire of Cotton: A Global History* (Vintage Books, 2014).

9. Simon P. Newman, *A New World of Labor: The Development of Plantation Slavery in the British Atlantic* (University of Pennsylvania Press, 2013); Russell R. Menard, *Sweet Negotiations: Sugar, Slavery, and Plantation Agriculture in Early Barbados* (University of Virginia Press, 2006).

10. Carey, *From Peace to Freedom,* 170–71.

11. Rediker, *The Fearless Benjamin Lay,* 32–36.

12. Rediker, *The Fearless Benjamin Lay,* 36–51.

13. Erik Loomis, *Out of Sight: The Long and Disturbing Story of Corporations Outsourcing Catastrophe* (The New Press, 2015).

14. Rediker, *The Fearless Benjamin Lay,* 49–54.

15. Rediker, *The Fearless Benjamin Lay,* 1–2.

16. Rediker, *The Fearless Benjamin Lay,* 54–70; Carey, *From Peace to Freedom,* 147–64.

17. David Waldstreicher, *Runaway America: Benjamin Franklin, Slavery, and the American Revolution* (Hill and Wang, 2004).

18. Rediker, *The Fearless Benjamin Lay,* 114–16.

19. William Cronon, *Changes in the Land: Indians, Colonists, and the Ecology of New England* (Hill and Wang, 1983).

20. Carey, *From Peace to Freedom.*

21. Rediker, *The Fearless Benjamin Lay,* 71–94.

22. Rediker, *The Fearless Benjamin Lay,* 109.

23. Rediker, *The Fearless Benjamin Lay,* 119–20.

24. Carey, *From Peace to Freedom,* 1.

25. Jean R. Soderlund, *Quakers and Slavery: A Divided Spirit* (Princeton University Press, 1985); Carey, *From Peace to Freedom.*

2. Lydia Maria Child: Not All White Suffragists

1. For the earlier view of Jackson, see Arthur M. Schlesinger Jr., *The Age of Jackson* (Little, Brown, 1945). For a more recent view, see Claudio Saunt, *Unworthy Republic: The Dispossession of Native Americans and the Road to Indian Territory* (Norton, 2020).

2. Louise Michele Newman, *White Women's Rights: The Racial Origins of Feminism in the United States* (Oxford University Press, 1999); Cathleen

D. Cahill, *Recasting the Vote: How Women of Color Transformed the Suffrage Movement* (University of North Carolina Press, 2020); Laura E. Free, *Suffrage Reconstructed: Gender, Race, and Voting Rights in the Civil War Era* (Cornell University Press, 2015).

3. Carolyn L. Karcher, *The First Woman in the Republic: A Cultural Biography of Lydia Maria Child* (Duke University Press, 1994), 3.

4. Renée L. Bergland, *The National Uncanny: Indian Ghosts and American Subjects* (Dartmouth University Press, 2000), 63–82; Karcher, *The First Woman in the Republic,* 16–37.

5. John A. Andrew III, *From Revivals to Removal: Jeremiah Evarts, the Cherokee Nation, and the Search for the Soul of America* (University of Georgia Press, 1992); Theda Perdue and Michael D. Green, *The Cherokee Nation and the Trail of Tears* (Penguin, 2007).

6. Deborah Pickman Clifford, *Crusader for Freedom: A Life of Lydia Maria Child* (Beacon Press, 1992), 61–70.

7. Lori Kenschaft, *Lydia Maria Child: The Quest for Racial Justice* (Oxford University Press, 2002), 31–36; Samantha Seeley, *Race, Removal, and the Right to Remain: Migration and the Making of the United States* (University of North Carolina Press, 2021).

8. Ruth Schwartz Cohen, *More Work for Mother: The Ironies of Household Technology from the Open Hearth to the Microwave* (Basic Books, 1983); Virginia Bartlett, *Keeping House: Women's Lives in Western Pennsylvania, 1790–1850* (University of Pittsburgh Press, 1994); Karcher, *The First Woman in the Republic,* 126–36; Clifford, *Crusader for Freedom,* 76–81.

9. Charles Sellers, *The Market Revolution: Jacksonian America, 1815–1846* (Oxford University Press, 1994); Daniel Walker Howe, *What Hath God Wrought: The Transformation of America, 1815–1848* (Oxford University Press, 2007); Holly Jackson, *American Radicals: How Nineteenth-Century Protest Shaped the Nation* (Crown, 2019).

10. Henry Mayer, *All on Fire: William Lloyd Garrison and the Abolition of Slavery* (Norton, 1998).

11. Manisha Sinha, *The Slave's Cause: A History of Abolition* (Yale University Press, 2016); John Stauffer, *The Black Hearts of Men: Radical Abolitionists and the Transformation of Race* (Harvard University Press, 2009); Kellie Carter Jackson, *Force and Freedom: Black Abolitionists and the Politics of Violence* (University of Pennsylvania Press, 2019).

12. Robin C. Sager, *Marital Cruelty in Antebellum America* (Louisiana State University Press, 2016).

13. Stephanie E. Jones-Rodgers, *They Were Her Property: White Women as Slave Owners* (Yale University Press, 2019).

14. Michael D. Pierson, *Free Hearts and Free Homes: Gender and American Antislavery Politics* (University of North Carolina Press, 2003).

15. Kenschaft, *Lydia Maria Child,* 6.

16. Marcus Rediker, *The Fearless Benjamin Lay: The Quaker Dwarf Who Became the First Revolutionary Abolitionist* (Beacon Press, 2017), 5.

17. Karcher, *The First Woman in the Republic,* 125–38, 151–72, 270–94.

18. Karcher, *The First Woman in the Republic,* 220–29, 295–355.

19. Kristen Tegtmeier Oertel, *Bleeding Borders: Race, Gender, and Violence in Pre–Civil War Kansas* (Louisiana State University Press, 2009).

20. Williamjames Hull Hofer, *The Caning of Charles Sumner: Honor, Idealism, and the Origins of the Civil War* (Johns Hopkins University Press, 2010).

21. Tony Horwitz, *Midnight Rising: John Brown and the Raid That Sparked the Civil War* (Macmillan, 2011); Karcher, *The First Woman in the Republic,* 384–435.

22. Jean Fagan Yellin, *Harriet Jacobs: A Life* (Civitas Books, 2005), 140–42, 161–63, 223–25; Karcher, *The First Woman in the Republic,* 435–38.

23. Louis P. Masur, *The Sum of Our Dreams: A Concise History of America* (Oxford University Press, 2020), 92.

24. Karcher, *The First Woman in the Republic,* 443–86.

25. Karcher, *The First Woman in the Republic,* 101–25.

26. Karcher, *The First Woman in the Republic,* 10–12.

27. Karcher, *The First Woman in the Republic,* 542–46.

28. Quoted in Frederick E. Hoxie, *This Indian Country: American Indian Activists and the Place They Made* (Penguin Books, 2012), 162–63.

29. Carol Kort, *A to Z of American Women Writers* (Facts on File, 2021), 49.

3. Maggie Walker: Using the Tools of the Master

1. Andrés Reséndez, *The Other Slavery: The Uncovered Story of Indian Enslavement in America* (Houghton Mifflin Harcourt, 2016).

2. Sven Beckert, *Empire of Cotton: A Global History* (Knopf, 2014), is probably the best summary of these complex phenomena.

3. Walter Johnson, *River of Dark Dreams: Slavery and Empire in the Cotton Kingdom* (Harvard University Press, 2013); Jennifer Morgan, *Laboring Women: Reproduction and Gender in New World Slavery* (University of Pennsylvania Press, 2004); Edward E. Baptist, *The Half That Has Never Been Told: Slavery and the Making of American Capitalism* (Basic Books, 2014).

4. Mark Fiege, *The Republic of Nature: An Environmental History of the United States* (University of Washington Press, 2012), 100–155.

5. Willie Lee Nichols Rose, *Rehearsal for Reconstruction: The Port Royal Experiment* (Oxford University, 1976); Bruce E. Baker and Brian Kelly, eds., *After Slavery: Race, Labor, and Citizenship in the Reconstruction South* (University Press of Florida, 2013); Julie Saville, *The Work of Reconstruction: From Slave to Wage Laborer in South Carolina, 1860–1870* (Cambridge University Press, 1994); Scott Reynolds Nelson, *Iron Confederacies: Southern Railways,*

Klan Violence, and Reconstruction (University of North Carolina Press, 1999); Amy Dru Stanley, *From Bondage to Contract: Wage Labor, Marriage, and the Market in the Age of Slave Emancipation* (Cambridge University Press, 1998).

6. Tera Hunter, *To 'Joy My Freedom: Southern Black Women's Lives and Labors After the Civil War* (Harvard University Press, 1997), 74–97.

7. Elsa Barkley Brown, "Constructing a Life and a Community: A Partial Story of Maggie Lena Walker," *OAH Magazine of History* 7, no. 4 (Summer 1993): 28–31.

8. Gertrude Woodruff Marlowe, *A Right Grand Worthy Mission: Maggie Lena Walker and the Quest for Black Economic Empowerment* (Howard University Press, 2003), 1–20.

9. Brown, "Constructing a Life and a Community."

10. Eric Foner, *Reconstruction: America's Unfinished Revolution, 1863–1877* (Harper & Row, 1988); Rod Andrew Jr., *Wade Hampton: Confederate Warrior to Southern Redeemer* (University of North Carolina Press, 2008).

11. David S. Cecelski and Timothy B. Tyson, eds., *Democracy Betrayed: The Wilmington Race Riot of 1898 and Its Legacy* (University of North Carolina Press, 1998).

12. Hunter, *To 'Joy My Freedom.*

13. Joseph Gerteis, *Class and the Color Line: Interracial Class Coalition in the Knights of Labor and Populist Movement* (Duke University Press, 2007).

14. Shennette Garrett-Scott, *Banking on Freedom: Black Women in U.S. Finance Before the New Deal* (Columbia University Press, 2019), 41–55.

15. Garrett-Scott, *Banking on Freedom,* 69–72; Marlowe, *A Right Worthy Grand Mission,* 27–47.

16. Garrett-Scott, *Banking on Freedom,* 74.

17. Mehrsa Baradaran, *The Color of Money: Black Banks and the Racial Wealth Gap* (Harvard University Press, 2019).

18. Garrett-Scott, *Banking on Freedom,* 7.

19. Marlowe, *A Right Worthy Grand Mission,* 54–62.

20. Glenda Elizabeth Gilmore, *Gender and Jim Crow: Women and the Politics of White Supremacy* (University of North Carolina Press, 1996).

21. Garrett-Scott, *Banking on Freedom,* 87–111.

22. Brown, "Constructing a Life and a Community," 29.

23. Garrett-Scott, *Banking on Freedom,* 150–91.

24. Jacqueline Jones, *Goddess of Anarchy: The Life and Times of Lucy Parsons, American Radical* (Basic Books, 2017).

25. Ned Oliver, "Richmond Mulls Historic Cemetery Takeover," *Axios Richmond,* February 27, 2023, https://www.axios.com/local/richmond/2023/02/27/enrichmond-cemetery-takeover-richmond.

26. Marlowe, *A Right Worthy Grand Mission,* xiii.

4. Ida B. Wells: Intersectionality Pioneer

1. Beth Kruse et al., "Remembering Ida, Ida Remembering: Ida B. Wells-Barnett and Black Political Culture in Reconstruction-Era Mississippi," *Southern Cultures* 26, no. 3 (Fall 2020): 20–41.

2. Hilary Green, *Educational Reconstruction: African American Schools in the Urban South, 1865–1890* (Fordham University Press, 2016); James D. Anderson, *The Education of Blacks in the South, 1860–1935* (University of North Carolina Press, 1988).

3. James West Davidson, *They Say: Ida B. Wells and the Question of Race* (Oxford University Press, 2008), 34–52.

4. Stephen V. Ash, *A Massacre in Memphis: The Race Riot That Shook the Nation One Year After the Civil War* (Hill and Wang, 2013); Brian D. Page, " 'In the Hands of the Lord': Migrants and Community Politics in the Late Nineteenth Century," in *An Unseen Light: Black Struggles for Freedom in Memphis, Tennessee,* ed. Adam Goudsouzian and Charles W. McKinney Jr. (University Press of Kentucky, 2018), 13–38.

5. Davidson, *They Say,* 64–75; Patricia A. Schechter, *Ida B. Wells-Barnett and American Reform, 1880–1930* (University of North Carolina Press, 2001), 71–72.

6. Schechter, *Ida B. Wells-Barnett and American Reform,* 59–63, 71–75; Davidson, *They Say,* 100–123.

7. Schechter, *Ida B. Wells-Barnett and American Reform,* 75–79; Davidson, *They Say,* 124–36; W. Fitzhugh Brundage, *Lynching in the New South: Georgia and Virginia, 1880–1930* (University of Illinois Press, 1993); Terence Finnegan, *A Deed So Accursed: Lynching in Mississippi and South Carolina, 1881–1940* (University of Virginia Press, 2013); Charles Seguin and David Rigby, "National Crimes: A New National Data Set of Lynchings in the United States, 1883 to 1941," *Socius* 5 (2019), https://journals.sagepub.com/doi/10.1177/2378023119841780.

8. Quoted in Linda K. Kerber et al., eds., *Women's America: Refocusing the Past* (Oxford University Press, 2016), 323–29. Also, see Davidson, *They Say,* 137–50; Schechter, *Ida B. Wells-Barnett and American Reform,* 81–85.

9. Davidson, *They Say,* 151–58.

10. Davidson, *They Say,* 159–67.

11. Lisa G. Materson, *For the Freedom of Her Race: Black Women and Electoral Politics in Illinois, 1877–1932* (University of North Carolina Press, 2009), 27–59.

12. Rebecca Hill, *Men, Mobs, and Law: Anti-lynching and Labor Defense in U.S. Radical History* (Duke University Press, 2008), 117–28; Schechter, *Ida B. Wells-Barnett and American Reform,* 81–88, 112–20.

13. Sarah L. Silkey, *Black Woman Reformer: Ida B. Wells, Lynching, and Transatlantic Activism* (University of Georgia Press, 2015).

14. Schechter, *Ida B. Wells-Barnett and American Reform,* 103–10.

15. Davidson, *They Say,* 171–73; Robert J. Norrell, *Up from History: The Life of Booker T. Washington* (Harvard University Press, 2009).

16. Schechter, *Ida B. Wells-Barnett and American Reform,* 174–82.

17. Robyn Muncy, *Creating a Female Dominion in American Reform, 1890–1935* (Oxford University Press, 1991); Kathryn Kish Sklar, *Florence Kelley and the Nation's Work: The Rise of Women's Political Culture, 1830–1900* (Yale University Press, 1995).

18. Chaebong Nam, "Civic Friendship in the Wild: A Historic Example of Ida B. Wells-Barnett and Jane Addams," *Schools* 20, no. 2 (September 2023): 448–68; Wanda A. Hendricks, *Gender, Race, and Politics in the Midwest: Black Club Women in Illinois* (Indiana University Press, 1998).

19. Schechter, *Ida B. Wells-Barnett and American Reform,* 186–214.

20. Schechter, *Ida B. Wells-Barnett and American Reform,* 138–41.

21. Michelle Mitchell, *Righteous Propagation: African Americans and the Politics of Racial Destiny After Reconstruction* (University of North Carolina Press, 2004), 48, 52, 75.

22. Faye E. Dudden, *Fighting Chance: The Struggle over Woman Suffrage and Black Suffrage in Reconstruction America* (Oxford University Press, 2011).

23. Hendricks, *Gender, Race, and Politics in the Midwest,* 79–95; Cathleen D. Cahill, *Recasting the Vote: How Women of Color Transformed the Labor Movement* (University of North Carolina Press, 2020).

24. Susan Ware, *Why They Marched: Untold Stories of the Women Who Fought for the Right to Vote* (Harvard University Press, 2019), 99–110.

25. Schechter, *Ida B. Wells-Barnett and American Reform,* 149–68; "Elaine Massacre," *Encyclopedia of Arkansas,* https://encyclopediaofarkansas.net/entries/elaine-massacre-of-1919-1102/.

26. Schechter, *Ida B. Wells-Barnett and American Reform,* 215–46.

27. Michael D. Shear, "Biden Signs Bill to Make Lynching a Federal Crime," *The New York Times,* March 29, 2022.

28. Lawrie Balfour, "Ida B. Wells and 'Color Line Justice': Rethinking Reparations in Feminist Terms," *Perspectives on Politics* 13, no. 3 (September 2015): 680–96.

5. Eugene Debs: The American Path to Socialism

1. Mark Aldrich, *Safety First: Technology, Labor, and Business in the Building of American Work Safety, 1870–1939* (Johns Hopkins University Press, 1997); Mark Aldrich, *Death Rode the Rails: American Railroad Accidents and Safety, 1828–1965* (Johns Hopkins University Press, 2006).

2. Nick Salvatore, *Eugene V. Debs: Citizen and Socialist* (University of Illinois Press, 1982), 45.

3. Salvatore, *Eugene V. Debs,* 23–55, specifically 29, 36.

4. Salvatore, *Eugene V. Debs,* 40–41.

5. Matthew Hild, *Greenbackers, Knights of Labor, and Populists: Farmer-Labor Insurgency in the Late-Nineteenth-Century South* (University of Georgia Press, 2010).

6. Alexander Saxton, *The Indispensable Enemy: Labor and the Anti-Chinese Movement in California* (University of California Press, 1971); Beth Lew-Williams, *The Chinese Must Go: Violence, Exclusion, and the Making of the Alien in America* (Harvard University Press, 2018).

7. Edward O'Donnell, *Henry George and the Crisis of Inequality: Progress and Poverty in the Gilded Age* (Columbia University Press, 2015).

8. James Green, *Death in the Haymarket: A Story of Chicago, the First Labor Movement and the Bombing That Divided Gilded Age America* (Pantheon Books, 2006); Kim Voss, *The Making of American Exceptionalism: The Knights of Labor and Class Formation in the Nineteenth Century* (Cornell University Press, 1993).

9. Richard White, *Railroaded: The Transcontinentals and the Making of Modern America* (Norton, 2011).

10. Theresa Ann Case, *The Great Southwest Strike and Free Labor* (Texas A&M Press, 2010); Salvatore, *Eugene V. Debs,* 69–70.

11. Salvatore, *Eugene V. Debs,* 73–82.

12. Salvatore, *Eugene V. Debs,* 88–113.

13. Salvatore, *Eugene V. Debs,* 105.

14. Salvatore, *Eugene V. Debs,* 118–25.

15. William H. Carwardine, *The Pullman Strike* (Charles H. Kerr and Company, 1894), 25, 49.

16. Salvatore, *Eugene V. Debs,* 125–28.

17. Troy Rondinone, *The Great Industrial War: Framing Class Conflict in the Media, 1865–1950* (Rutgers University Press, 2011), 82–83.

18. David Ray Papke, *The Pullman Case: The Clash of Labor and Capital in Industrial America* (University Press of Kansas, 1999).

19. Salvatore, *Eugene V. Debs,* 149–55.

20. Salvatore, *Eugene V. Debs,* 169–77.

21. Charles Pierce LeWarne, *Utopias on Puget Sound, 1885–1915* (University of Washington Press, 1975).

22. Salvatore, *Eugene V. Debs,* 208–9.

23. Rebecca N. Hill, *Men, Mobs, and Law: Anti-lynching and Labor Defense in U.S. Radical History* (Duke University Press, 2008), 136–37.

24. Frank Stricker, *American Unemployment: Past, Present, and Future* (University of Illinois Press, 2020), 35.

25. Louis L. Gould, *Four Hats in the Ring: The 1912 Election and the Birth of Modern American Politics* (University Press of Kansas, 2008).

26. Salvatore, *Eugene V. Debs,* 245.

27. Salvatore, *Eugene V. Debs,* 226–28.

28. Geoffrey R. Stone, *Perilous Times: Free Speech in Wartime from the Sedition Act of 1798 to the War on Terrorism* (Norton, 2004).

29. Ernest Freeberg, *Democracy's Prisoner: Eugene V. Debs, the Great War, and the Right to Dissent* (Harvard University Press, 2008).

6. Clara Lemlich: A Revolutionary Life

1. John Bodnar, *The Transplanted: A History of Immigrants in Urban America* (Indiana University Press, 1985).

2. Hasia R. Diner, *Roads Taken: The Great Jewish Migrations to the New World and the Peddlers Who Forged the Way* (Yale University Press, 2015).

3. Daniel E. Bender and Richard A. Greenwald, eds., *Sweatshop USA: The American Sweatshop in Historical and Global Perspective* (Routledge, 2003).

4. Annelise Orleck, *Common Sense and a Little Fire: Women and Working-Class Politics in the United States, 1900–1965* (University of North Carolina Press, 1995), 18, 219.

5. Orleck, *Common Sense and a Little Fire,* 21–22.

6. Orleck, *Common Sense and a Little Fire,* 25.

7. Orleck, *Common Sense and a Little Fire,* 48–49.

8. David Von Drehle, *Triangle: The Fire That Changed America* (Grove Press, 2003), 58.

9. Nan Enstad, *Ladies of Labor, Girls of Adventure: Working Women, Popular Culture, and Labor Politics at the Turn of the Twentieth Century* (Columbia University Press, 1999), 140–42, 146–48.

10. Von Drehle, *Triangle.*

11. Quoted in Orleck, *Common Sense and a Little Fire,* 91.

12. Orleck, *Common Sense and a Little Fire,* 92.

13. Orleck, *Common Sense and a Little Fire,* 95–96.

14. Orleck, *Common Sense and a Little Fire,* 95–99.

15. "Miss Clara Lemlich, Shirt-Waist Maker, Replies to New York Senator on Relieving Working Women of the Burdens and Responsibility of Life" (Wage Earners' Suffrage League, [1912?]).

16. Orleck, *Common Sense and a Little Fire,* 118.

17. Orleck, *Common Sense and a Little Fire,* 217.

18. Orleck, *Common Sense and a Little Fire,* 220–23.

19. Orleck, *Common Sense and a Little Fire,* 231–40.

20. Orleck, *Common Sense and a Little Fire,* 227–28.

21. Michelle Markel and Melissa Sweet, *Brave Girl: Clara and the Shirtwaist Strike of 1909* (Balzer + Bray, 2013).

7. Frank Little: The Martyr

1. Jane Little Botkin, *Frank Little and the IWW: The Blood That Stained an American Family* (University of Oklahoma Press, 2017), 28–37; Michael J. Hightower, *1889: The Boomer Movement, the Land Run, and Early Oklahoma City* (University of Oklahoma Press, 2018).

2. Botkin, *Frank Little and the IWW,* 50–77.

3. David R. Berman, *Radicalism in the Mountain West, 1880–1920: Socialists, Populists, Miners, and Wobblies* (University Press of Colorado, 2007); Eric L. Clements, "Pragmatic Revolutionaries?: Tactics, Ideologies, and the Western Federation of Miners in the Progressive Era," *Western Historical Quarterly* 40, no. 4 (Winter 2009): 450–67.

4. Andrew B. Arnold, *Fueling the Gilded Age: Railroads, Miners, and Disasters in Pennsylvania Coal Country* (New York University Press, 2014); James Green, *The Devil Is Here in These Hills: West Virginia's Coal Miners and Their Battle for Freedom* (Atlantic Monthly Press, 2015); David Brody, *Steelworkers in America: The Nonunion Era* (University of Illinois Press, 1960).

5. J. Anthony Lukas, *Big Trouble: A Murder in a Small Western Town Sets Off a Struggle for the Soul of America* (Simon & Schuster, 1997), 98–154; Ileen A. DeVault, *United Apart: Gender and the Rise of Craft Unionism* (Cornell University Press, 2004).

6. Mark Wyman, *Hard Rock Epic: Western Miners and the Industrial Revolution, 1860–1910* (University of California Press, 1979); Elizabeth Jameson, *All That Glitters: Class, Conflict, and Community in Cripple Creek* (University of Illinois Press, 1998).

7. Botkin, *Frank Little and the IWW,* 78–89.

8. Melvyn Dubofsky, *We Shall Be All: A History of the Industrial Workers of the World,* 2nd ed. (University of Illinois Press, 1988), especially 81–87, 105–19.

9. Botkin, *Frank Little and the IWW,* 103–4.

10. Botkin, *Frank Little and the IWW,* 104.

11. David M. Rabban, *Free Speech in Its Forgotten Years* (Cambridge University Press, 1997), 77–109; Botkin, *Frank Little and the IWW,* 106–21.

12. Botkin, *Frank Little and the IWW,* 122–30.

13. Botkin, *Frank Little and the IWW,* 131–92.

14. Michael Cohen, " 'The Ku Klux Government': Vigilantism, Lynching, and the Repression of the IWW," *Journal for the Study of Radicalism* 1,

no 1 (Spring 2007): 31–56; Botkin, *Frank Little and the IWW,* 193–205; Arnold Stead, *Always on Strike: Frank Little and the Western Workers* (Haymarket Books, 2014), 69–85.

15. Nate Holdren, *Injury Impoverished: Workplace Accidents, Capitalism, and the Law in the Progressive Era* (Cambridge University Press, 2020), 137–74.

16. Botkin, *Frank Little and the IWW,* 222–43.

17. Joseph McCartin, *Labor's Great War: The Struggle for Industrial Democracy and the Origin of Modern American Labor Relations, 1912–1921* (University of North Carolina Press, 1997).

18. Dubofsky, *We Shall Be All,* 353–60.

19. Cohen, " 'The Ku Klux Government,' " 41.

20. "Still on Strike! Recollections of a Bisbee Deportee—Fred Watson," https://libcom.org/article/still-strike-recollections-bisbee-deportee-fred-watson.

21. Botkin, *Frank Little and the IWW,* 247–56.

22. Botkin, *Frank Little and the IWW,* 256–68; Katherine Benton-Cohen, *Borderline Americans: Racial Division and Labor War in the Arizona Borderlands* (Harvard University Press, 2011); James W. Byrkit, *Forging the Copper Collar: Arizona's Labor-Management War of 1901–1921* (University of Arizona Press, 2016).

23. Quoted in Stead, *Always on Strike,* 2.

24. Michael P. Malone, *The Battle for Butte: Mining and Politics on the Northern Frontier, 1864–1906* (University of Washington Press, 1981).

25. Arnon Gutfield, "The Speculator Disaster in 1917: Labor Resurgence in Butte, Montana," *Arizona and the West* 11, no. 1 (April 1969): 27–38.

26. Botkin, *Frank Little and the IWW,* 279–90.

27. Botkin, *Frank Little and the IWW,* 295–311.

28. William M. Adler, *The Man Who Never Died: The Life, Times, and Legacy of Joe Hill, American Labor Icon* (Bloomsbury, 2011); David S. Reynolds, *John Brown, Abolitionist: The Man Who Killed Slavery, Sparked the Civil War, and Seeded Labor Rights* (Knopf Doubleday, 2005).

8. Elizabeth Gurley Flynn: A Rebel Life

1. Heather Mayer, *Beyond the Rebel Girl: Women and the Industrial Workers of the World in the Pacific Northwest, 1905–1924* (Oregon State University Press, 2018), 32–33; Lara Vapnek, *Elizabeth Gurley Flynn: Modern American Revolutionary* (Westview Press, 2015), 9–14.

2. Vapnek, *Elizabeth Gurley Flynn,* 15–18.

3. Ralph Darlington, *Syndicalism and the Transition to Communism: An International Comparative Analysis* (Ashgate Publishing, 2008).

4. Vivian Gornick, *Emma Goldman: Revolution as a Way of Life* (Yale University Press, 2011); Jean H. Baker, *Margaret Sanger: A Life of Passion* (Hill & Wang, 2011); Sharon E. Wood, *The Freedom of the Streets: Work, Citizenship, and Sexuality in a Gilded Age City* (University of North Carolina Press, 2005).

5. Vapnek, *Elizabeth Gurley Flynn,* 26–27, 43–46.

6. Matthew S. May, *Soapbox Rebellion: The Hobo Orator Union and the Free Speech Fights of the Industrial Workers of the World, 1909–1916* (University of Alabama Press, 2013), 12–41.

7. Vapnek, *Elizabeth Gurley Flynn,* 19–34; Mayer, *Beyond the Rebel Girl,* 36.

8. Vapnek, *Elizabeth Gurley Flynn,* 1, 40.

9. Vapnek, *Elizabeth Gurley Flynn,* 37–45; Bruce Watson, *Bread & Roses: Mills, Migrants, and the Struggle for the American Dream* (Penguin, 2005); Ardis Cameron, *Radicals of the Worst Sort: Laboring Women in Lawrence, Massachusetts, 1860–1912* (University of Illinois Press, 1993).

10. Steve Golin, *The Fragile Bridge: Paterson Silk Strike, 1913* (Temple University Press, 1998); Anne Huber Tripp, *The I.W.W. and the Paterson Silk Strike of 1913* (University of Illinois Press, 1987); Vapnek, *Elizabeth Gurley Flynn,* 47–51; Melvyn Dubofsky, *We Shall Be All: A History of the Industrial Workers of the World,* 2nd ed. (University of Illinois Press, 1988), 266–87.

11. Rebecca Hill, *Men, Mobs, and Law: Anti-lynching and Labor Defense in U.S. Radical History* (Duke University Press, 2008), 142–44; William M. Adler, *The Man Who Never Died: The Life, Times, and Legacy of Joe Hill, American Labor Icon* (Bloomsbury, 2011); Vapnek, *Elizabeth Gurley Flynn,* 62–63.

12. Vapnek, *Elizabeth Gurley Flynn,* 63–65; Dubofsky, *We Shall Be All,* 331–33.

13. Jeffrey A. Johnson, *The 1916 Preparedness Day Bombing: Anarchy and Terrorism in Progressive Era America* (Routledge, 2017).

14. Mary Anne Trasciatti, "Elizabeth Gurley Flynn, the Sacco-Vanzetti Case, and the Rise and Fall of the Liberal-Radical Alliance, 1920–1940," *American Communist History* 15, no. 2 (2016): 191–92; Vapnek, *Elizabeth Gurley Flynn,* 53–55, 70–86.

15. Bruce Watson, *Sacco & Vanzetti: The Men, the Murders, and the Judgment of Mankind* (Viking, 2007).

16. Trasciatti, "Elizabeth Gurley Flynn, the Sacco-Vanzetti Case, and the Rise and Fall of the Liberal-Radical Alliance, 1920–1940," 191–216; Samuel Walker, *In Defense of American Liberties: A History of the ACLU,* 2nd ed. (Southern Illinois University Press, 1990).

17. Vapnek, *Elizabeth Gurley Flynn,* 87–102; Lara Vapnek, "The Rebel Girl Revisited: Reading Elizabeth Gurley Flynn's Life Story," *Feminist Studies* 44, no. 1 (2018): 13–42.

18. Trasciatti, "Elizabeth Gurley Flynn, the Sacco-Vanzetti Case, and the Rise and Fall of the Liberal-Radical Alliance, 1920–1940"; Vapnek, *Elizabeth Gurley Flynn,* 103–21.

19. Vapnek, *Elizabeth Gurley Flynn,* 122–37.

20. Vapnek, *Elizabeth Gurley Flynn,* 138–62.

21. Vapnek, *Elizabeth Gurley Flynn,* 163–78.

9. Myles Horton: Organizing the South for Justice

1. Stephen Hahn, *The Roots of Southern Populism: Yeoman Farmers and the Transformation of the Georgia Upcountry, 1850–1890* (Oxford University Press, 1983), remains a classic text on how this platform could be implemented in an area not far from Horton's hometown.

2. John M. Glen, *Highlander: No Ordinary School, 1932–1962* (University of Kentucky Press, 1988), 6–7.

3. Richard Whiteman Fox, *Reinhold Niebuhr: A Biography* (Cornell University Press, 1985).

4. Jon N. Hale, "Myles Horton and Critical Education in the Deep South," *American Educational History Journal* 34, no. 2 (2007): 315–29.

5. Dale Jacobs, ed., *The Myles Horton Reader: Education for Social Change* (University of Tennessee Press, 2003), xxiv.

6. Frank Adams, *Unearthing Seeds of Fire: The Idea of Highlander* (John F. Blair, 1975), 1–10.

7. Adams, *Unearthing Seeds of Fire,* 18–19.

8. Tobias Higbie, *Labor's Mind: A History of Working-Class Intellectual Life* (University of Illinois Press, 2019), 66–84.

9. Karen A. Shapiro, *A New South Rebellion: The Battle Against Convict Labor in the Tennessee Coalfields, 1871–1896* (University of North Carolina Press, 1998); Glen, *Highlander,* 17–18.

10. Jane Addams, *Twenty Years at Hull-House* (Macmillan, 1911).

11. W. Calvin Dickinson, "Radical Hillbillies: Socialism in Tennessee," in *Rural Life and Culture in the Upper Cumberland,* ed. Michael E. Birdwell and W. Calvin Dickinson (University Press of Kentucky, 2004), 211–26.

12. Adams, *Unearthing Seeds of Fire,* 37–38.

13. Adams, *Unearthing Seeds of Fire,* 47; Glen, *Highlander,* 21–47.

14. Adams, *Unearthing Seeds of Fire,* 54–71.

15. David Lewis Coleman, *Race Against Liberalism: Black Workers and the UAW in Detroit* (University of Illinois Press, 2008); Bruce Nelson, *Divided We Stand: American Workers and the Struggle for Black Equality* (Princeton University Press, 2001); Ruth Needleman, *Black Freedom Fighters in Steel:*

The Struggle for Democratic Unionism (Cornell University Press, 2003); Robert Rodgers Korstad, *Civil Rights Unionism: Tobacco Workers and the Struggle for Democracy in the Mid-Twentieth-Century South* (University of North Carolina Press, 2003).

16. Adams, *Unearthing Seeds of Fire,* 84; Glen, *Highlander,* 47–69.

17. Beth Anne English, *A Common Thread: Labor, Politics, and Capital Mobility in the Textile Industry* (University Press of Georgia, 2006).

18. James Green, *The Devil Is Here in These Hills: West Virginia's Coal Miners and Their Battle for Freedom* (Atlantic Monthly Press, 2015).

19. William P. Jones, *The Tribe of Black Ulysses: African American Lumber Workers in the Jim Crow South* (University of Illinois Press, 2005); Scott Reynolds Nelson, *Steel Drivin' Man: John Henry, The Untold Story of an American Legend* (Oxford University Press, 2006); Peter Rachleff, *Black Labor in the South: Richmond, Virginia, 1865–1890* (University of Illinois Press, 1984); Talitha L. LeFlouria, *Chained in Silence: Black Women and Convict Labor in the New South* (University of North Carolina Press, 2015); James D. Ross Jr., *The Rise and Fall of the Southern Tenant Farmers Union in Arkansas* (University of Tennessee Press, 2018).

20. Glen, *Highlander,* 71–86.

21. "Zilphia Mae Johnson Horton," *Encyclopedia of Arkansas,* https://encyclopediaofarkansas.net/entries/zilphia-mae-johnson-horton-6857/.

22. Stuart Stotts, *We Shall Overcome: The Song That Changed the World* (Houghton Mifflin, 2010).

23. Elizabeth Fones-Wolf and Ken Fones-Wolf, *Struggle for the Soul of the Postwar South: White Evangelical Protestants and Operation Dixie* (University of Illinois, 2015); Glen, *Highlander,* 87–106.

24. Glen, *Highlander,* 129–54.

25. Adams, *Unearthing Seeds of Fire,* 118–20; Glen, *Highlander,* 155–72.

26. Adams, *Unearthing Seeds of Fire,* 122.

27. Glen, *Highlander,* 173–209.

28. Adams, *Unearthing Seeds of Fire,* 133.

29. Francesca Polletta, *Freedom Is an Endless Meeting: Democracy in American Social Movements* (University of Chicago Press, 2002), 61–67.

30. Myles Horton and Paulo Freire, *We Make the Road by Walking: Conversations on Education and Social Change* (Temple University Press, 1990), 136.

10. Lucy Randolph Mason: To Win These Rights

1. Louise W. Knight, *Citizen: Jane Addams and the Struggle for Democracy* (Norton, 2005); Louise W. Knight, *Jane Addams: Spirit in Action* (Norton, 2010).

2. Robyn Muncy, *Relentless Reformer: Josephine Roche and Progressivism in Twentieth-Century America* (Princeton University Press, 2015); Kristin Downey, *The Woman Behind the New Deal: The Life of Frances Perkins, FDR's Secretary of Labor and His Moral Conscience* (Nan A. Talese, 2009); Frances Perkins, *The Roosevelt I Knew* (Viking Press, 1946); Bill Severn, *Frances Perkins: A Member of the Cabinet* (Hawthorn Books, 1976).

3. John A. Salmond, *Miss Lucy of the CIO: The Life and Times of Lucy Randolph Mason, 1882–1959* (University of Georgia Press, 1988), 8.

4. Salmond, *Miss Lucy of the CIO,* 17.

5. Nancy Marie Robertson, *Christian Sisterhood, Race Relations, and the YWCA, 1906–46* (University of Illinois Press, 2007); Sarah Heath, "Negotiating White Womanhood: The Cincinnati YWCA and White Wage-Earning Women," in Nina Mjagkij and Margaret Spratt, eds., *Men and Women Adrift: The YMCA and YWCA in the City* (New York University Press, 1997), 86–110.

6. Salmond, *Miss Lucy of the CIO,* xi.

7. Salmond, *Miss Lucy of the CIO,* 42.

8. Noralee Frankel and Nancy S. Dye, eds., *Gender, Class, Race, and Reform in the Progressive Era* (University of Kentucky Press, 1991); Robyn Muncy, *Creating a Female Dominion in American Reform, 1890–1935* (Oxford University Press, 1991); Kathryn Kish Sklar, *Florence Kelley and the Nation's Work: The Rise of Women's Political Culture, 1830–1900* (Yale University Press, 1995).

9. Nancy Woloch, *Muller v. Oregon: A Brief History with Documents* (Bedford-St. Martin's, 1996); Rebecca DeWolf, *Gendered Citizenship: The Original Conflict over the Equal Rights Amendment, 1920–1963* (University of Nebraska Press, 2021).

10. J.D. Zahniser and Amelia R. Fry's biography *Alice Paul: Claiming Power* (Oxford University Press, 2014) notably ends in 1920, simply leaving out Paul's controversial and often depressing last half century of life.

11. Salmond, *Miss Lucy of the CIO,* 21–24.

12. Nancy Schrom Dye, *As Equals and as Sisters: Feminism, the Labor Movement, and the Women's Trade Union League of New York* (University of Missouri Press, 1980).

13. Lucy Randolph Mason, *Standards for Workers in Southern Industry* (National Consumers League, 1931).

14. Betsy Wood, *Upon the Altar of Work: Child Labor and the Rise of a New American Sectionalism* (University of Illinois Press, 2020).

15. Salmond, *Miss Lucy of the CIO,* 50–74.

16. Bruce Nelson, *Workers on the Waterfont: Seaman, Longshoremen, and Unionism in the 1930s* (University of Illinois Press, 1988); Philip A. Korth, *The Minneapolis Teamsters Strike of 1934* (Michigan State University Press, 1995); Elizabeth Faue, *Community of Suffering and Struggle: Women, Men,*

and the Labor Movement in Minneapolis, 1915–1945 (University of North Carolina Press, 1991); Janet Irons, *Testing the New Deal: The General Textile Strike of 1934 in the American South* (University of Illinois Press, 2000); Robert W. Cherny, *Harry Bridges: Labor Radical, Labor Legend* (University of Illinois Press, 2023); Colin Gordon, *New Deals: Business, Labor, and Politics in America, 1920–1935* (Cambridge University Press, 1994).

17. Ira Katznelson, *Fear Itself: The New Deal and the Origins of Our Time* (Liveright, 2013); Jason Scott Smith, *A Concise History of the New Deal* (Cambridge University Press, 2014).

18. Robert H. Zieger, *The CIO, 1935–1955* (University of North Carolina Press, 1995).

19. Beth English, *A Common Thread: Labor, Politics, and Capital Mobility in the Textile Industry* (University of Georgia Press, 2006); Erik Loomis, *Out of Sight: The Long and Disturbing Story of Corporations Outsourcing Catastrophe* (The New Press, 2015).

20. Lucy Randolph Mason, *To Win These Rights: A Personal Story of the CIO in the South* (Harper, 1952); Michelle Brattain, *The Politics of Whiteness: Race, Workers, and Culture in the Modern South* (Princeton University Press, 2001).

21. Salmond, *Miss Lucy of the CIO,* 75–100.

22. Salmond, *Miss Lucy of the CIO,* 101–6.

23. Salmond, *Miss Lucy of the CIO,* 107–23.

24. Salmond, *Miss Lucy of the CIO,* 124–45; Timothy J. Minchin, *What Do We Need a Union For? The TWUA in the South, 1945–1955* (University of North Carolina Press, 1997); Robert Rodgers Korstad, *Civil Rights Unionism: Tobacco Workers and the Struggle for Democracy in the Mid-Twentieth-Century South* (University of North Carolina Press, 2003).

11. Clint Jencks: El Palomino

1. James J. Lorence, *Palomino: Clinton Jencks and Mexican-American Unionism in the American Southwest* (University of Illinois Press, 2013), 7–9.

2. Lorence, *Palomino,* 13–20.

3. Lorence, *Palomino,* 25–28.

4. James J. Lorence, "Mexican-American Workers, Clinton Jencks, and Mine-Mill Social Activism in the Southwest, 1945–52," in *Labor's Cold War: Local Politics in a Global Context,* ed. Shelton Stromquist (University of Illinois Press), 206–7.

5. Lorence, "Mexican-American Workers, Clinton Jencks, and Mine-Mill Social Activism in the Southwest," 207.

6. John Lewis Gaddis, *The Cold War: A New History* (Penguin Books, 2006).

7. Mary Stanton, *Red, Black, White: The Alabama Communist Party, 1930–1950* (University of Georgia Press, 2019); Robin D.G. Kelley, *Hammer and Hoe: Alabama Communists During the Great Depression* (University of North Carolina Press, 1990).

8. Lorence, "Mexican-American Workers, Clinton Jencks, and Mine-Mill Social Activism in the Southwest," 207–8.

9. I go into this history in detail in Erik Loomis, *A History of America in Ten Strikes* (The New Press, 2018).

10. Lorence, "Mexican-American Workers, Clinton Jencks, and Mine-Mill Social Activism in the Southwest, 1945–52," 205; Lorence, *Palomino,* 36–41.

11. Lorence, *Palomino,* 45–62.

12. Lorence, *Palomino,* 21–22, 41–43.

13. Jake Rosenfeld, *What Unions No Longer Do* (Harvard University Press), 10–31.

14. James Gross, *Broken Promise: The Subversion of U.S. Labor Relations* (Temple University Press, 1995), 42–71.

15. Lorence, *Palomino,* 65–68.

16. Lorence, *Palomino,* 97.

17. Lorence, *Palomino,* 99–104.

18. Lorence, *Palomino,* 71–72.

19. James J. Lorence, *The Suppression of* Salt of the Earth*: How Hollywood, Big Labor, and Politicians Blacklisted a Movie in Cold War America* (University of New Mexico Press, 1999).

20. Lorence, *Palomino,* 102–6.

21. Richard M. Fried, *Nightmare in Red: The McCarthy Era in Perspective* (Oxford University Press, 1990).

22. Lorence, *Palomino,* 86.

23. Raymond Caballero, *McCarthyism vs. Clinton Jencks* (University of Oklahoma Press, 2019), 86–123.

24. Caballero, *McCarthyism vs. Clinton Jencks,* 124–66.

25. Caballero, *McCarthyism vs. Clinton Jencks,* 188–94.

12. Mike Quill: The Power of a Union

1. L.H. Whittemore, *The Man Who Ran the Subways: The Story of Mike Quill* (Holt, Rinehart and Winston, 1968), 8–14.

2. Stephen H. Norwood, *Strikebreaking and Intimidation: Mercenaries and Masculinity in Twentieth-Century America* (University of North Carolina Press, 2002), 50–64; Joshua B. Freeman, *In Transit: The Transport Workers Union in New York City, 1933–1966* (Oxford University Press, 1989), 3–15.

3. Sarah M. Henry, "The Strikers and Their Sympathizers: Brooklyn in the Trolley Strike of 1895," *Labor History* 32, no. 3 (1991): 329–53.

4. Whittemore, *The Man Who Ran the Subways,* 14–25; Freeman, *In Transit,* 39–50.

5. Austen Morgan, *James Connolly: A Political Biography* (Manchester University Press, 1988).

6. Whittemore, *The Ran Who Ran the Subways,* 33–37.

7. Freeman, *In Transit,* 83.

8. Freeman, *In Transit,* 84.

9. Nelson Lichtenstein, *State of the Union: A Century of American Labor,* revised and expanded edition (Princeton University Press, 2013), 45.

10. Freeman, *In Transit,* 102–14.

11. Jennifer Luff, *Commonsense Anticommunism: Labor and Civil Liberties Between the World Wars* (University of North Carolina Press, 2012); Whittemore, *The Man Who Ran the Subways,* 71–144; Freeman, *In Transit,* 128–61.

12. Freeman, *In Transit,* 104–8, 146–51.

13. Freeman, *In Transit,* 177–79. 192–200.

14. Freeman, *In Transit,* 286–317.

15. Ted Morgan, *A Covert Life: Jay Lovestone, Communist, Anticommunist, and Spymaster* (Random House, 1999).

16. Whittemore, *The Man Who Ran the Subways,* 201–6; Jefferson Cowie, *Stayin' Alive: The 1970s and the Last Days of the Working Class* (The New Press, 2010).

17. Ronan Burtenshaw, "Mike Quill: The Greatest Irish American," *Jacobin,* March 17, 2024. https://jacobin.com/2024/03/mike-quill-irish-american-twu-civil-rights.

18. Whittemore, *The Man Who Ran the Subways,* 187–200, 214–28, 251–58.

19. Whittemore, *The Man Who Ran the Subways,* 265–98.

20. Joseph P. Viteritti, ed., *Summer in the City: John Lindsay, New York, and the American Dream* (Johns Hopkins Press, 2014).

21. Ronan Burtenshaw, "Mike Quill: The Greatest Irish American," *Jacobin,* March 17, 2024, https://jacobin.com/2024/03/mike-quill-irish-american-twu-civil-rights.

13. Robert Williams: Organizing Through Armed Self-Defense

1. Charles E. Cobb Jr., *This Nonviolent Stuff'll Get You Killed: How Guns Made the Civil Rights Movement Possible* (Basic Books, 2014), 7.

2. Cobb, *This Nonviolent Stuff'll Get You Killed,* 10.

3. Timothy B. Tyson, *Radio Free Dixie: Robert F. Williams and the Roots of Black Power* (University of North Carolina Press, 1999), 1, 15–20.

4. Rachel Marie-Crane Williams, *Run Home If You Don't Want to Be Killed: The Detroit Uprising of 1943* (University of North Carolina Press, 2021).

5. Jonathan Cutler, *Labor's Time: Shorter Hours, the UAW, and the Struggle for American Unionism* (Temple University Press, 2004).

6. Tyson, *Radio Free Dixie,* 39–48.

7. Manfred Berg, *The Ticket to Freedom: The NAACP and the Struggle of Political Integration* (University of Florida Press, 2007); Patricia Sullivan, *Lift Every Voice: The NAACP and the Making of the Civil Rights Movement* (The New Press, 2010); Mark V. Tushnet, *The NAACP's Legal Strategy Against Segregated Education, 1925–1950* (University of North Carolina Press, 1987).

8. Dan T. Carter, *Scottsboro: A Tragedy of the American South* (Louisiana State University Press, 1999).

9. Tyson, *Radio Free Dixie,* 49–50.

10. Tyson, *Radio Free Dixie,* 62–79.

11. Tyson, *Radio Free Dixie,* 79–88.

12. Cobb, *This Nonviolent Stuff'll Get You Killed,* 107.

13. Tyson, *Radio Free Dixie,* 88–89; Cobb, *This Nonviolent Stuff'll Get You Killed,* 109–11.

14. Tyson, *Radio Free Dixie,* 90–101.

15. Mary L. Dudziak, *Cold War Civil Rights: Race and the Image of American Democracy* (Princeton University Press, 2000).

16. Tyson, *Radio Free Dixie,* 102–36.

17. Tyson, *Radio Free Dixie,* 148–52.

18. Grif Stockley, *Daisy Bates: Civil Rights Crusader from Arkansas* (University Press of Mississippi, 2005).

19. Tyson, *Radio Free Dixie,* 189–219.

20. Tyson, *Radio Free Dixie,* 255.

21. Raymond Arsenault, *Freedom Riders: 1961 and the Struggle for Racial Justice* (Oxford University Press, 2006).

22. Tyson, *Radio Free Dixie,* 273.

23. Tyson, *Radio Free Dixie,* 262–86.

24. Simon Balto, *Occupied Territory: Policing Black Chicago from Red Summer to Black Power* (University of North Carolina Press, 2019), 190–221.

25. Angela D. Dillard, *Faith in the City: Preaching Radical Social Change in Detroit* (University of Michigan Press, 2007), 232.

26. Teishan A. Latner, *Cuban Revolution in America: Havana and the Making of a United States Left, 1968–1992* (University of North Carolina Press, 2018), especially 15–19.

27. Robert Williams, *Negroes with Guns* (Marzani and Munsell, 1962).

28. Thomas J. Sugrue, *Sweet Land of Liberty: The Forgotten Struggle for Civil Rights in the North* (Random House, 2009); Peniel E. Joseph, *Waiting 'Til the Midnight Hour: A Narrative History of Black Power in America* (Henry Holt, 2007).

29. Tyson, *Radio Free Dixie,* 3.

14. Ella Baker: Give People Light and They Will Find Their Own Way

1. Veronica Coptis, "Organizing Coal Country," in *Power Lines: Building a Labor-Climate Justice Movement,* ed. Jeff Ordower and Lindsay Zafir (The New Press, 2024), 91–99.

2. Barbara Ransby, *Ella Baker and the Black Freedom Movement: A Radical Democratic Vision* (University of North Carolina Press, 2003), 13–45.

3. Ransby, *Ella Baker and the Black Freedom Movement,* 46–63; Joy James, *Transcending the Talented Tenth: Black Leaders and American Intellectuals* (Routledge, 1997); David Levering Lewis, *W.E.B. Du Bois: Biography of a Race, 1868–1919* (Henry Holt, 1993).

4. Ransby, *Ella Baker and the Black Freedom Movement,* 64–91; Adam Ewing, *The Age of Garvey: How a Jamaican Activist Created a Mass Movement and Changed Global Black Politics* (Princeton University Press, 2014); Troy R. Saxby, *Pauli Murray: A Personal and Political Life* (University of North Carolina Press, 2020).

5. Ransby, *Ella Baker and the Black Freedom Movement,* 98–101; James A. Miller, *Remembering Scottsboro: The Legacy of an Infamous Trial* (Princeton University Press, 2021).

6. Dan T. Carter, *Scottsboro: A Tragedy of the American South,* rev. ed. (Louisiana State University Press, 2007); Patricia Sullivan, *Lift Every Voice: The NAACP and the Making of the Civil Rights Movement* (The New Press, 2009).

7. Ransby, *Ella Baker and the Black Freedom Movement,* 105–46.

8. Mary L. Dudziak, *Cold War Civil Rights: Race and the Image of American Democracy* (Princeton University Press, 2000); Erik S. Gelman, *Death Blow to Jim Crow: The National Negro Congress and the Rise of Militant Civil Rights* (University of North Carolina Press, 2012); Kevin M. Kruse and Stephen Tuck, eds., *Fog of War: The Second World War and the Civil Rights Movement* (Oxford University Press, 2012).

9. Ransby, *Ella Baker and the Black Freedom Movement,* 147–71; Adam Fairclough, *To Redeem the Soul of America: The Southern Christian Leader-*

ship Conference and Martin Luther King, Jr. (University of Georgia Press, 1987).

10. Mie Inouye, "Starting with People Where They Are: Ella Baker's Theory of Political Organizing," *American Political Science Review* 116, no. 2 (2022): 538–39, 541.

11. Ransby, *Ella Baker and the Black Freedom Movement,* 172–94.

12. Christopher W. Schmidt, *The Sit-Ins: Protest and Legal Change in the Civil Rights Era* (University of Chicago Press, 2018); William H. Chafe, *Civilities and Civil Rights: Greensboro, North Carolina, and the Black Struggle for Freedom* (Oxford University Press, 1980).

13. Clayborne Carson, *In Struggle: SNCC and the Black Awakening of the 1960s* (Harvard University Press, 1981).

14. Ransby, *Ella Baker and the Black Freedom Movement,* 195–219.

15. Henry Hampton and Steve Fayer, *Voices of Freedom: An Oral History of the Civil Rights Movement from the 1950s Through the 1980s* (Bantam Books, 1990), 63.

16. Keisha N. Blain, *Until I Am Free: Fannie Lou Hamer's Enduring Message to America* (Beacon Press, 2021), 43–46.

17. Ransby, *Ella Baker and the Black Freedom Movement,* 273–341.

18. Ransby, *Ella Baker and the Black Freedom Movement,* 342–52.

19. Ransby, *Ella Baker and the Black Freedom Movement,* 353–56.

15. Bob Moses: The Organizer of Mississippi

1. Eric Burner, *And Gently He Shall Lead Them: Robert Parris Moses and Civil Rights in Mississippi* (New York University Press, 1994), 9–16.

2. Burner, *And Gently He Shall Lead Them,* 16–19.

3. John D'Emilio, *Lost Prophet: The Life and Times of Bayard Rustin* (Free Press, 2003).

4. Burner, *And Gently He Shall Lead Them,* 20–31.

5. Quoted in Clayborne Carson, *In Struggle: SNCC and the Black Awakening of the 1960s* (Harvard University Press, 1981), 13.

6. Akinyele Omowale Umoja, *We Will Shoot Back: Armed Resistance in the Mississippi Freedom Movement* (New York University Press, 2013), 55–59.

7. Carson, *In Struggle,* 46–48.

8. "History of Lynching in America," NAACP, https://naacp.org/find-resources/history-explained/history-lynching-america; Charles M. Payne, *I've Got the Light of Freedom: The Organizing Tradition and the Black Freedom Struggle* (University of California Press, 1995), 111–14.

9. Carson, *In Struggle,* 48–49.

10. Emilye Crosby, *A Little Taste of Freedom: The Black Freedom Strug-*

gle in Claiborne County, Mississippi (University of North Carolina Press, 2005), 79–83.

11. Payne, *I've Got the Light of Freedom,* 118–31.

12. Quoted in Carson, *In Struggle,* 78.

13. Burner, *And Gently He Shall Lead Them,* 76.

14. Carson, *In Struggle,* 88–89.

15. John Dittmer, Jeff Konick, and Leslie Burl-McLemore, *Freedom Summer: A Brief History with Documents* (Bedford/St. Martin's, 2017), 8–9, 62–87.

16. Howard Ball, *Murder in Mississippi:* United States v. Price *and the Struggle for Civil Rights* (University Press of Kansas, 2004).

17. Taylor Branch, *At Canaan's Edge: America in the King Years, 1965–68* (Simon & Schuster, 2006), 41.

18. Hasan Kwame Jeffries, *Bloody Lowndes: Civil Rights and Black Power in Alabama's Black Belt* (New York University Press, 2009), 56–58.

19. Burner, *And Gently He Shall Lead Them,* 2–3.

20. Lerone Bennett Jr., "SNCC: Rebels with a Cause," *Ebony,* July 1965, 148.

21. Branch, *At Canaan's Edge,* 277–79.

22. Laura Visser-Maessen, *Robert Parris Moses: A Life in Civil Rights and Leadership at the Grassroots* (University of North Carolina Press, 2016), 294–96.

23. Visser-Maessen, *Robert Parris Moses,* 296.

24. David Dennis Jr., *The Movement Made Us: A Father, a Son, and the Legacy of a Freedom Ride* (Harper Collins, 2022).

25. Robert P. Moses and Charles E. Cobb Jr., *Radical Equations: Civil Rights from Mississippi to the Algebra Project* (Beacon Press, 2001). For a great summary of Moses's work and his book, see David Levine, "Radical Equations," https://rethinkingschools.org/articles/radical-equations/.

16. Yuri Kochiyama: The Late-Life Organizer

1. Ellen D. Wu, *The Color of Success: Asian Americans and the Origins of the Model Minority* (Princeton University Press, 2014).

2. Alexander Saxton, *The Indispensable Enemy: Labor and the Anti-Chinese Movement in California* (University of California Press, 1971); Tomás Almaguer, *Racial Fault Lines: The Historical Origins of White Supremacy in California* (University of California Press, 1994).

3. Roger Daniels, *Asian America: Chinese and Japanese in the United States since 1850* (University of Washington Press, 1988); Beth Lew-Williams, *The Chinese Must Go: Violence, Exclusion, and the Making of the Alien in America* (Harvard University Press, 2018).

4. Juliana Pegues, "Strategies from the Field: Organizing the Asian American Feminist Movement," in *Dragon Ladies: Asian American Feminists Breathe Fire,* ed. Sonia Shah (South End Press, 1997), 15–16.

5. Mark Gallicchio, *The African American Encounter with Japan and China: Black Internationalism in Asia, 1895–1945* (University of North Carolina Press, 2000); Chris Dixon, *African Americans and the Pacific War, 1941–1945: Race, Nationality, and the Fight for Freedom* (Cambridge University Press, 2020).

6. Connie Y. Chiang, *Nature Behind Barbed Wire: An Environmental History of the Japanese American Incarceration* (Oxford University Press, 2018); Stephanie Himmershitz, *Japanese American Incarceration: The Camps and Coerced Labor During World War II* (University of Pennsylvania Press, 2021).

7. Diane C. Fujino, *Heartbeat of Struggle: The Revolutionary Life of Yuri Kochiyama* (University of Minnesota Press, 2005), 70–77.

8. Fujino, *Heartbeat of Struggle,* 77–109.

9. "May 19, 1921: Yuri Kochiyama Born," Zinn Education Project, https://www.zinnedproject.org/news/tdih/yuri-kochiyama-was-born/.

10. Fujino, *Heartbeat of Struggle,* 107–9.

11. Fujino, *Heartbeat of Struggle,* 115–18.

12. Fujino, *Heartbeat of Struggle,* 119–22.

13. Fujino, *Heartbeat of Struggle,* 123–34.

14. Fujino, *Heartbeat of Struggle,* 135–36.

15. Manning Marable, *Malcolm X: A Life of Reinvention* (Penguin Books, 2011), 340.

16. Fujino, *Heartbeat of Struggle,* 135–61; Marable, *Malcolm X,* 439.

17. Timothy B. Tyson, *Radio Free Dixie: Robert F. Williams and the Roots of Black Power* (University of North Carolina Press, 1999).

18. David Cunningham, *There's Something Happening Here: The New Left, the Klan, and FBI Counterintelligence* (University of California Press, 2004).

19. Johanna Fernández, *The Young Lords: A Radical History* (University of North Carolina Press, 2019).

20. Fujino, *Heartbeat of Struggle,* 234–38.

21. Fujino, *Heartbeat of Struggle,* 239–40.

22. Fujino, *Heartbeat of Struggle,* 243–44.

23. Fujino, *Heartbeat of Struggle,* 260–71.

17. Daniel Berrigan: The Power of Religious Example

1. Pew Research Center, "About Three-in-Ten U.S. Adults Are Now Religiously Unaffiliated," December 14, 2021, https://www.pewresearch .org/religion/2021/12/14/about-three-in-ten-u-s-adults-are-now-religiously

-unaffiliated/; "Age Distribution," Pew Research Center, https://www.pewresearch.org/religion/religious-landscape-study/age-distribution/.

2. Robert D. Putnam, *Bowling Alone: The Collapse and Revival of American Community* (Simon and Schuster, 2000).

3. Simone Pathe and Kelly Mena, "Black Faith Leaders Push Back After Elimination of Sunday Voting in One Georgia County," CNN, May 21, 2022, https://www.cnn.com/2022/05/21/politics/voting-2022-primary-georgia/index.html/.

4. Mary Patrice Erdmans, "The Poles, the Dutch, and the Grand Rapids Furniture Strike of 1911," *Polish American Studies* 62, no. 2 (2005): 5–22.

5. Ronald W. Schatz, "American Labor and the Catholic Church, 1919–1950," *International Labor and Working-Class History* 20 (1981): 46–53.

6. Nancy L. Roberts, *Dorothy Day and the Catholic Worker* (State University of New York Press, 1984); James H. Forest, *Love Is the Measure: A Biography of Dorothy Day* (Paulist Press, 1986).

7. Luke Hansen, "The Peacemaking Legacy of Daniel Berrigan, S.J.," *America Magazine,* April 30, 2016.

8. James J. Farrell, *The Spirit of the Sixties: Making Postwar Radicalism* (Routledge, 1997), 48–49.

9. Seth Jacobs, *America's Miracle Man in Vietnam: Ngo Dinh Diem, Religion, Race, and U.S. Intervention in Southeast Asia* (Duke University Press, 2004).

10. Farrell, *The Spirit of the Sixties,* 181.

11. Phillip Berryman, *Liberation Theology: Essential Facts About the Revolutionary Movement in Latin America and Beyond* (Pantheon Books, 1987); Christian Smith, *The Emergence of Liberation Theology: Radical Religion and Social Movement Theory* (University of Chicago Press, 1991).

12. Charles A. Meconis, *With Clumsy Grace: The American Catholic Left, 1961–1975* (Continuum Press, 1979).

13. Bruce Dancis, *Resister: A Story of Protest and Prison During the Vietnam War* (Cornell University Press, 2014).

14. Brett Beemyn, "The Silence Is Broken: A History of the First Lesbian, Gay, and Bisexual College Student Groups," *Journal of the History of Sexuality* 12, no. 2 (April 2003): 205–23.

15. Sharon Erickson Nepstad, *Religion and War Resistance in the Plowshares Movement* (Cambridge University Press, 2008), 47.

16. Hansen, "The Peacemaking Legacy of Daniel Berrigan, S.J."

17. Benjamin Halligan, " 'This Is Father Berrigan Speaking from the Underground': Daniel Berrigan SJ and the Conception of a Radical Theatre," *TDR: The Drama Review* 62, no. 2 (2018): 97–114.

18. Christopher Reed, "Father Daniel Berrigan Obituary," *Guardian,* May 2, 2016, https://www.theguardian.com/world/2016/may/02/father-daniel-berrigan-obituary.

19. Anne Klejment, "War Resistance and Property Destruction: The Catonsville Nine Draft Board Raid and Catholic Worker Pacifism," in *A Revolution in the Heart: Essays on the Catholic Worker,* ed. Patrick G. Coy (Temple University Press, 1988), 272–312.

20. Halligan, " 'This is Father Berrigan Speaking from the Underground.' "

21. Sharon Erickson Nepstad, "Persistent Resistance: Commitment and Community in the Plowshares Movement," *Social Problems* 51, no. 1 (February 2004): 43–60.

22. Randy Shilts, *And the Band Played On: People, Politics, and the AIDS Epidemic* (St. Martin's Press, 1987).

23. Daniel Berrigan, *Sorrow Built a Bridge: Friendship and AIDS* (Wipe & Stock, 1989).

24. Stephen Settle, "Daniel Berrigan, Pro-Lifer," *New Oxford Review,* October 1984.

25. Keisha N. Blain, *Until I Am Free: Fannie Lou Hamer's Enduring Message to America* (Beacon Press, 2021), 65–76.

26. Dan Clendenin, "As If the Truth Were True: Remembering Daniel Berrigan," *Medium,* May 11, 2016, https://danclend.medium.com/as-if-the-truth-were-true-remembering-daniel-berrigan-aad147241235.

27. Chris Hedges, *Death of the Liberal Class* (Knopf, 2010), 159.

18. Barbara Gittings: The Mother of the Gay Civil Rights Movement

1. Erik Kojola, *Mining the Heartland: Nature, Place, and Populism on the Iron Range* (New York University Press, 2023), provides an excellent window into these developments in northern Minnesota, as one example.

2. Arlene Stein, *The Stranger Next Door: The Story of a Small Community's Battle over Sex, Faith, and Civil Rights, or, How the Right Divides Us* (Beacon Press, 2001); Amy L. Stone, *Gay Rights at the Ballot Box* (University of Minnesota Press, 2012).

3. Doug Meyer, *Violence Against Queer People: Race, Class, Gender, and the Persistence of Anti-LGBT Discrimination* (Rutgers University Press, 2015).

4. Lillian Faderman, *Harvey Milk: His Lives and Death* (Yale University Press, 2018); Randy Shilts, *The Mayor of Castro Street: The Life and Times of Harvey Milk* (Macmillan, 1982).

5. Wendy L. Rouse, *Public Faces, Secret Lives: A Queer History of the Women's Suffrage Movement* (New York University Press, 2022).

6. "Marsha Johnson, Sylvia Rivera, and the History of Pride Month,"

Smithsonian, June 7, 2021, https://www.si.edu/stories/marsha-johnson-sylvia-rivera-and-history-pride-month.

7. Bernadette Barton, *Pray the Gay Away: The Extraordinary Lives of Bible Belt Gays* (New York University Press, 2012): Frédéric Martel, *In the Closet of the Vatican: Power, Homosexuality, Hypocrisy* (Bloomsbury, 2019).

8. Marcia M. Gallo, *Different Daughters: A History of the Daughters of Bilitis and the Rise of the Lesbian Rights Movement* (Basic Books, 2007), 12.

9. Tracy Baim, *Barbara Gittings: Gay Pioneer* (Prairie Avenue Productions, 2015), 14–15.

10. George Chauncey, *Gay New York: Gender, Urban Culture, and the Making of the Gay Male World, 1890–1940* (Basic Books, 2008).

11. Allen Bérubé, *Coming Out Under Fire: The History of Gay Men and Women in World War Two* (Free Press, 1990).

12. Margot Canaday, *The Straight State: Sexuality and Citizenship in Twentieth-Century America* (Princeton University Press, 2009).

13. Kay Tobin and Randy Wicker, *The Gay Crusaders* (Arno Press, 1975), 208.

14. Kay Tobin Lahusen, "Barbara Gittings: Independent Spirit," in *Before Stonewall: Activists for Gay and Lesbian Rights in Historical Context,* ed. Vern L. Bullough (Routledge, 2002), 242.

15. John D'Emilio, *Sexual Politics, Sexual Communities: The Making of a Homosexual Minority in the United States, 1940–1970* (University of Chicago Press, 1983); Gallo, *Different Daughters;* Nan Alamilla Enstad, *Wide-Open Town: A History of Queer San Francisco to 1965* (University of California Press, 2003).

16. Lauren Jae Gutterman, *Her Neighbor's Wife: A History of Lesbian Desire Within Marriage* (University of Pennsylvania Press, 2019), 78–80.

17. Eric Marcus, *Making Gay History: The Half-Century Fight for Lesbian and Gay Equal Rights* (Perennial, 2002), 61–62.

18. Baim, *Barbara Gittings,* 25–34.

19. Gutterman, *Her Neighbor's Wife,* 81–85.

20. Baim, *Barbara Gittings,* 27–28.

21. Ronald Bayer, *Homosexuality and American Psychiatry: The Politics of Diagnosis* (Princeton University Press, 1987), 87–88.

22. Lillian Faderman, *The Gay Revolution: The Story of the Struggle* (Simon & Schuster, 2015), 142–45.

23. Alex Williams, "Lilli Vincenz, Lesbian Crusader When Few Dared to Be One, Dies at 85," *New York Times,* July 19, 2023.

24. David K. Johnson, *The Lavender Scare: The Cold War Persecution of Gays and Lesbians in the Federal Government* (University of Chicago Press, 2004), 123–24.

25. Annelise Orleck, *Rethinking American Women's Activism* (Routledge, 2014), 175.

26. Marcus, *Making Gay History,* 135–37.

27. Marcus, *Making Gay History,* 178–80.

28. Jessamyn, "Barbara Gittings, That Lady in the 'Hug a Homosexual' Booth," March 30, 2013, https://www.librarian.net/stax/4070/barbara-gittings-that-lady-in-the-hug-a-homosexual-booth/.

29. "A Pioneer Passes; the Work Goes On," *Congressional Record,* February 28, 2007, https://www.congress.gov/congressional-record/volume-153/issue-34/extensions-of-remarks-section/article/E416-4.

30. Orleck, *Rethinking American Women's Activism,* 176.

31. Kevin Jennings, "Fighting for Freedom in Philadelphia: Barbara Gittings, 1932–2007," *Huffington Post,* April 29, 2007, https://www.huffpost.com/entry/fighting-for-freedom-in-p_b_47208.

19. Richard Oakes: The Fight for Indigenous Justice

1. Dennis Banks with Richard Erdoes, *Ojibwa Warrior: Dennis Banks and the Rise of the American Indian Movement* (University of Oklahoma Press, 2005); Troy R. Johnson, *Red Power: The Native American Civil Rights Movement* (Chelsea House Publishers, 2007); Bradley G. Shreve, *Red Power Rising: The National Indian Youth Council and the Origins of Native Activism* (University of Oklahoma Press, 2011).

2. Katherine Wiltenburg Todrys, *Black Snake: Standing Rock, the Dakota Access Pipeline, and Environmental Justice* (University of Nebraska Press, 2021).

3. Stephanie Woodard, "The Police Killings No One Is Talking About," *In These Times,* October 17, 2016, https://inthesetimes.com/features/native_american_police_killings_native_lives_matter.html; Cheryl Platzman Weinstock, "Native American Communities Have the Highest Suicide Rates, Yet Interventions Are Scarce," CNN, January 26, 2024, https://www.cnn.com/2024/01/22/health/native-american-communities-suicide-rates-interventions-kff-health-news/index.html.

4. Kent Blansett, *A Journey to Freedom: Richard Oakes, Alcatraz, and the Red Power Movement* (Yale University Press, 2018), 12–74.

5. Laurie Arnold, *Bartering with the Bones of Their Dead: The Colville Confederated Tribes and Termination* (University of Washington Press, 2012); Donald L. Fixico, *Termination and Relocation: Federal Indian Policy, 1945–1960* (University of New Mexico Press, 1986); Roberta Ulrich, *American Indian Nations from Termination to Reservation, 1953–2006* (University of Nebraska Press, 2010).

6. Blansett, *A Journey to Freedom,* 83, 88–96; Kent Blansett, Cathleen D.

Cahill, and Andrew Needham, eds., *Indian Cities: Histories of Indigenous Urbanization* (University of Oklahoma Press, 2022); Douglas K. Miller, *Indians on the Move: Native American Mobility and Urbanization in the Twentieth Century* (University of North Carolina Press, 2019).

7. Blansett, *A Journey to Freedom,* 3–5.

8. Blansett, *A Journey to Freedom,* 75–96.

9. Blansett, *A Journey to Freedom,* 9; Gerald W. Haslam with Janice E. Haslam, *In Thought and Action: The Enigmatic Life of S.I. Hayakawa* (University of Nebraska Press, 2011).

10. Blansett, *A Journey to Freedom,* 106–8.

11. Robyn C. Spencer, *The Revolution Has Come: Black Power, Gender, and the Black Panther Party in Oakland* (Duke University Press, 2016); Curtis J. Austin, *Up Against the Wall: Violence in the Making and Unmaking of the Black Panther Party* (University of Arkansas Press, 2006); Mario T. García, ed., *The Chicano Movement: Perspectives from the Twenty-First Century* (Routledge, 2014); Peter Braunstein and Michael Doyle, eds., *Imagine Nation: The American Counterculture of the 1960s and '70s* (Routledge, 2002).

12. Blansett, *A Journey to Freedom,* 113–16.

13. Blansett, *A Journey to Freedom,* 5.

14. Blansett, *A Journey to Freedom,* 135–44.

15. Donald L. Fixico, *Bureau of Indian Affairs* (Bloomsbury, 2012).

16. Blansett, *A Journey to Freedom,* 138–43.

17. Blansett, *A Journey to Freedom,* 144–62.

18. Blansett, *A Journey to Freedom,* 162–68; Troy R. Johnson, *The Occupation of Alcatraz Island: Indian Self-determination and the Rise of Indian Activism* (University of Illinois Press, 1996).

19. Blansett, *A Journey to Freedom,* 170–85; Trova Heffernan, *Where the Salmon Run: The Life and Legacy of Billy Frank Jr.* (University of Washington Press, 2012); Charles Wilkinson, *Messages from Frank's Landing: A Story of Salmon, Treaties, and the Indian Way* (University of Washington Press, 2000).

20. Jeffrey Craig Sanders, *Seattle and the Roots of Urban Sustainability: Inventing Ecotopia* (University of Pittsburgh Press, 2010), 99–130; Blansett, *A Journey to Freedom,* 185–200.

21. Blansett, *A Journey to Freedom,* 201–5.

22. Blansett, *A Journey to Freedom,* 205–16.

23. Blansett, *A Journey to Freedom,* 216–22.

24. Blansett, *A Journey to Freedom,* 223–41.

25. Blansett, *A Journey to Freedom,* 240–46.

26. Blansett, *A Journey to Freedom,* 246–64.

27. Jason Fagone and Julie Johnson, "The Killing of Richard Oakes," *San Francisco Chronicle,* September 19, 2023.

20. Dolores Huerta: A Living Legend

1. Vicki Ruiz, *Cannery Women, Cannery Lives: Mexican Women, Unionization, and the California Food Processing Industry, 1930–1950* (University of New Mexico Press, 1987).

2. Frank Bardacke, *Trampling Out the Vintage: Cesar Chavez and the Two Souls of the United Farm Workers* (Verso, 2011), 118–19.

3. Gabriel Thompson, *America's Social Arsonist: Fred Ross and Grassroots Organizing in the Twentieth Century* (University of California Press, 2016).

4. Lori A. Flores, *Grounds for Dreaming: Mexican Americans, Mexican Immigrants, and the California Farmworkers Movement* (Yale University Press, 2016), 113.

5. Miriam Pawel, *The Crusades of Cesar Chavez: A Biography* (Bloomsbury Press, 2014), 67.

6. Alberto Garcia, *Abandoning Their Beloved Land: The Politics of Bracero Migration in Mexico* (University of California Press, 2023); Mireya Loza, *Defiant Braceros: How Migrant Workers Fought for Racial, Sexual, and Political Freedom* (University of North Carolina Press, 2016); Don Mitchell, *They Saved the Crops: Labor, Landscape, and the Struggle over Industrial Farming in Bracero-Era California* (University of Georgia Press, 2012).

7. Bardacke, *Trampling Out the Vintage,* 119–20.

8. Quoted in Bardacke, *Trampling Out the Vintage,* 120.

9. Matt Garcia, *From the Jaws of Victory: The Triumph and Tragedy of Cesar Chavez and the Farm Worker Movement* (University of California Press, 2012), 27–28.

10. Alicia Chávez, "Dolores Huerta and the United Farm Workers," in *Latina Legacies: Identity, Biography, and Community,* ed. Vicki L. Ruiz and Virginia Sánchez Korrol (Oxford University Press, 2005), 241.

11. Pawel, *The Crusades of Cesar Chavez,* 65–68.

12. Bardacke, *Trampling Out the Vintage,* 112–13.

13. Garcia, *From the Jaws of Victory,* 30–36; Pawel, *The Crusades of Cesar Chavez,* 40–73.

14. Pawel, *The Crusades of Cesar Chavez,* 105–16, 143–56.

15. For a great insider's look at the often conflicted relationship between the Filipinos and the Mexican American farmworker leaders in the UFW, including Huerta, see Craig Scharlin and Lilia V. Villanueva, *Philip Vera Cruz: A Personal History of Filipino Immigrants and the Farmworker Movement* (University of Washington Press, 2000).

16. Garcia, *From the Jaws of Victory,* 47–49.

17. John Gregory Dunne, *Delano: The Story of the California Grape Strike* (University of California Press, 1967).

18. Garcia, *From the Jaws of Victory,* 62–66, 129.

19. Chávez, "Dolores Huerta and the United Farm Workers," 251–52.

20. Garcia, *From the Jaws of Victory,* 145–77.

21. Pawel, *The Crusades of Cesar Chavez,* 350–89.

22. Bardacke, *Trampling Out the Vintage,* 713–16; Garcia, *From the Jaws of Victory,* 233.

23. Carlos Andres López, "Dolores Huerta: 'We Have to Keep on Marching,' " *New York Times,* October 7, 2020.

Conclusion

1. Robyn Magalit Rodriguez and Diane C. Fujino, eds., *Contemporary Asian American Activism: Building Movements for Liberation* (University of Washington Press, 2022), 1–34, quote on 22.

2. Mariame Kaba, *We Do This 'Til We Free Us: Abolitionist Organizing and Transforming Justice* (Haymarket Books, 2021), 33.

Index

About the Author

Erik Loomis is professor of history at the University of Rhode Island. He blogs at *Lawyers, Guns and Money* on labor and environmental issues, past and present. His work has also appeared in the *New York Times*, the *Washington Post*, *Dissent*, and the *New Republic*. The author of *Out of Sight* and *A History of America in Ten Strikes* (both from The New Press) as well as *Empire of Timber*, he lives in Warwick, Rhode Island.

Publishing in the Public Interest

Thank you for reading this book published by The New Press; we hope you enjoyed it. New Press books and authors play a crucial role in sparking conversations about the key political and social issues of our day.

We hope that you will stay in touch with us. Here are a few ways to keep up to date with our books, events, and the issues we cover:

- Sign up at www.thenewpress.com/subscribe to receive updates on New Press authors and issues and to be notified about local events
- www.facebook.com/newpressbooks
- www.x.com/thenewpress
- www.instagram.com/thenewpress

Please consider buying New Press books not only for yourself, but also for friends and family and to donate to schools, libraries, community centers, prison libraries, and other organizations involved with the issues our authors write about.

The New Press is a 501(c)(3) nonprofit organization; if you wish to support our work with a tax-deductible gift please visit www.thenewpress.com/donate or use the QR code below.